S0-AIO-985

The Psychology of the Physically Handicapped

begun with four general chapters on personality, mental hygiene, the nervous system, and psychological tests. If the student has already studied general and educational psychology, he may use these chapters as a kind of review, or as a reorientation. Chapter IV gives practical information as to the types of tests suitable for the various handicapped groups.

Chapters V to XII deal with the several handicapped groups. The chapters in this part vary greatly in length because of the fragmentary aspect of our psychological knowledge of some of these groups. It is to be hoped that the near future will see these large gaps in our knowledge rapidly filled in.

The responsibility for the various chapters is as follows: Dr. Stanton has written Chapters IX and X; Dr. Eisenson, Chapters I, II, III, XI, and XII; Dr. Pintner, Chapters IV, V, VI, VII, and VIII.

R. P.
J. E.
M. S.

Preface

This book has been designed by us as a textbook for the ever-increasing number of courses in colleges and universities devoted to a study of the psychology of the physically handicapped, as well as for those professionally engaged in work with the physically handicapped in some form or other. It is an attempt to bring together in one volume the very scattered information that has slowly been accumulating in very diverse periodicals and journals and reports, and to make this information useful to all those who are actually dealing with physically handicapped children or adults in schools, hospitals, psychological clinics, guidance bureaus, rehabilitation centers, and convalescent homes.

In one sense there is no special psychology of the physically handicapped individual as contrasted with the individual without any serious physical impairment. The same psychological mechanisms are at work in all cases. But any physical defect, whether major or minor, presents problems to the individual in addition to the problems common to all individuals as such. Furthermore, it is valuable for the psychologist and educator to be aware of the facts concerning the deaf or the blind or any other handicapped group in order to advise more competently with regard to their education and vocational adjustment. Some of the problems of blindness and deafness are of interest and value to normal psychology.

Because we have planned our book as a textbook, we have

THE PSYCHOLOGY OF THE PHYSICALLY HANDICAPPED

RUDOLF PINTNER
Late of Teachers College,
Columbia University

JON EISENSON
Queens College

MILDRED STANTON
Department of Education
State of Connecticut

NEW YORK
APPLETON-CENTURY-CROFTS, INC.

MANUFACTURED IN THE
UNITED STATES OF AMERICA

561

Contents

GENERAL

I	Personality Development	1
II	Mental Hygiene	19
III	The Internal Mechanisms of Behavior	37
IV	Psychological Tests for the Physically Handicapped	72

THE HANDICAPPED GROUPS

V	The Deaf	101
VI	The Hard of Hearing	188
VII	The Blind	207
VIII	The Partially Sighted	252
IX	The Crippled	262
X	Other Physically Handicapped Groups	284
XI	The Defective in Speech	319
XII	Speech Involvements of Special Types of the Physically Handicapped	364
	Index	383

CHAPTER I

Personality Development

What Is Personality? When we use the term personality we probably have in mind the effect an individual's total conduct has on us; we are probably thinking of the quality or pattern of a person's total behavior. We are, whether or not we are aware of it, reacting to the sum total effect of the behavior of another individual. We may define personality as the expression of the more or less integrated activity of the total forces of the individual. These forces include the individual's ideas, his feelings, his habits, and his purposes. Both his desirable traits and those which from a social point of view are less desirable go into the makeup of a personality.

A personality is not a disembodied essence emanating in some mysterious fashion from an individual. It exists only as an aspect of an organism behaving in an environment in relationship to other organisms. The personality concept which we have of ourselves is in an important way derived from others. The picture we form of ourselves as Selves is largely determined by the picture we believe others have of us. We are, or tend to become, what others think we are. The personal reactions of the individual are determined by interactions between himself and his environment; they are an expression of his complex organism reacting to a complex environment of which his own organism is a very important and integral part.

The Development of Personality. The development of personality consists essentially of the adjustments made by a person to his environment. A personality begins to take form when an infant makes his first adjustments into the world into which he is born. At the moment of birth, when he makes his first response to our environment by crying, the infant is beginning the long series of reactions which in time will form his personality. At first his personality is rather nebulous and nondescript. The crying of one infant sounds much like the crying of another. The infant's responses to stimuli are characteristically undifferentiated. His total organism enters into and responds alike to every stimulus without regard to its particular nature or source. Later, as the infant matures, he responds differently according to the nature of the stimulus situation. As the reactions become differentiated, a distinct personality arises.

FACTORS OF PERSONALITY

The factors of personality—the powers that determine the nature of adjustments—lie partly in the individual and partly in the environment. The inherited factors that lie within the individual have only potential power; their actual value can be appreciated only when there is some interplay between them and environmental influences. Among the inherited factors that determine the nature of our adjustments and hence our personality are mental capacity or intellect, bodily build and general appearance, and temperament. We must recognize and realize that each of these factors is highly complex and that these terms are really nothing more than convenient headings which include many elements somehow related so that they can properly be included under one rather than another classification. Let us now consider the roles played by each of the innate factors of personality.

Intellect. The intelligence or mental capacity of a person is of fundamental importance in the development of his personality. The intelligent individual can control and direct his behavior before others by imagining or anticipating the effects of his acts before the acts are performed. He is better able to understand what people expect of him and to behave, if he cares, in the light of such expectations. Though a less intelligent person, and even a person of definitely inferior intelligence, may be trained to react in certain socially acceptable ways in given situations, the training will not result in generalizations and modifications of behavior such as are needed in meeting new or altered situations.

Bodily Build and General Appearance. A handsome or a tall person, regardless of what he may do or say, will cause people to respond to him in ways which are not the same were he homely or short. The attitudes which are assumed toward us because of our physical appearances affect our adjustment tendencies to the people in our environment. If people expect us to assume leadership because we look tall and strong, we may try consciously or unconsciously to play the role of leader. On the other hand, people of small physique and those with obvious physical handicaps are generally expected to submit to others, and are apt therefore to become submissive unless, as a compensatory mechanism, they become aggressively assertive. In any event, the factor of physical appearance is influential in determining behavior tendencies.

Temperament. The ancient Greeks and medieval physiologists believed man to be made up of four humors or liquids, sanguis, phlegm, melanchole or black bile, and chole or bile. If the humors were tempered in equal parts man was of even temperament; but if one humor exceeded the others, the individual was held to be somewhat peculiar. If, for example, *sanguis* or blood predominated, man was considered sanguine; if *phlegm* prevailed, man was considered phlegmatic; if *melanchole* was disproportionately present, he was believed to be melancholic; if *chole* prevailed, he was deemed choleric. In time the term humor came to mean eccentricity, a personality type determined by the physiological make-up of the individual.

Though today we consider the explanation of temperament in terms of "humors" inadequate and unscientific, we still are in search of a physiological basis for temperament. Some of us believe we have found the explanation in the glandular products of the human organism. The endocrine glands which discharge the products known as hormones directly into the blood stream are believed to be of fundamental importance in controlling behavior. Hormones are said to determine not only the physiological functions of the organism, but also the personality make-up of the individual. An ever-increasing amount of experimental evidence is being accumulated which tends to prove that the endocrine glands are responsible for maintaining the internal dynamic equilibrium of the individual. Proper glandular functioning is necessary for the balanced functioning of the organs of the body. We do not as yet know the exact nature or the specific function of each endocrine gland. Precisely what contribution each glandular product makes to the welfare and efficient operation of the integrated organism is still not entirely clear. But we do have evidence to show that the personality of the individual is decidedly modified if variations occur in the functions of the endocrine glands. For example, disturbances in the functioning of the pituitary gland, a small organ situated in the base of the skull, have marked effects on the growth of the organism. A reduction in the activity of the thyroid gland brings about metabolic changes leading to decreased bodily activity, depression, and intellectual dullness. An overactive thyroid, on the other hand, tends to make an individual extremely active, restless, irritable, and tense. Malfunctioning of the parathyroid glands which are concerned with the regulation of the calcium content of the system, may alter the emotional behavior of the individual. Any interference with the normal functioning of the gonads or sex glands, which influence bodily changes at puberty, will have marked effects on the behavior of the individual to his environment and of persons in his environment to him. These effects will be considered in some detail in our discussion of the internal mechanisms of behavior (pp. 62–69).

Environmental Factors in Personality Development. The most striking environmental adjustment the individual ever has to make takes place at the moment of birth. The change from the life within the womb to the life outside is made easy for the individual because he is not expected to do anything about it himself and the people in the infant's environment do everything they can to help him. His wants, needs, and recognized desires are fulfilled with almost no effort on the part of the infant. As the child matures, less is done for him and more is expected of him. Other children, and even adults, oppose their wills to his. In this opposition of wills, adaptations have to be made. The nature of these adjustments is determined by the inherited and developed tendencies of the child and in a large part also by the way older members in the child's world assist him in the process of adjustment.

With developing maturity, continued adaptations have to be made. Entrance into primary school, and later into higher educational institutions, perhaps away from home, require difficult adjustments. The choice of and entrance into a vocation is another milestone of adjustment. Marriage and parenthood necessitate changes in life organization on the part of the individual which are extremely difficult and not always successful. In all these types of adjustments the environment of the individual may make demands which conflict with his own. It may happen, especially in cases involving the physically handicapped, that the environmental requirements are too severe; also it frequently happens that the individual's demands of his environment are excessive. Adaptation takes place only when there is some equalization of demand, and this obviously may necessitate certain compromises. Fundamentally, the ability to make adjustments will be determined by the traits one has developed as a result of the interaction of one's innate capacities and impulses and the environment.

Social-Cultural Factors. The society in which we live lays down patterns which we are expected to follow in the government of our behavior. Much of what we do is done because it is expected of us. Though each of us may individually decide to conform to the expectations and anticipations of society or rebel against them, the social forces at play are significant in the moulding of the personality. Young (14) points out that: "The demand or requirement to follow the patterns laid down for us by our fellows is a phase of social interaction which is found everywhere. The fact of *social expectancy* is basic both to playing of roles and to social control. In all groups, apparently, and in hundreds of common situations, the expectations of others determine largely how we behave. . . . The images of expectancy of what others will do and of what you will do yourself are important in the whole field of anticipatory behavior."

In the case of physically handicapped persons, the nature of the social participation of the individual is influenced in a profound way by the manner in which society indicates what the role and status of his behavior should be. The fat child *expects* that he will be the butt of jokes and the object of comments on the part of persons in his home, in school, and in his neighborhood. The crippled child *knows* that he will meet with oversentimentality and pity; the blind child *anticipates* oversolicitude and maudlin sympathy from the members of his environment. Vocational preparation and choice of occupation of physically handicapped persons are importantly influenced by society's limitations. All too often the blind child is thought of as a potential pencil peddler; few crippled persons can overcome preconceived biases, and achieve success as physicians or lawyers. Physically handicapped individuals are influenced by social stimuli to which they have become accustomed, and which they have finally learned to anticipate. The social group has indicated how it is likely to respond to the handicapped person, and by this indication it has defined the role and status the handicapped person is to assume in the group.

PERSONALITY TYPES

It would be pleasantly convenient if we could give way to our customary inclinations and classify people according to permanent personality types. Most of us like to classify; we think of people as good or bad, handsome or homely, stupid or bright.

However, though people tend to remain tall once they grow tall, and strive to remain handsome if they are so born, they do not seem to be content to have their personalities remain quite so definite in character and permanent in structure. The personality pattern is ever changing, though the nature and direction of the changes are influenced and largely controlled by the innate factors that determine adjustments: intellect, physique, and temperament.

We may, if we wish, think of personality types as ideal abstractions under which we can classify individuals if their personality patterns are at any time in keeping with the characteristics of the type. Let us bear in mind, however, that any individual may at one time present one personality pattern and at another time, under altered circumstances, present a different pattern. At the same time we should realize that there is a marked tendency for many individuals, especially those living in a fairly static environment, to persist in an established pattern so that generally the total effect of his behavior makes classification, if it is not too rigid, more possible than it might otherwise seem.

Introversion and Extroversion. Perhaps the most widely spoken-of personality types are those known as the introvertive and the extrovertive. The introvertive person is one whose interests are inwardly directed, who is largely concerned with his own thoughts and his desires. He is likely to be moody, reserved, and highly introspective. Further, the introvertive individual is apt to be absent-minded and given to day dreaming. The extrovertive individual, on the other hand, is supposed to be interested in external things, in objects outside of himself. The extrovert is not given to introspection and day dreaming but rather to action. In between the two extremes of extrovert and introvert is a group much larger than either of these—the ambiverts. The ambiverts are neither introvertive nor extrovertive, but a little of each, some tending more to one extreme than others.

Cycloid and Schizoid Types. Another classification of individuals is into cycloid and schizoid types. Kretschmer (7) believes that there is an inherent correlation between body build or physique and personality type. He believes that the well-rounded, heavy-built pyknic type is more apt to be extrovertive and, in extreme cases, manic; the thin, tall, frequently weak individual is apt to belong to the introvertive type and, in extreme cases, be schizophrenic. The normal cycloid's behavior is suggestive of the behavior of the manic-depressive. Cycloids go from a lively stage to a depressed stage, with a frequently long intervening level stage of behavior. The normal introvert's behavior may also be said to suggest the behavior of the schizoid. The introvert is a withdrawn person, but his withdrawal is never as complete as that of the schizoid, who apparently pays little or no attention to his environment and frequently sets up mental barriers which make ordinary social contact impossible.

Perseveration. Perseveration is the tendency of ideas to persist or remount into consciousness spontaneously after they have once occurred. All of us perseverate on occasion, usually when we are tired. The persistence of a tune or jingle in our minds, the tendency to repeat words when we are writing or speaking, are common and normal examples of the perseverating tendency. In some persons, however, mental processes tend to persist for an abnormally long time after the cessation of the stimuli which gave rise to them. Spearman (11), who has investigated the perseverating phenomenon, believes that perseveration tends to increase along the lines manic—normal—melancholic. He feels also that there is a greater tendency for the male sex to perseverate.

It is not difficult to see the possible relationship between perseveration and introverted behavior. Ewen (5), who investigated the perseverating phenomenon in normal and epileptic patients, found it to be a feature of the peculiar mental state of epileptics between attacks. Pinard (9) found that perseverators tend to be abnormally nervous and sensitive.

It is possible for us to continue adding to the list of personality types under which people might be classified. Little will be gained by such additions. It is probably of greater importance for us to remember that pure personality types seldom if ever exist, or if they do, they seldom remain pure for any length of time. The same individual varies from time to time in his personality pattern. Under one set of circumstances he may seem to be depressed, markedly withdrawn, and a perseverator. In another situation the same person may tend toward the manic and behave like an extrovert. We may be able to stabilize the terms which characterize hypothetical personality types, but the individuals we place under each classification may not be reconciled to remaining fixed in type. This is fortunate for the educator and psychologist, because an important part of their work consists of helping unfortunate people to change their methods of adjustments and so to help form new and socially desirable personalities.

Normality and Abnormality of Personality. Though we have presented a tentative definition of personality and presented several broad classifications of personality types, we have not yet attempted to arrive at definitions of the normal and abnormal personality. Let us first decide what the term normal means. The normal is a range or a mode within which the greatest number of persons fall in regard to a given trait. In mathematical science the norm, or average, is considered the central tendency of a group of measures. For example, the average weight of children at birth is from 5 to 7 pounds. This means that most children weigh from 5 to 7 pounds at birth. Children deviating markedly either below or above this weight at birth are not considered normal in respect to this trait. In regard to personality, normality means that an individual behaves as most persons do in making his adjustments to his environment. This does not imply that an individual must conform in all things and be in all respects like the fellow members of his environment. Individual differences are present in all of us. It is only when the differences deviate markedly in number or degree and prevent the person from adjusting readily to his tasks as he functions in his environment that the individual personality ceases to be normal. Campbell (3) in characterizing a normal personality says: "The organism has the task of maintaining its integrity, of establishing a balance between conflicting tendencies, of utilizing its resources to compensate for original or acquired defects. It has the task of attaining satisfaction from the exercise of its varied functions with the external resources at its disposal. In this task of attaining satisfaction the individual is responsive to the attitude of his fellows, covets a feeling of personal value, strives to neutralize any disturbing feeling of personal inferiority."

Society and culture have a profound influence on our concept of normality. In determining what constitutes normal behavior we must consider the standards of thought and conduct which the dominant social group maintains, the expectations of the social group in regard to the individual, and the manner in which the individual modifies his behavior in the light of the standards of the group. In summary, we may say that a normal personality may be measured by the ability of the individual to make desirable adaptations from his own and society's point of view. Conversely, the criterion of an abnormal personality is the inability of the individual to make such adaptations.

PERSONALITY PROBLEMS ARISING FROM PHYSICAL DEFICIENCIES

We have indicated that a personality arises as a result of the interplay of conditions between the individual and his environment. Any condition which sets the individual apart from his environment, such as an extreme difference in physical constitution or appearance, may have a significant effect in the development of a personality which will deviate to a marked degree from others. Such defects as crippling conditions, chronic lowered vitality, glandular imbalance, blindness, and deafness isolate the individual from other persons in his environment.

Physical deviations from the norm profoundly influence the manner in which an individual reacts to his environment and in which persons in his environment react to him.

Physical defects which interfere with the normal sensory and motor capacities of the individual make special demands on his resources. These demands frequently result in strain, fatigue, and discouragement. Even when the individual's resources are equal to the demands the reaction of others to his efforts importantly influences his behavior. When a sensory or motor defect is recognized by others and proper allowance is made in the handicapped person's efforts to perform his tasks, adjustment is considerably aided. Unfortunately, society does not always recognize the existence of physical or sensory defects or always know how to make proper allowances. Irritability, impatience, condescension, and pity are all too apt to characterize normal persons' reactions to recognized sensory or motor defects.

A badly crippled child who becomes the object of pity and maudlin sentiment may develop, despite superficial signs of outward conformity, an intense resentment against his environment which may be expressed in a violent phantasy life. The deaf child who cannot readily communicate with his environment and who does not readily call forth sympathetic responses from other persons may develop marked antisocial tendencies. The large and overweight child whose condition may be a result of thyroid or pituitary disturbance may became the butt of jokes and the cause of much embarrassing comments from his playmates. Withdrawal behavior and indulgence in daydreaming, or marked aggressive behavior may be the outcome. A child with a weak heart who cannot participate fully in the social life which surrounds him may be compelled to live a life which does not include his active environment.

Our discussion can best be objectified by a more detailed consideration of the special factors that determine the development of the personality of blind persons. Because of the absence of vision, stimulation for the blind takes place primarily through the sense of touch. The only objects the blind infant can touch and react to are those which are close to him—the parts of his own body, his bedclothes, people and articles which are near him. Of these, the child's own body is probably the most important source of stimulation. As a result he becomes preoccupied with himself, a preoccupation that never ceases and is more extreme than for normal persons or for other types of physically handicapped persons. To prevent or overcome the blind child's absorption with himself it is necessary to supply him with tactual stimulation from other sources. Unfortunately, because of the element of danger, the blind child cannot readily explore his environment for stimulating objects. These must be *brought to him.* From the very beginning, therefore, the blind child's social world is organized to *center about him.* Generally, this type of organization continues throughout the life of the blind.

During childhood, if the blind child lives at home, social activities continue to center about him. It is much easier for other members of the family group to arrange themselves about the blind child than it is for him to join them. For the most part the family games, parties, and social activities in general are arranged for the convenience of the blind child. He is exempt from most household duties; errands are run for him, he is not expected to run them for others; gifts are bought and brought to him, very rarely does he buy things for others. Because social activities center about the blind child he has a very limited concept of the nature of social relationships. He knows little about how members of his own family act in social situations outside of his home. Even when he participates in extra-family social affairs he continues to be the center of the social group. If the physical arrangement of a room is unfamiliar the blind child does not move about to meet and talk to people. Of necessity he waits for people to come and talk to him.

As the blind child matures he may become aware of social problems which may arise in his family because of him. He probably realizes that he circumscribes family activities. His parents and his brothers and sisters are not free to do as they might wish. Some one member is expected to remain at home with him while others go out. This knowledge may cause the blind person much distress, yet there is little he can do to alleviate the situation. Another important factor tending to make for a peculiar social development in the blind person is the likelihood that members of the family will adopt an habitual attitude to him not adopted toward other members of the group. He is quite likely to be overindulged and spoiled and be relieved of responsibility even in matters he is capable of handling. The physical environment of the blind person tends to be static. It is arranged for his convenience around his special needs. Because the blind person is the center of his social milieu his entire personality development tends to be egocentric.

In this brief sketch of the personality development of a blind individual we may have noted that the sensory limitation tended to make him more dependent on his immediate environment than he otherwise might have been. This dependence was manifest in situations that were intimate and personal, social, and economic. A blind individual, we may generalize, is not as socially competent as one who is sighted. But this generalization need not be restricted to the blind. Any severe sensory or physical deficiency may constitute the basis for a social handicap. Crippled persons and deaf persons seldom are able to live alone. They do not travel as widely as physically normal persons because traveling entails a need to ask questions, with which the deaf have difficulty, and severely crippled persons find moving about somewhat difficult unless they are aided. In the economic sphere, we know that many types of occupation are closed to the deaf and the crippled. A limitation in occupational opportunity tends to result in a limitation of financial independence.

In a recent study, Bradway (2) raised the questions "To what extent are total deafness, total blindness, and severe physical crippling social handicaps, and which of these is the greatest handicap?" The subjects of Bradway's study were made up of three groups. One was composed of 92 pupils ranging in age from five to twenty-one years, deaf since birth or shortly afterwards, who were attending the New Jersey School for the Deaf. A second group consisted of 73 blind pupils ranging in age from five to twenty years, blind since birth or before the age of four years, who were attending the Pennsylvania School for the Instruction of the Blind. The third group was of 7 boys, between seven and twelve years of age, who were at Babbitt Hospital because of various degrees of crippling associated with intercranial damage at birth. The three groups were rather roughly equated for family background and intelligence.

The testing instrument was the Vineland Social-Maturity Scale devised by Dr. Edgar A. Doll. The scale, patterned in principle after the Binet scale for measuring intelligence, consists of a series of statements for various age levels in regard to types of performances which are intended to reflect the degree of social maturation of the individual to whom the statements are applied. The total score is expressed as an age value. A social quotient, similar in principle to an intelligence quotient, is obtained by dividing the social age by the life age and multiplying by 100.

The results of Bradway's study showed that the blind were inferior to the deaf in social competence, and that both the blind and the deaf were inferior to persons not so handicapped.

The average social quotient for the deaf was 80 compared with an average of 62 for the blind. Perhaps a more significant finding than is revealed by a mere statement of social quotient was that ". . . in general neither deafness nor blindness constituted a permanent bar to successful performance on the items, but rather resulted in a delay in successful performance." The older deaf and blind children tested passed the items which the younger children failed. In an item comparison between the deaf and the blind, the deaf were found to be superior to the blind in the majority of items for each category except that of communication. The general conclusion may be drawn that blindness is a greater social handicap than is deafness.

The results of the comparisons of the crippled group with the blind and deaf must be accepted very tentatively because of the small number of crippled children involved in the study. The social quotients of four extremely crippled children were about 30. The remaining three children, less severely crippled, had social quotients of about 70.

In general we may observe that blindness or any other significant physical deviation is likely to result in a limitation of free interaction between the handicapped individual and other persons in his social environment. In the education and training of physically handicapped persons a personality concept must be built up which will make it possible for them to interact freely with physically normal people. While the physically handicapped must view the limitations imposed by their handicaps objectively and realistically, there must be no injury to their self-esteem. This will only be possible if the physically normal persons in the environment of the handicapped react to them understandingly but without maudlin sentiment or morbid curiosity. No person, whether physically normal or handicapped, can develop a socially desirable personality entirely through his own efforts. The training of the handicapped and the education of the members of his environment must take place simultaneously. The handicapped and the normal must learn how to react to one another. Out of this interreaction and learning the personalities of both will evolve.

In the development of the personality of the physically handicapped the forces at play, the mechanisms of adjustment, are essentially the same as for physically normal persons. We will observe later (pp. 26–34) that certain mechanisms, unfortunately not always of a socially desirable nature, are more likely to be used by the handicapped than by the normal. These mechanisms will be considered in the next chapter.

BIBLIOGRAPHY

1. Allport, G. W., *Personality* (Holt, N.Y., 1937).
2. Bradway, L. M., "Social Competence of Exceptional Children—III," *J. Except. Child.*, IV: 3 (Dec., 1937), 64–69.
3. Campbell, C. F., *Human Personality and the Environment* (Macmillan, N.Y., 1934).
4. Eisenson, J., *Psychology of Speech* (Crofts, N.Y., 1938), Ch. XII.
5. Ewen, J. H., "Perseveration in the Insane Epileptics," *J. Ment. Sci.*, LXXVI (1930), 537–40.
6. Haggard, H. W., and C. C. Fry, *Anatomy of Personality* (Harper, N.Y., 1936).
7. Kretschmer, E., *Physique and Character* (Harcourt Brace, N.Y., 1925).
8. Murphy, G., and F. Jensen, *Approaches to Personality* (Coward-McCann, N.Y., 1932).
9. Pinard, J. W., "Tests of Perseveration—II," *Brit. J. Psychol.*, XXIII (1932), 114–26.
10. Shaffer, L. F., *Psychology of Adjustment* (Houghton Mifflin, Boston, 1936).
11. Spearman, C. E., *The Abilities of Man* (Macmillan, N.Y., 1927), Ch. XVII.

12. Stockard, C. R., *The Physical Basis of Personality* (Norton, N.Y., 1931).
13. Thorpe, L. P., *Psychological Foundations of Personality* (McGraw-Hill, N.Y., 1938).
14. Young, K., *Personality and Problems of Adjustment* (Crofts, N.Y., 1940).

CHAPTER II

Mental Hygiene

What Is Mental Hygiene? Mental hygiene may be thought of as a method or approach which aims at the attainment of mental health. A person is mentally healthy if he can adjust himself to his environment so that he establishes and maintains adequate and satisfactory relationships. "He is mentally healthy if he adjusts himself so as to avoid undue conflicts, stresses, and strains, and if he adjusts himself to the world of people, things, and events about him so as to be highly effective both socially and personally, and at the same time to find much satisfaction in life. He achieves the most his abilities allow, secures for himself and society the greatest amount of satisfaction, but with the least strain and friction." (3, p. 495) Mental health is not an absolute state which an individual either reaches or fails to attain. Persons vary in their degree of mental health from time to time. None of us is always completely adjusted to his environment because no environment is completely static. The state of a person's mental health can be measured only by the adequacy of his adjustments to the environment in which he finds himself.

What Are the Aims of a Mental-Hygiene Program? A mental-hygiene program should be preventive and so must be positive in its approach. It should aim to assist the individual to make adequate initial adjustments to his environment rather than to make corrections because of original maladjustments. A mental-hygiene program should aim to prevent the all too common manifestations of maladjustment which include inferiority feelings, defensive mechanisms such as extreme aggression, attention-seeking mechanisms such as the perseveration of infantile behavior, the adoption of habitual negative attitudes, daydreaming, lying, etc. In addition, a mental-hygiene program must aim to prevent the less frequent but more severe forms of maladjustment in the form of definite psychotic (insane) behavior. Though the causes of insanity are not always known, it is generally agreed that some forms of psychoses arise as a result of habitual recourse to inadequate and inappropriate methods of adjusting to the motivating drives of life. A mental-hygiene program, then, must assist each individual in making those adjustments which are adequate and proper for him. The individual's physical condition, his intelligence, his predispositions and traits (so far as they can be determined), as well as the physical and social environment in which he is to adjust, must be considered. To assist an individual in making adjustments, his limitations as well as his special talents must be considered. Physical and mental shortcomings must not be overlooked; we must deal with the individual as we find him, and not as we would like him to be.

The Special Problems of a Mental-Hygiene Program for the Physically Handicapped. A mental-hygiene program for the physically handicapped is not inherently different from that for the physically normal. The physically handicapped are motivated by the same drives and respond to the drives with the same mechanisms used by the physically normal. Some of these mechanisms of adjustment are proper and socially acceptable; others are not. The physically handicapped do not have a monopoly of socially unacceptable mechanisms of adjustment.

However, because adjustments in general tend to be more difficult for the physically handicapped than for the normal, they are more likely to resort to the use of mechanisms which are less desirable than are the normal. The essential difference is not in kind but rather in frequency and in degree of intensity in the use of socially unacceptable mechanisms of adjustment. Before these are considered we will first review briefly the motivating drives of normal human behavior. These drives are no less fundamental for the physically handicapped than for the physically normal.

Fundamental Human Drives.

1. Human beings direct their activities to the satisfaction of biological wants and general physical well-being. When possible, they avoid situations that may result in physical deprivation, including pain, hunger, thwarting of sex demands, etc. Any one of these deprivations, however, may be suffered temporarily for the sake of ultimate satisfaction.

2. Human beings normally behave in ways that will lead them toward a degree of success, mastery, and achievement. The intensity of the degree is largely an individual matter. People try to avoid situations that are likely to result in thwarting, frustration, and disappointment. Occasionally, however, most people are compelled to accept temporary disappointment for a promise of future success or achievement.

3. Most human beings behave in ways that will help them to gain recognition, admiration, respect, and approval. They avoid moves that may result in their being ignored, or looked down upon, or merely tolerated. We recognize, however, that temporary disdain may be suffered by some people for the possibility of ultimate more lasting respect.

4. Human beings generally act in ways which will lead toward their being loved, and the realization of a feeling of being wanted. They tend to avoid the unwanted, belonging-to-

nobody feeling. Most people prefer, for a part of the time at least, to be with other persons rather than to be alone, and to be in the company of familiar persons rather than strange ones. Exceptions, however, are notable and important. The lone aviator flying to distant lands and strange people, the recluse who flees from all human society, are motivated in their actions by other drives which may for them be more fundamental —at least at the moment of the initiation of their activities.

5. Most persons act in ways that will bring about peace of mind, security, and a feeling of release from worry and anxiety. They generally avoid bringing about situations that are likely to result in worry, anxiety, or fear. People who knowingly borrow trouble seldom borrow real ones. Those of us who enjoy listening to the woes of others rarely treat them as seriously as our own.

6. Human beings indicate by their behavior that they seek some adventure, new experiences, and zestful living. They tend to avoid boring or monotonous situations. The amount of adventure, the number of new experiences, sought by a person is necessarily a highly individual matter. Special considerations, economic pressure and social responsibilities, the desire to be with familiar people, frequently come into conflict with our craving for the unusual in life. Too much of the new, however, may be just as assiduously avoided as too much of the old. Completely new situations require adjustments which are difficult and frequently painful. In general individuals tend to seek a life that presents enough novelty of situation to prevent monotony, and yet not so much novelty of situation that living becomes difficult because of the necessity for making continuous adjustment to rapidly and frequently changing situations.

As we have indicated, the drives we have just considered are fundamental to both the normal and the physically handicapped. Of necessity, however, some of these drives cannot be satisfied by the physically handicapped as readily and as easily as they can by physically normal individuals. Some, indeed, may never directly be adequately satisfied. Vicarious adventure trips experienced through reading may have to suffice the blind and the severely crippled individual. Yet, in general, most of these drives can be met and at least partially satisfied.

Mechanisms of Adjustment to the Motivating Drives.

1. Trial Behavior. This is the most fundamental and general method of making adjustments. From early infancy the individual tries out modes of behavior which tend to be reinforced and fixed according to their success in meeting situations. The small child learns through direct experience that crying brings him food even though the child cried originally because he was hungry and not because he knew crying would result ultimately in the satisfaction of his hunger. Thorndike and his associates have demonstrated in many experiments both with animals and human beings that random behavior in no way logically related to a given result may be repeated to bring about a desired result without the individual's being aware of his activity and the associations made. With awareness of the nature of associations and their consequent effects the likelihood for the repetition of an act tends to be increased. Thus, behavior which brings about a desired result, whether it be socially desirable or not, or logically connected with the end result or not, is likely to result in repetition of that behavior. A child faced with a new situation to which he must make some response will attempt to meet it in some way which resulted in a satisfactory solution before. If an old pre-established way fails of success an alternate will be tried. If the alternate is successful it may later be used to meet similar situations. For example, a boy moving into a new neighborhood may try to make friends by asking directly whether he may become a friend of other children in the neighborhood. If he is not immediately accepted he may show off his

athletic skills, or boast about his abilities, or put his toys on review, or perhaps just wait until overtures are made to him. What he attempts will in a large sense be determined by his success in like situations with certain measures used in the past and the progress of results in his present situation.

Direct trial behavior is time-consuming and not always practical when a situation permits of only one opportunity for adjustment. Fortunately, intelligent human beings need not actually try out a method to realize that it will not be adequate and will result in failure. Trial behavior may consist of thinking or reasoning, in which direct motor exploration is replaced by mental explorations. A mode of behavior may be tried out covertly and tentatively. The reasoning individual projects himself and his tentative response in a given "mental" situation before he tries it in an actual situation. If, in the light of the past experience of the individual, a given mode of behavior is considered as likely to meet with success, it will then be tried; if it is deemed likely to be unsuccessful it will be discarded without actually having been tried. In thinking or reasoning the individual is testing behavior in a not actually existent social situation. He anticipates the effects of his covert responses upon others and controls and directs his overt behavior in the light of these effects. A hungry child may feel an urge to steal the cookies and the jam, but a covert preliminary trial of such behavior may cause him to react painfully, and to change and try another mode of response (asking for a slice of bread) which will be ultimately if not immediately satisfying.

2. Sublimation. Most intelligent individuals realize fairly early in their lives that many of their desires and impulses cannot ever be satisfied in their original form. The reasons for such realization are many and varied. Perhaps the original desire was of too primitive a nature and one not normally satisfied in civilized society. Other responses to the desire, more socially

acceptable, may have been made instead. Many desires which do not meet with social disapproval are frequently just out of question in regard to their possible fulfillment. The cardiac boy simply cannot become a football player, though he may become a sports writer or a team manager. Whenever an original response to a desire is replaced by an acquired one which is more possible in the light of the circumstances involved, we have the adjustment mechanism known as sublimation. Many of our life's activities are sublimations; frequently they are made without the individual's being aware of it. It is obvious that the physically handicapped must make many more substitutions than physically normal individuals. The problem of sublimation is increasingly difficult for the physically handicapped because their choice of substitute activities is necessarily limited.

3. Compensation. The use of the mechanism of compensation implies that an individual is possessed of a shortcoming which he is trying to offset by the development of a special ability. It is a balancing of success against failure. The mechanism of compensation * involves the use of substitute activities which afford the individual a pleasure where original activities meant necessary failure. A near-sighted boy who cannot partake in sports may compensate by becoming a bookworm and receiving the reward of good school grades plus the approval of his teachers; the crippled boy may develop an unusual degree of manual skill and so in part make up for the loss of his legs; a dull child may attempt to make up for his school failures by successes in athletics. All of us at some time compensate for our shortcomings. Sometimes we are aware that we are substituting an activity which affords us pleasure and avoiding one

* The Adlerian use of the term compensation differs from our use in that it presupposes the existence of an original weakness which the individual overcomes by developing it into a strength. No substitute response is involved in the Adlerian concept of compensation.

which will result in failure. Many of our compensations, however, have been unconsciously developed and practiced.

Compensation, essentially, is an attempt on the individual's part to build up or maintain his self-esteem. The child with a physical defect who employs compensation as an adjustment mechanism indicates by his behavior that he is not interested in maudlin sympathy or condescending pity. Often the physically defective individual resorts to compensation because society expects him to do something to "atone" for his deficiency. If the handicapped person were not impressed with the need for such "atonement," if he were not made to feel that he must do something to "make up" for his defect, the problem of adjustment would be considerably easier. The physically normal as well as the handicapped should be made to realize that we do what we can, according to our pattern of assets and liabilities. Comparisons between physically atypical and normal individuals are as annoying and odious as comparisons between normal and superior individuals. The crippled boy should feel no more need to compensate for not being able to high-jump than the physically normal boy for not being able to high-jump six feet or more.

4. Escape Reactions. One way of not having to face the problem of adjusting to difficult situations is to avoid or escape them. This may be done either by living a life of daydreaming and phantasy in which we find no difficult problems in life by the simple device of not entertaining them, or by living wholly in terms of a past life which we had found to be easier, or by living a future anticipated life which is ever moved forward so that the present is not permitted to catch up with it. Any method of gaining satisfaction in life by withdrawing from reality and entering into a nonexistent world is indicative of a desire to escape. Such a desire is in itself quite normal, and the mechanism of escape into reverie or Never-Never Lands is not

to be considered harmful if the individual maintains an ability to distinguish between the real and the unreal, and does not too often allow the easy unreal world to replace the harder and more arduous real world.

The tendency to substitute daydreaming and wishful thinking for overt activity is considered symptomatic of the withdrawn personality commonly referred to as the introvert. In extreme cases of introversion all contact with the social environment may be broken. The individual will regularly substitute phantasies or daydreams for direct social contact. A barrier will be set up which not only prevents the introvertive individual from making contacts with his environment but may also very effectively nullify members of the environment or prevent them from making contacts with him. The catatonic stage of schizophrenia, characterized by complete inactivity and speechlessness, is an extreme form of introversion.

Though withdrawn behavior is considered by many psychologists as an inborn tendency, it is undoubtedly true that such behavior may be forced upon an individual. If the environmental demands upon a person become excessive, if he is too frequently expected to attempt acts which are either distasteful or are likely to result in failure, introvertive behavior may be the result. A hard-of-hearing child whose deficiency is not appreciated by himself or others and who therefore finds himself failing in school and in making friends, may withdraw into himself and live in a world of his own which makes fewer demands and which demands only what he can successfully perform.

Regressive behavior is another form of escape reaction. As children we met with fewer demands than we do as adults. The tendency of an individual to revert to childish forms of behavior as a response to situations he meets as an adult is symptomatic of regression. In effect it is a substitution of the past for the present, a past that was kind because it demanded only what the individual could do for a present that may make demands which are for some reason not in keeping with the individual's likes or abilities. The adult person who indulges in a fit of hysterics or who throws a temper tantrum to gain an end is exhibiting a form of behavior which was probably successful when he was a child. Pouting, whining, resorting to baby talk, and destruction of objects which annoy us are examples of regressive behavior.

Regression denotes defeat. It indicates that the individual is unequal to the demands of his environment and is unwilling to accept failure or to accept his inequality objectively. An environment whose demands equaled the individual's ability to meet demands would remove the necessity for regressive behavior. A child with weak physique, a cardiac for example, may indulge in regression because he cannot take part in physical activities and compete with other children of his age. The recognition and appreciation of such inability by the child and by the persons in his environment and the presentation of opportunities to perform in games as a scorekeeper or team manager would give the physically weak child a socially approved behavior outlet and would go far in preventing recourse to regression.

5. Identification. Whenever an individual adopts the mannerisms and habits of another person or community of people we have an example of the mechanism of identification. An individual may also identify himself with spiritual movements, business organizations, or special types of social activities. In the process of identification he consciously or unconsciously assumes the attitudes and feelings, the customs and mores, of the individual, group, or movement concerned. The earliest form of identification is that of a child with a parent, brother, or sister. Later the child may come to identify himself with a

friend, teacher, or well-known person. Adolescent girls frequently identify themselves with moving-picture actresses whose behavior and speech mannerisms they attempt to imitate. Boys are likely to identify themselves with baseball or football heroes, or the currently famous aviator.

The danger of this frequently used and for the most part normal mechanism of behavior is that the individual may substitute the activity of the person with whom he has identified himself for his own direct activity. A physically defective child may become attached to and identify himself with a physically normal or superior child. The satisfaction he has learned to derive from vicarious accomplishments may be sufficient to relieve him of the need to try to do things for himself.

6. Projection. A mechanism allied in a negative way to identification is projection. It consists of attributing to others thoughts, feelings, and attitudes which are our own, but which we may refuse to recognize as belonging to us. Projection is a commonplace of behavior. The child who couldn't do his homework because his pen would not write properly for him, the college student who is flunked by the instructor because the instructor did not like him, are evidencing the mechanism of projection. An extreme example of projection on the pathological level is exhibited by the paranoiac. His delusions of persecution most likely arise out of his own abnormal desires to harass and inflict pain upon others. Thus also a blind or deaf person may decide that the members of his environment are talking about him and are feeling annoyed with him. He may develop an ardent dislike for certain people because he is convinced or pretends to be convinced that they do not like him. Projection as a mechanism is frequently resorted to by people who are insecure, who therefore attribute to others traits, attitudes, and wishes which they possess and feelings which they experience but to which they are, because of social pressures,

unwilling to admit. Projection is essentially a method of adjustment which consists of blaming others for our own shortcomings.

7. Rationalization. When we present socially acceptable and therefore good reasons in place of the real reasons to explain our behavior we are adjusting by means of the mechanism called rationalization. Frequently we are not aware that we are rationalizing because the real reasons motivating our behavior may be unconsciously hidden or repressed. Occasionally the real reasons for our behavior are on the margin of our consciousness but in presenting the good reasons for our acts we partly succeed in deceiving ourselves if we do not wholly succeed in deceiving others for whom the explanation was supposedly intended. The need we feel to select and present socially acceptable reasons to explain our conduct indicates that we are not really satisfied with our behavior and that, unconsciously at least, we suspect that the adjustment we are making is not adequate.

The rationalizing mechanism is frequently developed in children because adults in the environment insist on intellectual explanations for emotionally motivated behavior. The girl who breaks a dish because she rebels against the idea of washing dishes when she might be doing something else more pleasant learns that she cannot have her true reason accepted. She therefore presents a more acceptable reason—the water was too hot and she burned her hand. The child with poor vision who does poorly in his school work will insist that other children distract him when he tries to study. If children could have their real reasons accepted there would be little need to invent good reasons. If environmental demands on an individual were not to exceed his physical and mental capacities, excuses for limitations would not have to be found.

8. Repression. An adjustment mechanism much emphasized

by psychoanalysts of the Freudian school is repression, which may be defined as complete unconscious inhibition of unpleasant memories. The person who is repressing is not consciously aware that he is trying to forget what would be painful to remember. Many of us react unpleasantly to people we have never seen before and to places we have never before visited. The Freudian explanation for our unpleasant reactions is that some element or feature in the person or place recalls to our unconscious mind a past experience, possibly long forgotten to our conscious minds, which we found undesirable. The individual may somehow resemble a person who once punished us for a misdeed of which we were or should have been ashamed. The exact nature of our misdeed may have been forgotten, but the unpleasantness associated with it is still unconsciously remembered. A place we dislike may resemble the scene of a misdeed; perhaps we were frightened, or felt that we should have been punished for visiting the place.

Repressed memories may account for many peculiarities of our behavior. In part it undoubtedly explains our tendency to rationalize our activities. We take a long and indirect way home and so go out of our way to avoid passing a certain street, or meeting a person, but we explain the situation to ourselves and to others by saying that we need fresh air and exercise. An adult may refuse to go swimming and explain his refusal by insisting that he is susceptible to colds whereas the basic and perhaps forgotten cause for his refusal is that he is afraid of water because, as a small child, he was almost drowned. Fear is the basic reason, but one he is not willing to acknowledge; susceptibility to catching colds is a good reason and one that he need not be ashamed to admit. Many hard-of-hearing children, and their parents as well, are unwilling to admit to a hearing incapacity because of a pervading feeling of shame associated with the deficiency. They may shun social contacts to avoid facing the difficulties of social situations, but explain their actions on other grounds. They, and their parents for them, may decide that the neighborhood children are too dull, or too rough, or otherwise undesirable as playmates.

Memory distortion (essentially repression is just that) may be avoided if unpleasant occurrences are faced objectively. If the basic causes of fears and shames are understood there will be little need for either conscious or unconscious memory distortions.

9. Fears and Phobias. A phobia may be defined as a fear reaction to a situation which, normally, should be responded to without fear. A given act of behavior cannot be characterized as a phobia unless the nature of the reaction indicates that it is inappropriate and inadequate for adjusting the individual to the situation. The child who refuses to cross the street alone because he has been admonished by his parents not to do so is behaving appropriately and adequately. The child who crosses the street alone, but rushes across as if terrified, is exhibiting fear. The child who is permitted to cross the street alone, but refuses, and trembles at the very suggestion of it, is exhibiting a phobia. His reaction is no longer appropriate for the situation.

Phobias are actually learned reactions to situations or types of situations. At one time in the history of the individual he may have had due cause for responding with fear. The original cause, the particular set of circumstances which brought about the fear response may have been forgotten, but the fear remains. Thus, in the case of the child who refuses to cross the street, there may actually have been danger of an accident. Perhaps the child was run down by a moving car. By his refusal to cross the street the child avoids meeting a situation that once was extremely unpleasant. Unfortunately, the unpleasant reaction continues. Many adults exhibit fears which had their foundation in early childhood. There are grownups who refuse to ride in subways, some refuse to look out of windows, others will not ride up in elevators, and still others will refuse to walk up or down flights of stairs. In some cases fears are learned through vicarious experiences or by indirect suggestion. Some children learn to be afraid of the dark because other members of the family exhibit fears of the dark and talk about such fears. A youngster who is praised for his courage for entering a dark room may wonder at the cause for such praise, and after a time decide that perhaps such courage is foolhardy.

Occasionally, what one actually fears is not the situation which calls forth the fear response but something else for which the situation stands and has become a symbol. A child who is afraid of the sound of rushing water and so refuses to enter a bathroom alone, may actually, though unconsciously, be associating the sound of rushing water with the roar of the ocean. Perhaps the child was lost at the beach and is reacting to the water in the bathroom in terms of the original fear of being lost at the seashore.

Until some attempt is made to meet the situation which brings forth the fear response, phobias are likely to persist. An analysis of the irrationality of fear may help, but analysis alone is not enough. Most adults will admit that they are unwise in their phobias, and can present no good reason for indulging in them. But unless the analysis is accompanied by an attempt to meet the situation, and unless the attempt meets with success, the phobia will remain. Where phobias are deep seated and have their origin in early childhood, specialized techniques for their removal calling for a psychologist or psychiatrist may be necessary.

10. Compulsion Neurosis. A compulsion neurosis manifests itself in an obsessive desire or impulse to perform a specific act. Most persons are prone to compulsive acts of a sort at one time or another. Some children make it a point to step on every crack

of a sidewalk while walking; others may make it a point to avoid stepping on a crack. Some college students insist on wearing a tie of a given color when taking an examination; others insist that they can use only one pen, or must have a special kind of blotter. Compulsive and seemingly trivial and purposeless acts of this sort become significant when the inhibition of their performance leaves the individual uncomfortable; when the individual dreads the possibilities of failing to execute the act, the compulsion becomes serious.

Determinants of a Choice of Adjustment Mechanisms. We trust that the reader has not formed the impression that an individual consciously and habitually chooses one mechanism in making adjustments to his environment. Initially, the choice of mechanism may be entirely a chance affair. The cardiac college student who becomes a sports writer for his school newspaper probably did not deliberately decide that because he could not participate actively in sports, writing would constitute an excellent outlet for his interests and limited energies. The greater likelihood is that circumstances, consisting of time on his hands and some writing ability, caused him to find himself on his school's newspaper staff, and an interest in athletics, or perhaps an arbitrary editor's assignment, started him writing about athletics. Similarly, another student who perhaps identifies himself with the football team's leading ground-gainer, did not make up his mind that such identification would be gratifying and an excellent substitute for active participation. Persons tend to drift into the use of an adjustment mechanism for meeting a given situation. Once an individual has drifted into the use of a mechanism for meeting a given situation, subsequent situations similar in type may result in the use of the same adjustment mechanism. Thus, if rationalization, projection, identification, daydreaming, etc., has each been a successful if not entirely a socially desirable mechanism of adjustment on occasion, each will tend to be used again when the same or a similar occasion arises.

To some extent the personality traits of an individual will predetermine the choice of an adjustment mechanism. Thus, a strongly introvertive person will tend to adjust to many different situations by withdrawing and resorting to daydreams. On the other hand, a markedly extrovertive individual is likely to be aggressive and seek to overcome all difficulties actively, even when direct action is not immediately required.

When Does a Mechanism of Adjustment Become Undesirable? At first blush it may seem that some mechanisms are more desirable than others; more careful consideration will show that only a fairly complete knowledge of a given situation and the individual involved can really indicate the relative adequacy or inadequacy of a given adjustment mechanism. Though, for example, identification may seem a more desirable and adequate means of adjustment than daydreaming, a child who identifies himself so completely with the country's current public enemy number one that he makes his companions pay him tribute is really in greater need of psychiatric attention than the child who resorts to daydreaming to imagine himself as potent a person as he would like to be.

To evaluate properly the various mechanisms of adjustment in order of their desirability one must not only know the given situation but also the frequency with which the mechanism has been used and its likely effect upon the individual personality and the environment. To grade or classify mechanisms in a social vacuum may be of interest but it will not be of any particular value. A mechanism of adjustment becomes undesirable when the situation is not solved by its use. The mechanism becomes actually harmful when its use makes it increasingly difficult for a more appropriate and more adequate mechanism to be tried.

BIBLIOGRAPHY

1. Anderson, H., "Conflicts in Personality Development," *Ment. Hyg.*, XXII (1936), 605–13.
2. Barraclough, W., "Mental Reactions of Normal Children to Physical Illness," *Am. J. Psychiat.*, XCIII (1937), 865–77.
3. Brooks, F. D., *Child Psychology* (Houghton Mifflin, Boston, 1937).
4. Cattell, R., *Crooked Personalities in Childhood and After* (Appleton-Century, N.Y., 1938).
5. Crothers, B., *A Pediatrician in Search of Mental Hygiene* (Commonwealth Fund, N.Y., 1937).
6. Groves, E. R., and P. Blanchard, *Introduction to Mental Hygiene* (Holt, N.Y., 1930).
7. Jordan, P., "The Role of the Pediatrician in Mental Hygiene," *J. Pediat.* (July, 1939), 121–9.
8. Lawton, G., "Fears: Their Cause and Prevention," *Child Develop.* (June, 1938), 151–9.
9. Morgan, J., *The Psychology of the Unadjusted School Child* (Macmillan, N.Y., 1937).
10. Rivlin, H., *Educating for Adjustment* (Appleton-Century, N.Y. and London, 1936).
11. Symonds, P., *Mental Hygiene of the School Child* (Macmillan, N.Y., 1935).
12. Wallin, J. E., *Personality Maladjustment and Mental Hygiene* (McGraw-Hill, N.Y., 1935).
13. Wile, I. S., "Integration of the Child: The Goal of the Educational Program," *Ment. Hyg.*, XXII (1936), 249–61.

CHAPTER III

The Internal Mechanisms of Behavior

THE NERVOUS SYSTEM

Earlier in this text, we considered the social drives and environmental forces which to a large extent were responsible for the motivation of human behavior. Now we will consider another form of adaptation which takes place within the living organism and without which no form of external or environmental adjustments could be possible. The organization and correlation of the many different parts of the body are carried on by two great integrating mechanisms, namely, the endocrine and nervous systems. In this chapter we shall consider the nature of these mechanisms, and the effects of deficiencies of these systems on the behavior of the individual.

GENERAL TOPOGRAPHY OF THE NERVOUS SYSTEM

The principal divisions of the nervous system are: (1) the central nervous system, (2) the cerebrospinal nervous system, and (3) the autonomic nervous system. These divisions, however, are not to be considered independent in their functionings. A true understanding of any one division requires a knowledge of the activities of the others. In our presentation we wish to emphasize functional relationships and so shall consider the cerebrospinal nerves together with the central nervous system.

The Central Nervous System. This division of the nervous system comprises the brain, the spinal cord, and the cerebrospinal nerves. The brain is enclosed within three layers of membranes called meninges and is protected by the bony structure of the skull. The spinal cord extends down the back. Like the brain, it is covered by meninges and is protected by a structure of bony arches which are part of the spinal column. The series of cerebrospinal nerves emerge from the brain and spinal cord and extend to all parts of the body, but principally to the skin and voluntary muscles. Figure 1 is a diagrammatic presentation of the central nervous system as a whole.

The most important functional divisions of the brain are the cerebrum, the cerebellum, and the brain stem. The *cerebrum* is the anterior and largest part of the brain and may be said to "top off" the entire nervous system (see Fig. 1). It is divided into right and left hemispheres by a deep longitudinal fissure. Folds (sulci) and grooves (gyri) divide the cerebrum into areas which can be easily recognized. The *cerebellum* (small brain) lies below and is partly covered over by the cerebrum. The cerebrum and the cerebellum are both connected with the brain stem, the posterior part of which consists of a bulblike or cone-shaped mass called the *medulla oblongata* or the "bulb." The medulla is continuous with the spinal cord and extends into it through an opening (Foramen Magnum) in the base of the skull. The medulla and spinal cord should not, however, be thought of as one structure. Structurally and functionally there are important differences.

The cerebrospinal nerves extend from either the brain or the spinal cord. Twelve pairs of irregularly placed cranial nerves arise from the brain, mostly from the medulla. Except for the tenth, or vagus nerve, which extends down the neck and into the chest and abdomen, the cranial nerves are distributed over

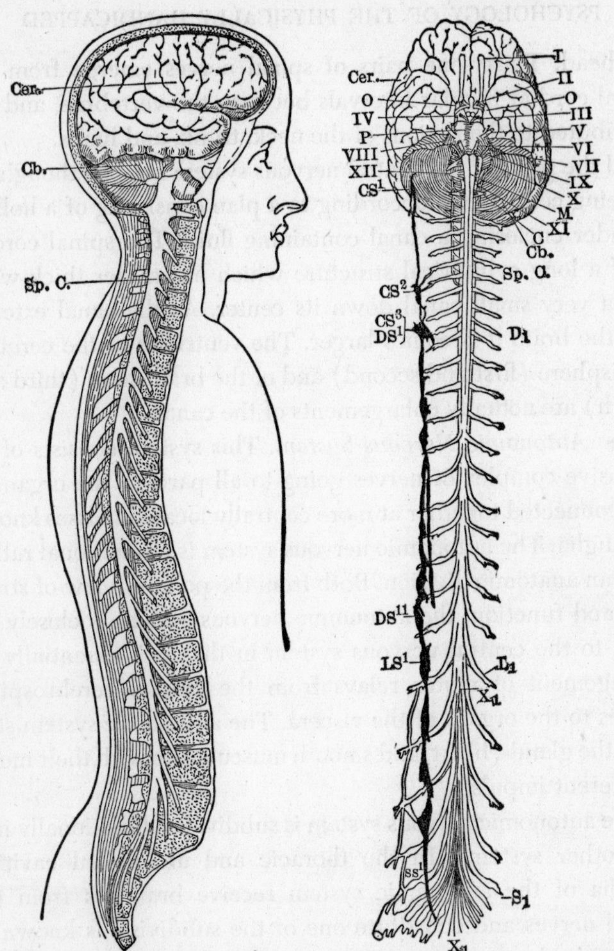

FIG. 1. THE CENTRAL NERVOUS SYSTEM AS A WHOLE

Left: seen from side in position in the vertebral column. Right: exposed and seen from front. *Cer,* cerebrum; *Cb,* cerebellum; *M,* medulla; *Sp. C,* spinal cord. The 12 cranial nerves designated by Roman numerals. Spinal nerves designated in part: *C,* first of the 8 cervical; D_1, first of the 12 thoracic; L_1, first of the 5 lumbar; S_1, first of the 5 sacral; X_1 (lower figure), the coccygeal. Ganglia and connections of autonomic division shown in solid black; *CS*¹, *CS*², *CS*³, superior, middle, inferior cervical ganglia; *DS*¹–*DS*¹¹, thoracic ganglia; *LS*¹, first lumbar ganglion; *SS*¹, sacral ganglion. (From J. F. Dashiell's *Fundamentals of Objective Psychology,* Houghton Mifflin Company.)

the head. Thirty-one pairs of spinal nerves emerge from the spinal cord at regular intervals between the vertebrae, and are distributed to the regions of the neck, trunk, and limbs.

All the parts of the central nervous system may be thought of as being constructed according to a plan consisting of a hollow cylinder enclosing a canal containing fluid. The spinal cord is itself a long cylindrical structure which has rather thick walls and a very small canal down its center. As the canal extends into the brain it becomes larger. The ventricles of the cerebral hemisphere (first and second) and of the brain stem (third and fourth) are actually enlargements of the canal.

The Autonomic Nervous System. This system consists of an extensive complex of nerves going to all parts of the organism and connected together at more centrally located masses known as ganglia. The autonomic nervous system is a functional rather than an anatomic division. Both from the point of view of structure and function, the autonomic nervous system is closely related to the central nervous system in that it is essentially an arrangement of motor relays from the cranial cerebrospinal nerves to the organs of the viscera. The autonomic system supplies the glands, heart, and smooth musculature with their motor or efferent impulses.

The autonomic nervous system is subdivided functionally into two other systems. In the thoracic and abdominal cavities, ganglia of the autonomic system receive branches from the spinal nerves and constitute one of the subdivisions known as the *sympathetic system.* The second subdivision, known as the *parasympathetic system* consists of those nerves which are connected with the tenth cranial nerve and with a few posterior spinal nerves. Both of these subdivisions control internal organs and structures which are not under voluntary control. The sympathetic and parasympathetic systems are generally opposed to one another in their activities in regard to any given set of organs. One system stimulates or accelerates activity; the other retards or inhibits the activity. For example, the sympathetic accelerates heart rate, decreases the flow of digestive juices, and inhibits movements of the digestive tract. The parasympathetic system, on the other hand, retards the heart rate, increases the flow of digestive juices, and increases the movements of the digestive tract.

ANATOMY OF THE NERVOUS SYSTEM

The Neuron. We shall begin our study of the physiology of the nervous mechanism with a study of the neuron, the basic structural unit of the entire nervous system. All nervous tissue is composed of specialized cells called neurons which, though varying greatly in size and shape, have common features and are built on a common plan. Typically, a neuron consists of a cell body, composed of a nucleus surrounded by a mass of cytoplasm, and branches of microscopic fineness called axons and dendrites. The branches may vary considerably in length; the axons of the peripheral nerves sometimes extend for several feet. Usually a neuron has but one axon. Dendrites are shorter and generally are more numerous than axons. Axons tend to run in bundles. In the periphery of the body these bundles constitute a *nerve;* in the central nervous system they constitute *tracts.*

The axon of a neuron or its branches may break up into an end brush, the parts of which dovetail and appear to be in contact with the dendrites of another neuron, or may make direct contact with the cell body of another neuron. The place of junction at which the impulse passes from axon to dendrite or cell body is called the *synapse.* A diagrammatic representation of a "typical" neuron is presented in Figure 2.

Nerve Fibers. Single axons are known as *nerve fibers.* Many axons are ensheathed by a fatty, glistening substance called myelin, which appears to serve as an insulating material for the

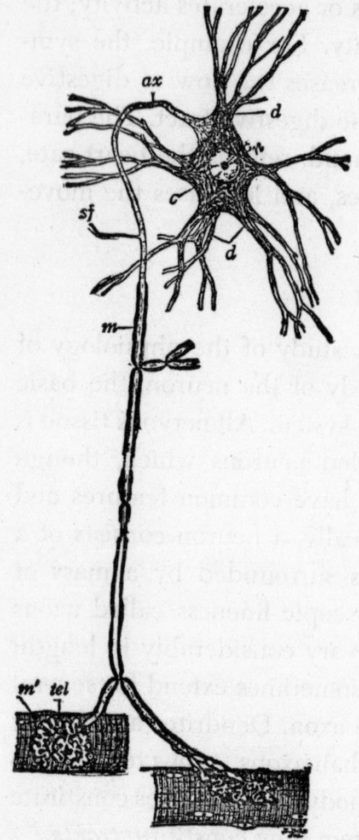

FIG. 2. PRIMARY MOTOR NEURON (DIAGRAMMATIC)

ax, axon; *c,* cytoplasm; *d,* dendrites; *m,* myelin sheath; *m',* striated muscles; *n,* nucleus; *sf,* collateral; *tel,* motor end plate (Barker, Bailey). (From Bailey's *Histology,* The Williams and Wilkins Company.)

fibers much as rubber covering does for electric wires. Axons which are ensheathed by myelin are known as *myelinated* or *medullated* fibers. These are to be found in the tracts of the central nervous system, in the peripheral nerves, and in the white matter of the brain.

The peripheral nerves, in addition to myelin, are covered by a thin outer sheath of structureless membrane called *neurilemma.* Like myelin, neurilemma is believed to be a protecting membrane. Whether neurilemma has any other function in the *normal* life of nerve fibers is not known. It is known, however, that the nuclei of the neurilemma play a very important part in the degeneration and the subsequent regeneration of injured nerve fibers and in the consequent restoration of normal function. Nerve fibers which do not contain neurilemma fail to regenerate once they have been injured by disease or accident. Fibers containing neurilemma, however, do regenerate and so are restored to normal function. Thus, if the nerve fibers of the spinal cord degenerate, as in poliomyelitis, regeneration does not take place, because the fibers of the central nervous system are devoid of neurilemma. On the other hand, in the event of injury to the fibers of the femoral nerve, which innervate the lower limb, regeneration is likely to take place because these peripheral nerve fibers contain neurilemma.

INTERCONNECTIONS OF NEURONS

Types of Neurons. There are three types of neurons classified according to structure and function (Fig. 3). *Afferent* or *sensory* neurons conduct impulses *toward* the central nervous system. An afferent fiber of a peripheral nerve may end nakedly, as in the skin, or may make contact with a special sense organ such as the ear. From either the skin or the special sense organ the afferent neuron receives the stimulation and conducts it centrally. Another class of neuron is *efferent* or *motor* in character. The processes of efferent neurons conduct impulses outward from the central nervous system. Nerve fibers of this class make direct contact with muscles or glands, which they stimulate into activity. Motor neurons are subdivided into two groups according to function. *Lower motor neurons* carry impulses directly to the effector organ; *upper motor neurons* carry the motor impulse to lower motor neurons. A third main class of neurons consists of the *internuncials* or *connectors.* Nerve fibers of this group relay the impulses received by the sensory neurons to the motor neurons or to other internuncial neurons. Without

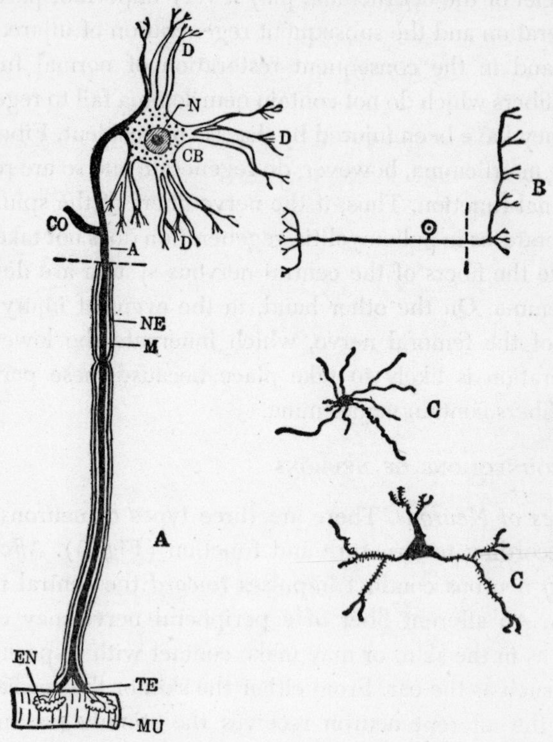

FIG. 3. TYPES OF NERVE FIBERS

A, typical efferent (motor) neuron; B, typical afferent (sensory) neuron, drawing more simplified than A; C, typical central (connecting) neurons, drawing more simplified than A.

Key: D, dendrites; *N,* nucleus; *CB,* central body; *CO,* collateral; *A,* axon; *NE,* neurilemma sheath; *M,* myelin; *EN,* motor end plate; *TE,* terminal arborization or end brush; *MU,* muscle. (Reprinted by permission from *Introduction to Psychology,* by Boring, Langfeld, and Weld, published by John Wiley & Sons, Inc.)

them the innumerable connections between the afferent and efferent neurons could not be made.

Reflex Arcs. Earlier in our discussion we characterized the neuron as the basic structural unit of the nervous system. The reflex arc may now be characterized as the basic *functional* unit. The simplest possible reflex arc would consist of two nerve cells,

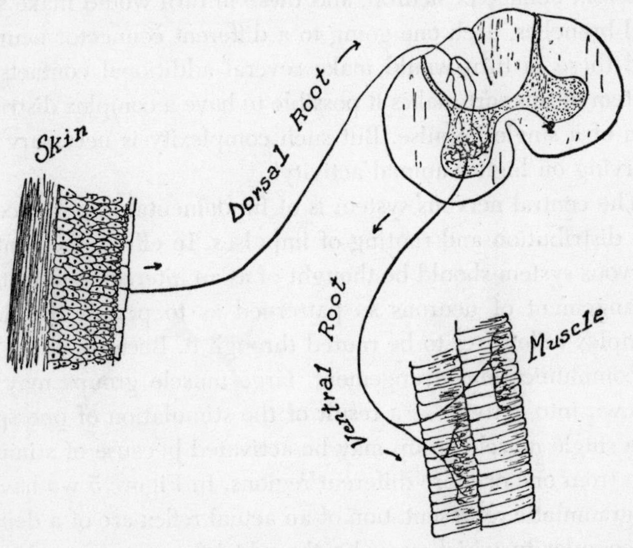

FIG. 4. DIAGRAMMATIC REPRESENTATION OF A SIMPLE SPINAL REFLEX ARC

(After Herrick's *Introduction to Neurology.* Drawn by Lee Eisenson.)

one sensory and one motor. In a two-celled reflex arc the nerve impulse would travel from the receptor end of a sensory fiber to a nerve center. There the nerve impulse would be transmitted by way of a synapse directly to a motor fiber which would carry the impulse to, and stimulate, some muscle or gland into activity. Such a reflex arc is diagrammatically represented in Figure 4. In higher animals, and especially in the human organism, it is very unlikely that a two-celled reflex arc ever exists. The greater likelihood is that an incoming impulse would pass from the sensory fiber to an internuncial or connector fiber which would distribute the impulse to other connector or to motor neurons. Furthermore, it is probable that the single sensory fiber would have several branches, each one going to a different connector neuron, and these in turn would make several branches, each one going to a different connector neuron, and these in turn would make several additional contacts. A system of this sort makes it possible to have a complex distribution of a single impulse. But such complexity is necessary for carrying on higher animal activity!

The central nervous system is of fundamental importance in the distribution and routing of impulses. In effect, the central nervous system should be thought of as an intercommunicating arrangement of neurons so patterned as to permit the most complex reflex arcs to be routed through it. Because of the intercommunicating arrangement, large muscle groups may be thrown into activity as a result of the stimulation of one spot, or a single muscle group may be activated because of stimulation from one or more different regions. In Figure 5 we have a diagrammatic representation of an actual reflex arc of a degree of complexity which may be thought of as more nearly approaching the characteristic reflex in a higher animal.

The Spinal Cord and its Tracts. An examination of a cross section of the spinal cord (see Fig. 6) reveals that it is composed of white and gray tissue. The region around the central canal of the cord is grayish in color; the periphery is a glistening white. The bulk of the gray matter is composed of cell bodies of the neurons and their dendrites. Synapses between axons and dendrites are made in the gray matter. The white matter consists mainly of axons with their myelin sheaths. It is the myelin which imparts the characteristic white color.

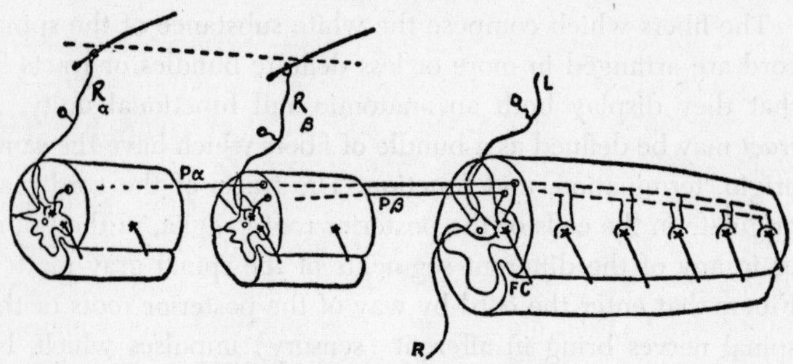

FIG. 5. DIAGRAM OF THE SPINAL ARCS INVOLVED IN SCRATCH REFLEX (DOG)

L, receptive or afferent nerve-path from the left foot; R, receptive nerve-path from the opposite foot; R^{α}, R^{β}, receptive nerve-paths from hairs in the dorsal skin of the left side; FC, the final common path, in this case the motor neuron to a flexor muscle of the hips; P^{α}, P^{β}, proprio-spinal neurons. (From C. S. Sherrington's *The Integrative Action of the Nervous System*, Yale University Press.)

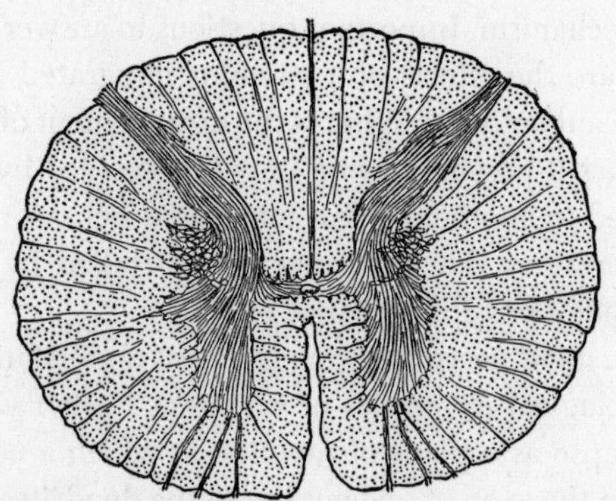

FIG. 6. CROSS SECTION OF SPINAL CORD

(From Gray and Wise, *The Bases of Speech*. Reproduced by permission of Harper & Brothers, the publishers.)

The fibers which compose the white substance of the spinal cord are arranged in more or less definite bundles or tracts so that they display both an anatomic and functional unity. A *tract* may be defined as a bundle of fibers which have the same origin, termination, and function. The tracts of the cord may originate in the cells of the posterior root ganglia, in the brain, or in any of the different segments of the spinal gray matter. Fibers that enter the cord by way of the posterior roots of the spinal nerves bring in afferent (sensory) impulses which, by definite tracts, may ultimately be relayed upward to some portion of the brain. On the other hand, efferent (motor) impulses may be conducted downward into the cord and find their outlets at one of the anterior roots of the spinal nerves. Tracts are characterized as ascending or descending according to the direction of their impulse. Later in this chapter we will consider some of the more important of these nerve pathways.

The Nature of the Synapse. In our discussion thus far we have tried to create an impression of the intricacy and complexity of the billions of neurons which make up the human nervous mechanism. Important questions to answer at this point are: How are the effects of a stimulus integrated into a useful and significant activity? What is the arrangement of the neurons which makes it possible for an impulse received by one neuron to be passed to another so that integrated behavior may result? What determines the particular course taken by an impulse from the many possibilities that exist?

To understand nervous action we must understand the nature and physiological properties of synapses. Earlier we characterized a synapse as a place of junction at which a nerve impulse passes from the axon of one neuron to the dendrites or cell body of another. One of the important physiological properties of the synapse is that it is polarized, that is, it will conduct an impulse *only in one direction,* from axon to dendrite. A second important property of synapses is that they have varied resistances. Thus, there is a path of least resistance through the potential synapses for each afferent neuron. This path would constitute the reflex aroused by a minimal stimulation, and would bring about a limited degree of response. A more vigorous stimulation, however, may make it possible for the stimulus to spread to additional neurons and so bring about a greater response. For example, a stimulus constituting a slight scratching of a finger may result in a mere withdrawal of the hand. A sudden, sharp cut, however, may cause the individual to jump away vigorously from the source of irritation. Once an impulse has succeeded in passing along a given pathway it reduces the resistances of the synapses along the pathway and it becomes easier for an impulse to be routed through it at a future time. The formation of neuron pathways or *neurograms* is the basic process in the training of the neuron system and thus of all learned behavior.

CO-ORDINATING CENTERS

Earlier in our discussion we learned that the basic reflex pattern of the central nervous system is complex to a degree which almost defies comprehension. Yet, the interconnections of neurons in reflex patterns are more or less direct, involving the lower motor neurons which directly innervate the reacting system. Superimposed upon the lower centers are higher centers of various degrees which are found in the brain. Those higher centers have as their function the bringing together of stimuli from all parts of the body in order to permit them to be organized into complex patterns which can then be sent to lower motor centers for proper distribution to the muscles, glands, etc., of the organism. The brain centers constitute an intricate hierarchy of control superimposed upon control. An illustration of activity on the levels of behavior may help to clarify the concept of hierarchy of control. A small object approaching the eye may evoke the relatively simple and localized reflex of winking. Such an act involves the lower neurons only. Let us suppose, however, that the approaching object is a ball and a cry of "Catch it" accompanies the ball in its flight. Blinking would hardly constitute an intelligent response. In such a case the visual and auditory stimuli which pass to higher centers in the brain would be integrated into a more complex and more appropriate response. An attempt would be made to catch the ball! In the discussion of the co-ordinating centers which follows we shall not attempt to present a detailed and minute analysis of the interconnections of these centers. We shall confine ourselves, rather, to a brief consideration of the physiological aspects of some of the most important centers which coordinate and control higher human behavior.

The Medulla Oblongata. The medulla, or bulb, we recall, is the first part of the central nervous system above the spinal cord. The medulla is the site of centers which are involved in the maintenance of vital functions. Through the respiratory center of the medulla rhythmic stimuli are sent out which regulate the breathing movements and modify the respiratory rate according to the needs of the organism. Afferent and efferent fibers from the heart, alimentary canal, lungs, pharynx, and tongue enter into and emerge from the medulla.

Because centers which control life-maintaining functions are localized in the medulla, lesions in this region are extremely serious. Injuries from a penetrating wound or a fracture dislocation involving a certain area are likely to result in death because of respiratory paralysis. An excellent example of the effects of nonfatal lesions of the medulla is presented in the fairly common disease called bulbar paralysis (polioencephalitis). The symptoms of this disease include disturbed articulation and voice production, difficulty in swallowing, weak and labored respiration, and rapid, weak, and irregular pulse. As the disease progresses there is likely to be a wasting of the affected muscles. Ordinarily, the trunk and limbs are not involved. However, if the underlying pathological process involves the pyramidal tracts which consist of motor fibers that originate in the motor area of the cerebral cortex and descend to the medulla, paralysis of the trunk and limbs will follow.

The Thalamus and Striate Bodies. Lying in the center of the cranium and surrounded by the mass of tissue which comprises the cerebrum are the thalamus and striate bodies. All nervous impulses from the lower centers which eventually reach the cortex pass into these regions and are here integrated. Clinical evidence seems to indicate that the integrations in the thalamic region are on a lower psychic level of behavior. In cases where the connections between the thalamus and cortex have been destroyed so that cortical control is lost, the behavior of the individual becomes characteristically violent and unrestrained. Emotional behavior such as crying, laughing, sneering, love, and hate are basically thalamic.

Although the function of the striate bodies (*corpus striatum*) is not entirely clear, it seems probable that they play an important part in regulating the posture and muscular movements of the body. Diseases of the corpus striatum such as *paralysis agitans* result in body rigidity and involuntary movement (tremor). The muscular disturbances are characterized by weakness, a limitation of movement, and an inability to maintain muscular contraction. Because the muscles which control laryngeal movements are involved, the voice becomes flat and is produced with insufficient variation of pitch and intensity.

The Hypothalamus. This region is situated directly beneath the thalamus. Here are located the centers for the control of the visceral organs which are involved in emotional responses. Hypothalamic control over the visceral organs in emotional responses is indirect, and is brought about through nerve fibers which interconnect the central nervous system with the parasympathetic division of the autonomic nervous system. In the emotion of anger, for example, the overt response of sneering is directly a result of the impulses which come from the thalamus and striate bodies. The covert responses, changes in the heart rate and blood pressure, are effected by the activities of the hypothalamic centers acting through the autonomic nervous system.

The Cerebellum. Morphologically, the cerebellum, like the cerebrum, is different from the other parts of the nervous system which we have thus far considered. In the cerebellum and cerebrum we find a reversal of the usual order in the neuron system for in these brain structures we observe that the gray matter with its neurons and synapses lie on the outer surface and the white medullary substance lies beneath. The cerebellum receives impulses, especially of muscle sense, from the lower centers in the brain stem as well as from higher centers through its connection with the cerebral hemisphere.

The most important function of the cerebellum is to effect co-ordination of muscular movement. The cerebellum seems to sort and arrange the impulses it receives from other centers and to correlate these impulses in such a manner as to bring about a *synergy* of muscular movements. *Synergy* refers to a co-operation of muscular activity, which may be exemplified in the production of a smooth and even flow of speech sounds. The cerebellum is also important in the regulation of muscle tone.

Injury to the cerebellum is likely to result in poorly coordinated, jerky muscular movements which are characteristic of *spastic paralysis.*

The Cerebrum. This is the highest of the integrating centers of the nervous mechanism. The physical basis for the human being's intelligence and conscious behavior is to be discovered in a study of the complex interrelationships of the billions of neurons of the cerebrum. The gray outer surface of the cerebrum, known as the cortex, consists of nerve cell bodies. Here synapses are made. Beneath the cortex we find the white matter which is composed of axons covered with myelin sheathing.

Areas of the Cortex. The cortex may be divided into different regions according to structural variations in thickness and arrangement of cell layers. Certain of these cortical regions which are known as *projection areas* receive fibers which are transmitted from lower centers. These fibers derive their impulses from individual sense organs such as the ear and the eye. Projection areas serve for the integration and conscious interpretation of the stimuli they receive. Figure 7 presents a diagrammatic representation of some of the cortical areas of special interest to us. This diagram, we should note, is of the *left* hemisphere of the cerebral cortex. We may observe that the visual center is located in the occipital lobe. On the upper edge of the temporal lobe we find the auditory center. The visual and auditory projection areas serve for the integration and conscious interpretation of the stimuli they receive. Further forward, on the posterior border of the frontal lobe, is the primary motor area which is involved in the conscious control of muscular movements. Just behind the motor area is the sensory or somesthetic area. This region is concerned with the reception and interpretation of sensations of pain, pressure, touch, heat, cold, and movement.

The sensory and motor projection regions occupy a comparatively small amount of the total surface of the cortex. The greater amount consists of association areas composed of fibers which connect them with the various sensory and motor projection areas. Some of the association areas appear to be directly and intimately linked with specific projection areas which they in part surround. A large part of the cortical area, however, especially of the frontal region, is made up of association areas which are less directly related to any specific projection center. It is likely that these nonspecific association areas are of especial significance in carrying on higher intellectual processes, such as speech, which distinguish man from other animals.

When we speak of localization of function in connection with projection areas we do not intend to give the impression that a given function is carried on only by means of a given area but rather that a given type of correlation is more effected in a given area than in others and that the particular function is the chief sufferer when there is destruction in a given area. For example, speech is most likely to be disturbed when there is some injury in the association center known as *Broca's area*, but speech may also be disturbed as a result of injury to almost any other part of the brain cortex, and other functions besides speech suffer as a result of injury to Broca's area.

The functional importance of the cortex can be made clear only by indicating the nature of the relationships existing between the cortex and lower centers. The cortex, as we have mentioned, receives impulses from all lower regions, integrates them, and sends forth controlling impulses to lower motor centers. These impulses may serve to stimulate lower centers to activity or to inhibit reflexes which might otherwise be carried on by the lower centers. In general, the sense organs of the body send impulses to sensory projection areas. But association neurons as well as sensory neurons are found in these projection areas. The association neurons connect the sensory neurons with one another and with other association neurons in the adjacent regions. In the association areas the path of the original impulse is further extended and complicated. The impulse may be spread to higher association centers where impulses from other sources may combine with it. At any one of these stages a connection may be made between an association neuron and a motor neuron. In the event of such a connection the

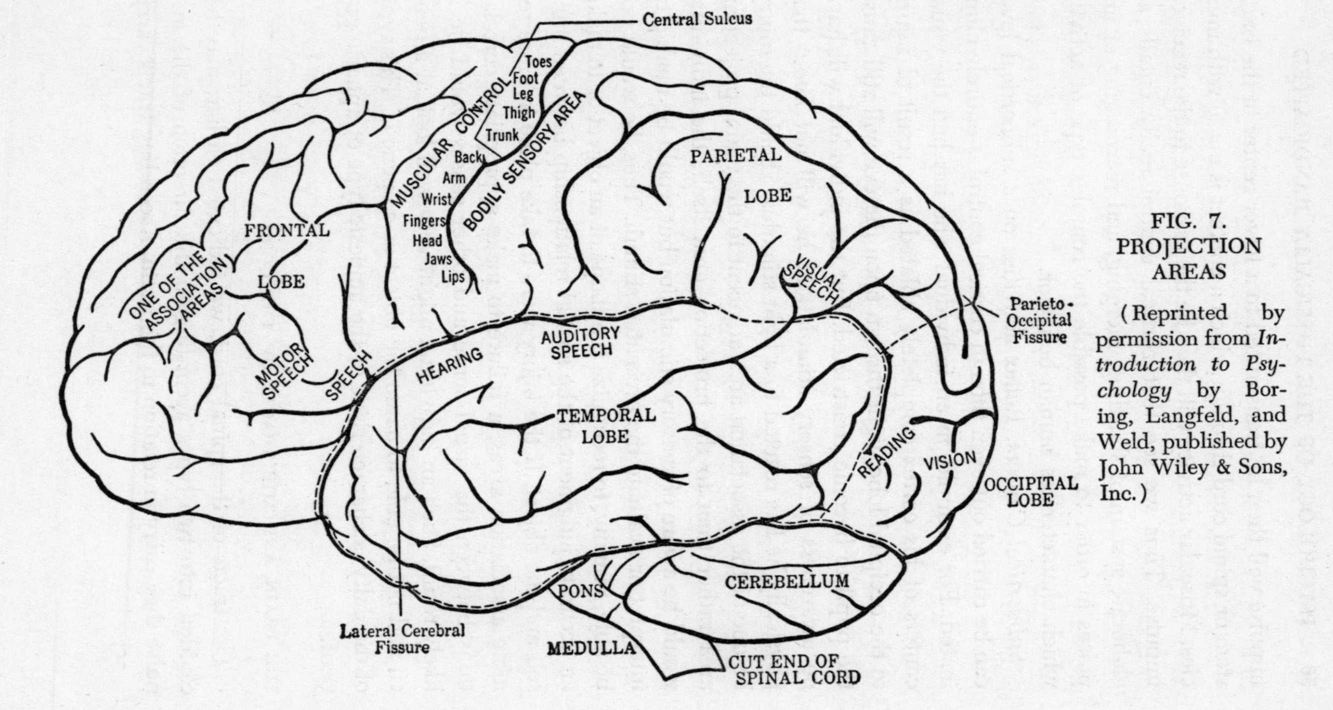

FIG. 7.
PROJECTION AREAS

(Reprinted by permission from *Introduction to Psychology* by Boring, Langfeld, and Weld, published by John Wiley & Sons, Inc.)

impulse will then be transmitted to a lower center in the brain stem or spinal cord through which a contact is made with muscles. Muscular activity will then be the response to the received impulse. Thus we see that cortical control really entails an elaborate system of shuttling, merging, and rearranging of impulses in order to make possible the complex type of activity which characterizes human behavior.

Subcortical Centers. Reflex activities on a subcortical level can be carried out even though cortical control is entirely eliminated. For example, in an individual who has had the visual centers of his cortex completely ablated as a result of injury to the occipital lobe, light thrown upon the eye will still cause the pupil to become constricted. But the individual will have no awareness of sensory stimulation; he will not *know* that physically he has reacted to a light stimulus. Should the injury be one of the association area adjacent to the visual projection area rather than to the projection area itself, the individual would be aware of sensory stimulation but would be unable to interpret or evaluate the presented stimuli. Thus, he would not be able, visually, to recognize the shape of an object or to make an accurate judgment of the spatial relationship between himself and the object. If the injury were to take place in more remote association areas, a failure to make appropriate correlations between the visual sense and other senses would be a likely result. Such an individual might very well look at a pencil and not be able to name the object as a "pencil." This type of difficulty is characteristic of the amnesic type of aphasic patient.

THE BRAIN AND THE TRACTS OF THE CORD

The tracts of the spinal cord, we indicated earlier, may be divided into two types according to the direction of the impulse they carry in relation to the brain. Ascending tracts carry sensory impulses *to* the brain; descending tracts convey motor impulses *away from* the brain. In the brief descriptions which follow we shall indicate the brain-spinal tract relationships and shall emphasize the functional roles of some of the more important tracts.

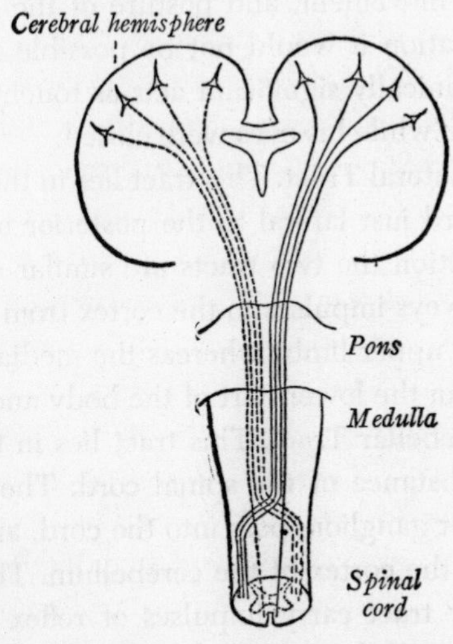

FIG. 8. DIAGRAM OF THE CORTICOSPINAL TRACTS

(From Ranson's *Anatomy of the Nervous System,* W. B. Saunders Company.)

Ascending or Sensory Tracts.

1. Posterior Medial Tract. This tract consists of axon fibers of cell bodies arising in the posterior nerve root of the cord. From their place of origin, fibers enter the gray matter of the cord and continue up in the posterior medial column until they reach their place of termination in the lower end of the medulla. Here a synapse is made and new axons cross over to the opposite side of the body to form the *sensory decussation* and then continue up, passing through the thalamus to reach the sensory area in

the posterior central gyrus of the cerebral cortex. This is the final station for sensations arising from the lower part of the body and lower limbs. The posterior medial tract conveys kinesthetic impulses pertaining to voluntary muscle sense. Kinesthetic impulses are those which give the individual awareness of the position, movement, and posture of the limbs. Without kinesthetic sensation it would not be possible for a person to perform such clinically significant acts as touching the tip of a finger to his nose while his eyes were closed.

2. Posterior Lateral Tract. This tract lies in the posterior part of the spinal cord just lateral to the posterior medial tract. In course and function the two tracts are similar except that the lateral tract conveys impulses to the cortex from the upper part of the body and upper limbs whereas the medial tract conveys the impulses from the lower part of the body and lower limbs.

3. Direct Cerebellar Tract. This tract lies in the lateral part of the white substance of the spinal cord. The fibers arise in the posterior root ganglion, pass into the cord, and continue up until they enter the cortex of the cerebellum. The fibers of the direct cerebellar tract carry impulses of reflex muscular tone and unconscious co-ordination from muscles, joints, and tendons to the cerebellum.

4. The Lateral Spinothalamic Tract. This tract is composed of three different bundles of fibers which lie in the anterior lateral part of the white matter of the cord. The fibers convey impulses of pain and temperature to the thalamus. From the thalamus the impulses are conveyed to the cerebral cortex.

Descending or Motor Tracts.

1. Crossed Pyramidal Tract. The fibers of this tract arise from pyramidal shaped cells in the anterior central gyrus of the cerebral cortex and pass through the lower levels of the brain to reach the spinal cord. Before entering the spinal cord proper, at the lower end of the medulla, the fibers cross over to the op-

posite side to take a lateral position in the cord. The crossing over of the fibers is known as the *decussation of the pyramids* or *motor decussation.* The fibers run down in the cord to the level which they serve, at which point they pass into the posterior horn of gray matter on the same side. Up to this point the fibers have been upper motor neurons. A synapse with an intermediate or connector neuron now takes place. The connector neuron passes to the anterior horn of the cord where a final synapse is made with another neuron. From the anterior horn of the cord the last (lower motor) neuron passes out to the muscles for the innervation of voluntary movement. By means of the crossed pyramidal tract, fibers that originate in the precentral motor area on the right side of the brain innervate the anterior horn cells which send fibers to muscles on the left side of the body.

2. Direct Pyramidal Tract. The fibers of this tract follow the same course as the fibers of the crossed pyramidal tract as far as the medulla. The fibers of the direct pyramidal tract do not cross in the medulla but continue downward as a distinct bundle near the anterior fissure of the cord. At various levels of the cord the axons turn off and cross over to the anterior horn of the opposite side where synapses are formed either with connector neurons or directly with lower motor neurons. By the midthoracic region all the fibers of the direct pyramidal tract have crossed over to the opposite side.

These two tracts which together constitute the *corticospinal tracts* are the main voluntary motor tracts of the body. Their fibers carry impulses from the motor region of the cerebral cortex to the cord and so serve to bring the spinal motor apparatus under voluntary control. The direct pyramidal tract serves only the upper part of the body whereas the fibers of the crossed pyramidal tract supply the entire body. Injury to the pyramidal system results first in a loss of voluntary movement of the parts affected followed after a time by an abnormal degree of increased tonus (spasticity) of the muscles because of the removal of cortical inhibition.

3. The Rubrospinal Tract. The fibers of this tract come from the red nucleus of the midbrain. By means of nerve cells which connect the midbrain with the cerebrum, the rubrospinal tract functions as an accessory to the main motor pathways. The tract conveys motor impulses concerned with automatic movements, such as walking, swinging the arms, etc., and the maintenance of body posture.

4. The Vestibulospinal Tract. This tract consists of fibers in the anterior lateral part of the white matter of the cord. It arises from the lateral nucleus of the eighth (auditory) nerve of the medulla and ends in the anterior gray matter. The fibers of this tract convey impulses concerned with the maintenance of equilibrium and body tonus.

5. The Tectospinal Tract. This tract is composed of fibers which arise in the roof (tectum) of the midbrain and continue down into the spinal cord to end in the gray matter of the anterior column. The fibers of the tract serve to innervate muscles concerned with optic and auditory reflexes. The tectospinal and vestibulospinal tracts are both parts of the *anterolateral descending tract*.

Decussation of the Fibers. In our discussion of the posterior medial sensory tract and the crossed and direct pyramidal motor tracts we indicated that the nerve fibers tended to cross over (decussate) from one side of the body to the other. With few exceptions, *all* sensory and motor fibers cross to the opposite side. The phenomenon of decussation explains how each of the cerebral hemispheres receives impulses from and controls the activities of the musculature of the opposite side of the body.

Effects of Lesions of the Spinal Cord. Specifically, the effects of a spinal cord lesion will be determined by the severity and exact site of the lesion. In the event of a hemisection of the spinal cord the patient will present a set of symptoms which will include the following:

1. Below the level of the lesion, and on the same side, the muscles of the body will display a spastic motor paralysis.
2. There will be a loss of sensation of the muscles, joints, and tendons below the level of, and on the same side as, the lesion.
3. The parts of the body supplied by the affected nerve segment will suffer from a flaccid motor paralysis.
4. On the opposite side of the body, beginning usually about one segment below the level of the lesion, there is a loss of sensation of pain and temperature.

THE DEVELOPMENT OF BEHAVIOR PATTERNS

According to early neurological concepts, behavior patterns were considered essentially to be the sum of localized individualized reflexes. Complex behavior emerged as a result of an increase in the total number of reflex arcs. A concept of this sort was quite consistent with the classical view of the reflex arc which we explained earlier and presented diagrammatically in Figure 4. We have pointed out, however, that this diagram is much more interesting for its naïve simplicity than significant for its accuracy, and so presented a more appropriate diagram based on the work of Sherrington (see Fig. 5).

The Emergence of Individualized Responses. Recent research concerning the development of behavior patterns in lower animals and in human infants has demonstrated that it is inadequate to consider behavior *a sum of reflexes.* Coghill (2) studied the problem of behavior patterns in a salamander. He found that the earliest behavior displayed by the animal involves mass responses of *all the muscles functioning at one time* rather than of localized reflexes. In the salamander this behavior assumes the form of swimming movements. When the legs develop they function first merely as part of the general swimming movement of the entire trunk and its appendages. Later, as the animal continues to mature, individualized control of the limbs, forearms, fingers, etc., is achieved. In neurological terms, we may say that stimuli tend to spread throughout the nervous system of an animal according to a pattern related to the organism as a whole. Later, pathways of progressively greater restriction appear individuated out of the mass pattern. It has not been possible, of course, to study the development of behavior in the human infant in any such detail. The available studies indicate that in the human fetus and in the newborn infant (8) the general interpretation of early mass behavior followed by progressive restriction and consequent individuation is confirmed.

Determinants of Individuation. We do not definitely know what factors actually determine differentiation of response. We know definitely that there is a relationship between the degree of neuron myelination and the development of specialized reflexive activity. It is not certain whether this relationship is one of causation or merely of concomitance. Myelination of the fiber tracts in the human infant begins at about the fifth month of intrauterine life and is not completed before the second year (9). We know that there is some reflexive behavior in the fetus before any myelination has taken place and that mass and diffuse behavior continues to be displayed in the new-born infant. Complex behavior, however, seems to develop only in connection with myelination of appropriate tracts.

THE ENDOCRINE SYSTEM

Nature of the Endocrine System. The endocrine system is composed of a number of different glands which produce chemically complex products known as hormones, or autacoid substances. The products of the endocrine glands are generally injected directly into the blood stream and are thus diffused throughout the entire body. Because of this diffusion of the products of the endocrine glands by the blood stream, the integration of the activities of many different and divergent organs of the body into a unified and co-ordinated response is made possible.

The hormones may be said to have a twofold influence on bodily activity. First, there is a general effect of either exciting or inhibiting muscular activity. Second, each gland produces chemicals to which special tissues of the body are responsive, and so specialized bodily functions are carried on. In general, the endocrine system is concerned with long-time, long-range responses which determine the disposition or "set" of the organism to changes in the environment. In this respect the endocrine system differs from the nervous system, which permits immediate, rapid, and localized responses to take place. Figure 9 presents the approximate localization of the major endocrine glands of the human organism. In our discussion we shall consider the pituitary, thyroid, parathyroid, adrenal, pancreas, pineal, thymus, and sex glands.

The Pituitary Gland or the Hypophysis. This gland, which is about the size of a pea, is located in the pituitary fossa, a little bony socket under the brain in the center of the skull. The gland is divided into four sections: (1) the anterior lobe, (2) the middle lobe or *pars intermedia,* (3) the *pars tuberalis,* and (4) the posterior lobe. The pituitary is often referred to as the master gland because it initiates and stimulates the activities of several of the other endocrine glands. The thyroid, the adrenal cortex, the parathyroids, and the sex glands are known to be regulated by pituitary action.

Directly, the pituitary gland is responsible for vital bodily functions. The hormone produced by the pituitary gland influ-

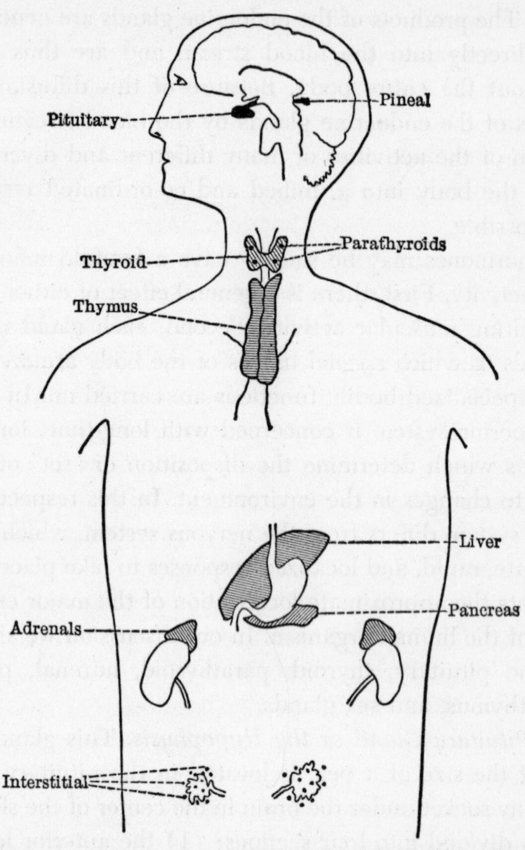

FIG. 9. THE PRINCIPAL ENDOCRINE GLANDS

(From J. F. Dashiell's *Fundamentals of Objective Psychology*, Houghton Mifflin Company.)

ences growth, temperature, and basal metabolism. *Prolactin*, a pituitary product, is believed to be responsible both for the "mental set" which is popularly known as the maternal instinct, and for the physical changes which enable the mother to nurse her child.

Dysfunctions of the pituitary gland are responsible for several abnormal conditions which are represented in well-recognized clinical pictures. Overactivity of the anterior lobe of the pituitary gland will result in a condition known as *gigantism* and *acromegaly*. The basic dysfunction for both conditions is the same. Gigantism results when the disturbance sets in before the growth of the long bones of the body has ceased. The picture is one of abnormally accelerated growth, typified by the giant of the circus. Acromegaly is a disease of maturity; the disease is characterized by continued growth of the hands, fingers, feet, and face. The facial features are markedly changed; the lower jaw and the ridges above the eyes are usually greatly enlarged and prominent; the face is broadened and elongated; the nostrils are wide, and the lips coarse and thickened.

Retarded skeletal growth may be associated with a deficiency of the growth hormone of the anterior lobe. Pituitary dwarfism of the "midget" circus type is characterized by the maintenance of relatively normal bodily proportions. The "midget" is slight of build, his skeletal undergrowth involves all the bones so that the individual presents a rather delicate and graceful picture.

Froelich's syndrome or *dystrophia adiposa-genitalis* is another common clinical picture associated with malfunctioning of the posterior lobe of the pituitary. The true Froelich's syndrome is characterized by three major symptoms: dwarfism, genital infantilism, and an increase of fatty tissue, which is distributed especially on the breasts, abdomen, and hips of the individual. The male patient is likely to develop female characteristics, including a broadened pelvis, rounded limbs, slender fingers, and a tendency to mammary development. The skin is likely to be smooth and rather dry. The pubic hair tends to take on the female distribution, even if the disorder is postadolescent and the male type of distribution has already been established.

The Thyroid Gland. This gland is situated at the base of the neck astride the windpipe. The size of the gland varies, especially with the adult individual, but it is not likely to weigh more than an ounce in the normal adult. The pathological enlargement of the gland is known as *goiter*. The thyroid gland manufactures an iodine-containing hormone called *thyroxin* which regulates the metabolic activities of all the cells of the organism. Though the principle function of the thyroid gland is that of regulating energy discharge, experimental evidence indicates that it also stimulates bodily growth and mental functions. In the female, the thyroid gland is fundamentally related to the sex apparatus.

A brief review of the results of the malfunctioning of the thyroid gland will help in an understanding of the specific effects it has on the organism. In general, an individual with an overactive thyroid gland (hyperthyroidism) is likely to be restive and irritable; the increased cellular activity is usually correlated with a loss of weight. In the opposite condition of reduced thyroid activity (hypothyroidism), the individual is likely to have a reduced metabolic rate, be overweight, and will tend to be sluggish in his behavior. In children, a marked thyroxin deficiency frequently manifests itself in the clinical picture of *cretinism* or *childhood myxedema*. The cretin is retarded in both his mental and physical development. He has been characterized as "a stunted, potbellied, bandy-legged imbecile." In adults, a marked lack of thyroxin gives rise to the condition called *myxedema*. The overt characteristics are like those of the cretin. The skin of the myxedema patient becomes rough, dry, and scaly; the hair is dry and brittle and falls out rather readily. Subcutaneous fatty pads develop over the clavicles and around the wrists and ankles. The speech of the myxedema patient, whether childhood or adult, is likely to be slow, thick, and lacking in precision. The voice reveals a characteristic monotony of pitch and intensity and sounds childishly immature.

The Parathyroids. These are four tiny glands which lie near or are imbedded within thyroid tissue. The hormone of the parathyroids regulates the concentration of calcium in the blood. The element calcium is essential for the maintenance of the proper degree of irritability of the muscular and nervous systems. Parathyroid deficiency results in hyperexcitability of the nervous system, and spasmodic muscular cramps, and a condition of tonic contractions of the muscles (tetany). In severe cases convulsions may appear.

The Adrenals. The adrenal glands are situated just above the kidney in the abdominal cavity. In size and shape they resemble large beans. The adrenal glands show two kinds of influence on bodily function. The *medulla,* or inner core of the adrenal, produces a hormone called *adrenalin* or *epinephrin* which has an action on body tissue similar to that arising from the stimulation of the sympathetic division of the autonomic nervous system (see pp. 40–41). Adrenalin accelerates cardiac activity, raises blood pressure, induces a release of sugar from the liver into the blood, inhibits the action of the digestive system, stimulates respiratory activity, and in general seems to supplement the nervous mechanism in preparing the organism for strenuous activity.

The cortex or outer portion of the adrenal glands produces a hormone, *cortin,* which is essential for the maintenance of life, although the chemical nature of the hormone or its mode of action is not definitely known. Cortin deficiency results in symptoms of fatigue, lethargy, changes in metabolism especially in regard to sugar, and a general loss of resistance to heat.

The Sex Glands. The gonads or sex glands not only produce the cells necessary for carrying on reproduction (*gametes*) but in addition produce important hormones associated with sexual behavior, with physical growth, and with the temperament of the individual.

The male gland *testis* produces the *spermatozoa,* the male sex cells necessary for reproduction. The *testis* also produces a hormone which promotes the development of the secondary sex characteristics including pubic hair, voice changes, and the general masculine appearance of the body. Gonad deficiency in the male results in a maintenance of infantile characteristics. The voice remains childlike in pitch and quality, the beard fails to develop, pubic hair tends to be scanty and to resemble the female's in pattern of distribution; the primary sex organs remain underdeveloped. In cases of precocious gonad development, early physical and sexual maturation is likely to occur.

The *ovaries* are the female sex glands. They produce the *ova* or female sex cells and at least two hormones which are associated with menstruation, gestation, lactation, and with the general bodily changes characteristic of the pubertal and postpubertal female. The sexual changes in the female are more complex than in the male. Other glands, especially the pituitary (see p. 63) play significant and important parts in female sex development and behavior.

The Pancreatic Islands. The pancreas produces several chemical products which function as aids to digestion. Imbedded within the pancreatic tissue are the Islets of Langerhans, which produce the important hormone insulin necessary for the proper metabolism of sugars and fats by the body. An absence or deficiency of the normal amount of insulin results in *diabetes mellitus,* a disease characterized by sugar in the urine, excessive excretion of urine, excessive hunger and thirst, muscular weakness, and general emaciation.

The Pineal Gland. This gland is a tiny cone-shaped organ suspended from the roof of the third ventricle of the cerebrum.

Evidence as to the influence of the pineal gland in the body, and even of its classification as a ductless gland, is not clear. Experimental work with the gland seems to indicate that it has an inhibitory effect upon the too rapid maturation of the body. There is some clinical evidence to demonstrate that pathological destruction of the gland may be associated with precocious physical and sexual maturation.

The Thymus Gland. The thymus, like the pineal, has not yet been fully accepted as a member of the endocrine system. The thymus gland lies near the apex of the chest and consists of two nearly separated lobes. The gland is a temporary organ; it attains its full size about the end of the second year when it normally ceases to grow and begins to atrophy. By puberty the thymus may have entirely disappeared. Although no specific chemical substance has been isolated from the thymus, there is some clinical evidence to indicate that the failure of the gland to atrophy is associated with the retention of infantile characteristics in the adult, including smooth skin, "baby face," little hair, genital underdevelopment, and a general disinclination for muscular activity.

Other Glands. Other tissues of the body also produce hormones. *Sympathin* is a product of the sympathetic nervous system and *acetylcholine* a product of the parasympathetic nerves. These hormones are believed to serve as the immediate stimuli of the tissues of the body which are activated by the autonomic nervous system. Several of the digestive organs produce hormones which aid in the digestive process. *Gastrin* is a hormone product of the stomach which aids in stimulating the flow of the gastric juices; *secretin* and *prosecretin* seem to aid in the stimulation of the pancreatic juices. It is believed also that the tissues of the stomach and upper intestine produce a hormone called *cholecystokinin* which influences the activity of the gall bladder to excrete bile.

BIBLIOGRAPHY

THE NERVOUS SYSTEM

1. Cannon, W. B., and A. Rosenblueth, *Autonomic Neuro-Effector Systems* (Macmillan, N.Y., 1937).
2. Coghill, G. E., *Anatomy and the Problem of Behavior*, (Cambridge Univ. Press, N.Y., 1929).
3. Ford, F. R., *Diseases of the Nervous System in Infancy, Childhood, and Adolescence* (C. C. Thomas, Springfield, Ill., 1937).
4. Herrick, C. J., *An Introduction to Neurology*, 5th ed. (Saunders, Phil., 1931).
5. Keiller, W., *Nerve Tracts of the Brain and Cord* (Macmillan, N.Y., 1927).
6. Kuntz, A., *A Textbook of Neuro-anatomy* (Lea and Febiger, Phil., 1936).
7. Lickley, J. D., *The Nervous System* (Longmans, Green, N.Y., 1931).
8. Pratt, K. C., A. K. Nelson, and K. H. Sun, *The Behavior of the Newborn Infant* (Ohio State Univ. Press, Columbus, 1930).
9. Ranson, S. W., *The Anatomy of the Nervous System*, 5th ed. (Saunders, Phil., 1935).
10. Sherrington, C. S., *The Integrative Action of the Nervous System* (Yale Univ. Press, New Haven, 1906).
11. Wechsler, I. S., *A Textbook of Clinical Neurology* (Saunders, Phil., 1939).

THE ENDOCRINE SYSTEM

12. Cameron, A. T., *Recent Advances in Endocrinology* (Blakiston, Phil., 1936).
13. Gregory, J., *The A.B.C. of the Endocrines* (Williams and Wilkins, Baltimore, 1935).
14. Ingle, D., "Endocrine Function and Personality," *Psychol. Rev.*, XLII (1935), 466–79.

15. Lurie, L., "Endocrinology and Behavior Disorders of Children," *Am. J. Orthopsychiat.*, V (1935), 141–53.
16. Mateer, F., *Glands and Efficient Behavior* (Appleton-Century, N.Y., 1935).
17. Stockard, C. R., *The Physical Basis of Personality* (Norton, N.Y., 1931).
18. Tredgold, A. F., *Mental Deficiency* (William Wood, N.Y., 1929).
19. Wilkins, W., "Pituitary Dwarfism and Intelligence," *J. Gen. Psychol.*, XVIII (April, 1938), 305–17.
20. Wolf, W., *Endocrinology in Modern Practice* (Saunders, Phil., 1937).

CHAPTER IV

Psychological Tests for the Physically Handicapped

GENERAL

The modern type of test for the measurement of mental characteristics received its great stimulus about the beginning of this century with the work of Binet, and particularly with the publication of the Binet-Simon Scale for the measurement of intelligence. There were, of course, many mental tests before this period, but they had not been used very much in actual school work. We must not, however, imagine that Binet "invented" or "discovered" mental testing. What he did was to produce the first workable scale for the measurement of intelligence, based upon much previous work of many other workers. Another powerful impetus to mental measurement was given about the same time by the work of Thorndike. He produced some of the earliest tests for the measurement of educational achievement, and stimulated his pupils to the production of many more. Thus we find intelligence testing and educational-achievement testing developing about the same time. Personality testing is a much later growth.

Binet's main interest in the construction of his intelligence scale was the differentiation between the normal and the feeble-minded child. He was studying feeble-mindedness and seeking a more objective method of diagnosis. His scale proved useful for this primary purpose and then its use rapidly spread, and later adaptations of the Binet scale soon came to be used for the measurement of the intelligence of all children. During this stage of rapid spread, it became obvious that certain groups of children, notably the physically handicapped groups, could not be tested by the standard Binet scales. Hence the need for special scales for these groups, which we describe later.

After much work with individual tests, group testing arose, and it was soon demonstrated that reliable and useful measures could be obtained by the group-testing procedure. Gradually these techniques of individual and group testing were applied to the measurement of personality. Let us now summarize briefly the various kinds of tests in common use at the present time and then turn to the particular adaptations that must be made for the measurement of the various physically handicapped groups.

KINDS OF TESTS

We may group mental tests under the four following headings: (1) Intelligence, (2) Educational achievement, (3) Personality, (4) Special abilities.

Intelligence. Our two main divisions here are Individual and Group Tests:

Individual tests	*Group tests*
1. Binet-type scales	1. Verbal
2. Performance scales	2. Nonverbal
	3. Nonlanguage

Individual intelligence tests of the Binet type are characterized by the miscellaneous character of the test items: oral items of the question and answer type, picture items, drawing items, performance items, memory items, reading items. The examination is in the nature of "an interview," with subject and examiner reacting one to the other. The examiner talks a lot, tells the subject what to do, and so the subject must be able to hear normally. The examiner shows the subject pictures and designs and expects the subject to draw, and so the subject must have normal vision. The examiner asks the subject questions and so the subject must be able to speak. This very miscellaneous character of the Binet-type test is one of the reasons why it has proved such a good test of general all-round ability.

Individual tests of the performance type stress the doing of something: putting blocks in a form board, constructing with blocks, arranging blocks to form a design, filling in parts to make a sensible picture, and the like. How well a subject can "do" or "perform," not how well he can describe or explain, is the criterion of ability here. Many of the tests do not require verbal directions, so hearing is not important. All, of course, assume normal vision.

Group tests of intelligence make certain assumptions as follows: Verbal tests assume a normal language development in the subject so that he can understand the oral or printed directions for doing the test. The test items are mostly language items and they assume a normal reading development on the part of the subject in accordance with the stage of development he is supposed to have reached. For example, an opposites test for the elementary grades includes words which elementary school pupils know and can read. The task is to find opposites of the words they know. If they did not know the words or could not read them, it would not be an opposites test for them.

Nonverbal tests assume a knowledge of language sufficient to understand the examiner's instructions for doing the test. The test material is all pictorial, so that no knowledge of reading is assumed.

Nonlanguage tests are those that make no assumptions with reference to language knowledge on the part of the subject. The directions for doing the test are given by pantomime and by examples on the blackboard. The content of the test is entirely pictorial, and so no assumption as to reading is made. Some nonlanguage tests assume a knowledge of numbers.

Educational Achievement. Such tests are almost always group tests. They are constructed to test the various aspects of school work. Their number is very great, probing into all the varied outcomes of school instruction. There are composite tests covering the common skills and informations which most schools teach their pupils. From such tests we can arrive at a general educational age or a grade-placement score for a pupil which shows how much he has learned of the basic content of instruction. Then there are specialized tests which go into much greater detail with reference to arithmetic or reading or Spanish or English literature or social science and the like. Some of these tests are diagnostic in the sense that they try to diagnose any particular difficulty which a pupil may be having. Finally there are tests which measure the more general outcomes of educational endeavor, such as ability to reason about given subject matter, knowledge of how to study effectively, and so on. The underlying assumption about all such educational-achievement tests is that the individual to be tested has developed more or less normally with reference to his language development. They are practically all printed verbal tests assuming greater or lesser amounts of reading ability.

Personality. We are at present in the midst of active experimentation in the testing of personality. What tests or what type of tests will eventually survive as the best tests of personality, no one can at present predict. Roughly we can group the present tests into group and individual. The group tests are largely of the inventory or questionnaire type. Questions are presented to the subject which he is required to check in some form or other. Naturally the assumption here is that the items or questions are understood by the subject. The language must not be too difficult for the level of development reached by the subject.

Individual tests of personality may consist of the showing of some picture or diagram to the subject for his reaction. Observation and ratings of subjects are also used.

Special Abilities. Here we have group and individual tests which attempt to measure some special ability or capacity such as musical capacity, mechanical ability, motor ability, aesthetic appreciation and the like. Some of them are supposed to be prognostic in the sense that they make no demand for any special knowledge, but presumably indicate a latent talent in some particular field. Each one of them makes specific assumptions with reference to hearing or vision or muscular development and we shall later discuss their value for the physically handicapped.

TESTS SUITABLE FOR THE DEAF

GENERAL REQUIREMENTS

Because the deaf individual cannot hear, all tests which assume normal hearing are unsuitable. Furthermore, because the deaf individual does not acquire language in the normal way because of his lack of hearing, all tests assuming this normal development of language are ruled out as tests of intelligence. In the case of educational-achievement tests, these can be used to test the actual level of educational achievement attained, provided that the directions for taking the test are understood by the pupils tested. If such directions are not properly understood, the results cannot be compared with the norms for the test. In the case of personality and special-ability tests, we must make sure that the language of the directions or of the tests themselves is well within the comprehension of the children tested, otherwise they become measures of language achievement primarily, plus whatever else the test is supposed to measure.

INTELLIGENCE

Individual scales that make no assumptions of language development and can be given without verbal directions are all of the performance type.

Pintner-Paterson Performance Scale. This scale was specifically constructed with the deaf in mind. The tests and their standardization are described in the book by Pintner and Paterson (32). A shortened form of the scale, called the Pintner-Paterson Short Performance Scale, is now generally used. It consists of the ten following subtests:

1. Mare and foal board. This is a picture board of a mare and foal with a number of cutouts which the subject has to put in the correct places. It is very simple and resembles a child's game and serves as a very good introduction for children. Time and number of errors are recorded.
2. Seguin form board. Ten blocks representing common geometrical forms are to be placed in their appropriate places. The time of the shortest of three trials is recorded.
3. Five-figure board. Five geometrical figures each divided into two or three pieces are to be placed in their appropriate places. Time and number of errors are recorded.
4. Two-figure board. Nine pieces are to be placed in two spaces. Time and number of moves are recorded.
5. Casuist board. A more difficult board, consisting of four

spaces into which have to be fitted twelve blocks. Time and number of errors are recorded.

6. Manikin test. Subject has to put together legs, arms, head and body to form a man. There is no board into which the pieces fit. Quality of performance is scored.

7. Feature-profile test. In the same manner as in the previous test, subject has to put together pieces to form a head. Time is recorded.

8. Ship test. This consists of the picture of a ship cut into ten pieces of the same size and shape which are to be fitted together properly in a rectangular frame. Quality of performance is scored.

9. Picture-completion test. Subject is required to select the appropriate block out of many possible blocks to complete the picture. Quality of performance is scored.

10. Cube test. Four cubes are tapped in a certain order and the subject is required to watch and then imitate the movement. Number of combinations correctly imitated is recorded.

Tests 6 and 7, the manikin and feature-profile tests, are used as one test because the norms for the former run from age four to eight and for the latter from age ten to fifteen. No language directions are needed. The tests are more or less self-explanatory. Only simple pantomime is necessary to start the deaf child off. Directions for giving and scoring the short scale are to be found in the manual by Hildreth and Pintner (19). This test is relatively simple to give and has been used with many deaf children. It is suitable for most deaf children in schools for the deaf with the exception of the youngest children.

The Drever-Collins Performance Scale. This scale has been constructed by Drever and Collins primarily for the testing of the deaf, but it has been used with hearing children as well. It consists of the following tests: (1) block design test (Kohs); (2) cube test (Knox and Pintner); (3) domino test (Drever and Collins); (4) size and weight test; (5) manikin and profile test (Pintner and Paterson); (6) form-boards test (Pintner's two-figure board and Healy's puzzle A); (7) cube construction; (8) picture-completion boards (Drever and Collins, and Healy's picture No. 1).

The tests are scored by an allotment of points for each test. The maximum score is 148. There are tentative age norms for both hearing and deaf children.

This scale was constructed in Great Britain by Drever and Collins (10) and has not been widely used in the United States. MacKane's (22) use of this scale would seem to raise the question as to whether it is adequately standardized for children in the United States (see Chapter V).

The Arthur Performance Scale. This scale has been constructed by Arthur (2, 3). It consists of the following ten tests: (1) Knox cube; (2) Seguin form board; (3) two-figure board; (4) casuist form board; (5) manikin; (6) feature-profile; (7) mare and foal; (2) Healy picture completion I; (9) Porteus-maze; (10) Kohs block design. The first eight tests are the same as in the Pintner-Paterson Scale and have been borrowed from that scale. The last two are additions which do not appear in the Pintner-Paterson Scale. Unlike the latter scale, the Arthur Scale allots points to each test performance. The sum of such points is then converted into a mental age. MacKane (22) seems to have made the only study with deaf children comparing the Arthur and Pintner-Paterson Scales. It would seem that the two scales give very similar results. Because the Pintner-Paterson is much simpler to score and to derive a mental age from, it would seem to be preferable for practical use in schools for the deaf at the present time.

Ontario School-Ability Examination is a performance scale by Amoss (1) constructed especially with the deaf in mind. It requires no language on the part of the examiner or subject. The mental level of the various items was determined by the mental ages on the Stanford Revision of the standardization group of hearing subjects. The scale consists of five sections or so-called examinations as follows: (1) manipulation, which includes a miscellaneous set of tests, such as paper-folding, block-building, tying knots, arranging weights, etc.; (2) color patterns, adapted from the Kohs Block-Design Test; (3) Knox cubes; (4) dominoes, a visual-memory test; (5) drawing, copying designs, and designs from memory; (6) tapping, a kind of number-sequence test. The total of the number of points earned on these various tests determines the mental age of the child. From the results so far published, this scale would seem to be well suited to the deaf. The box of materials is small and can be conveniently carried by the school psychologist.

Pintner Preschool Performance Scale. This is a scale in process of construction and standardization by Pintner and has not yet been published. It is designed for the lower levels of mentality not reached by the Pintner-Paterson Scale, and can be given entirely by pantomime directions. The scale consists of eleven subtests as follows: (1) pegboard with square and round pegs of two sizes; (2) cube construction—building various simple structures; (3) color assortment—three colored boxes into which chips of three different colors are to be put; (4) nest of boxes—triangular boxes to be placed into a square box; (5) picture recognition—matching pictures; (6) beads—stringing large beads in various patterns; (7) cups—nest of cups of various sizes to be assembled; (8) picture puzzles—eight pictures cut in pieces to be assembled; (9) box assembly—small boxes of various sizes to be assembled; (10) drawing—ten different geometrical figures; (11) form board—with two sets of pieces, one set undivided and the other divided into many parts.

As this scale is still in the process of standardization, no results are as yet available.

Porteus Maze Scale. This consists of a graded series of mazes standardized for ages 3 to 14 by Porteus (33, 34). It has been used with the deaf, but no standard set of instructions for the deaf has been published. It tests a very narrow aspect of behavior and should be used with caution as a measure of the general intelligence of the deaf.

Group intelligence tests for the deaf ought always to be strictly of the nonlanguage type, that is the content should be entirely nonverbal and in addition the directions for administering the test should be entirely pantomimic. Explanation of what is to be done should never be given in written or spoken language. Furthermore the standardization of the test, based on normal hearing subjects, should be made with the same pantomimic instructions as used with the deaf, if the test is to be considered a standard test. Since very few psychologists have been interested in the deaf, it is not surprising that only three group-intelligence tests come up to these requirements, namely the first three mentioned below.

Pintner Nonlanguage Mental Test. This was the first group test constructed with a view to the measurement of the intelligence of the deaf and it has been widely used for this purpose. There are numerous references to it in the literature (25, 26, 31), and the results of its use with the deaf together with the appropriate references are given in Chapter V. The test consists of the following six subtests: (1) movement imitation, i. e., reproducing the movements of a pointer after it has been moved from dot to dot in different ways on the blackboard (essentially the Knox cube test arranged for group purposes); (2) easy learning, i. e., a very simple digit-symbol test containing three elements. (3) hard learning, i. e., a more difficult digit-symbol test containing nine elements; (4) drawing completion, i. e., drawing in the missing parts of pictures; (5) reversed drawings, i. e., reproducing geometrical forms as they would be when turned upside-down; (6) picture reconstruction, i. e., indicating by numbers the positions of the parts of pictures so as to make a complete picture.

The test takes about thirty minutes to give, and has proved very serviceable, requiring, as it does, simply a blackboard and one demonstration picture. It has been well standardized on ordinary school children. The correlations with various verbal tests for various groups range from .25 to .72. Its validity coefficient with a composite criterion of intelligence is .78. This test is suitable for deaf children from age ten up. It is too difficult for the younger children.

Pintner Nonlanguage Primary Mental Test. This has been constructed by Pintner (28) and is suitable for younger deaf children. The directions are entirely in pantomime and have been very carefully described. To give it properly requires care and practice on the part of the examiner. As many children can be tested at the same time, as can be adequately controlled by the examiner and his assistants. Young children may need help in turning over the pages of the booklet and in keeping to the right item. The subtests consist of: (1) marking objects held up before the child; (2) completing unfinished geometrical forms; (3) completing unfinished faces; (4) manikin test for position of arms.

Chicago Nonverbal Examination. This test has been constructed by Brown (5), and it has both verbal and pantomime directions. It consists of ten subtests: (1) symbol-digit test; (2) cross out what does not belong; (3) cube counting; (4) recognition of parts to make a whole; (5) similarities; (6) picture reconstruction; (7) picture sequences; (8) picture absurdities; (9) associating parts with wholes; (10) hard symbol-digit.

This test has been tried out by Brown with deaf children of ages ten to twenty and evidently it works very well.

Goodenough Drawing Scale. Although this test (13) was not constructed specifically for the deaf, it has been used with the deaf in several studies. The instructions to the subjects are given orally as follows: "Make a picture of a man. Make the very best picture that you can." No remarks of any kind that might influence the nature of the drawings are allowed. The drawings are scored by an elaborate scoring scheme which allots points for the presence of certain items, e. g., legs present, legs attached to trunk, nose present, fingers present, etc. No attention is paid to the artistic quality of the drawing. Older deaf children can understand the instructions when given orally or written, but no worker has specifically standardized the directions for giving the test to the deaf. The test would seem to be suitable for deaf children in the middle age range. It does not have enough "top" to test the older children, and it is doubtful whether the younger deaf children fully understand the instructions. How good a test this is of the general intelligence of the deaf we do not know. It depends upon a very limited aspect of behavior and until we know more about it, it should be used with caution as a measure of the general intelligence of the deaf.

EDUCATIONAL ACHIEVEMENT

Theoretically any standard educational-achievement test, if given to deaf children, will allow us to make comparisons between the achievement of the deaf and the hearing. In this sense, therefore, there is no need for special educational achievement tests for the deaf. However, in order to measure educational achievement uncontaminated with ability to understand the directions for taking the test, we must make certain that such directions are understood equally well by the deaf and the hearing, and this is usually not the case. Further, because of the tremendous language handicap of the deaf, their educational achievement as measured by printed verbal tests lags far behind that of the hearing. Hence the desirability for educational-achievement tests constructed specifically for the deaf—tests which will keep close to the curriculum of deaf schools.

Pintner Educational-Survey Test. This test (31) has been used more than any other in surveys in schools for the deaf. It was not specifically constructed for the deaf, but the instructions for taking the test were drawn up with the deaf in mind. It has been successful in giving a general all-round index of achievement in the common branches.

The Stanford Achievement Test. This well-known test needs no description here. It has been used in some deaf schools. It is successful with the more advanced pupils who can understand the printed directions.

Keys-Pedersen Visual-Language Tests. These are tests of language constructed by Keys and Pedersen and described by Keys and Boulware (20). They have been constructed specifically for the deaf and are designed to cover the earlier stages of language learning among the deaf. The word-knowledge test is designed for classes in their first to fourth year of schooling. It consists of the matching of pictures of objects with the printed word. The sentence-completion test is designed for classes in their second to seventh year. It consists in recognizing the correct word to make a sensible sentence. The paragraph-reading test and the sentence-making test are designed for classes in their third to seventh years. The former consists of short paragraphs to be read, with questions in alternative answer form based on them. The latter consists of arranging jumbled words into a correct sentence.

PERSONALITY

Any personality test that can be understood by the deaf would theoretically be usable. Here again the stumbling block is language. In using the standard inventories and questionnaires we never can be absolutely sure that the deaf can interpret the meaning of the questions in the same manner as the hearing. Only one of the following inventories has been specifically constructed for the deaf.

Brunschwig Personality Inventory for the Deaf. Brunschwig (8) constructed this especially for the deaf child of school age. It consists of 67 items couched in very simple language. The questions attempt to get at the child's attitude toward his school, his playmates, and toward himself, and also how he feels with reference to many situations. The subject checks one of the three possible answers to each question. Some of the questions are:

4. Do other children like you?
   They like me a little.
   They like me very well.
   They do not like me.
12. Are you happy at home?
   I am not happy at home.
   Sometimes I am happy at home.
   I am very happy at home.
22. Are you smart?
   I am the same as other children.
   I am not smart.
   I am very very smart; I am smarter than other children.

The total score on this test gives a general estimate of general adjustment; partial scores can be obtained for school adjustment, home adjustment, and social adjustment. Percentile ratings are available, based upon results for 770 deaf boys and 560 deaf girls and are given in an article by Pintner and Brunschwig (29). This test is at present the only personality inventory standardized on the deaf. It is in general suitable for pupils in the intermediate and advanced departments of schools for the deaf.

Other personality scales which have been tried with the deaf, but were not originally constructed for the deaf, will be briefly mentioned.

Pupil Portraits. This is a general adjustment inventory couched in fairly simple language. It gives measures of school and home adjustment as well as a general over-all score of adjustment. The language does not seem to be too difficult for pupils in the intermediate and advanced departments of most schools for the deaf.

Aspects of Personality. This test gives a measure of three aspects of personality, namely, (1) ascendance-submission, (2) introversion-extraversion, (3) emotional stability. The language is fairly simple and the test should be useful in the intermediate and advanced departments.

Bernreuter Personality Inventory. This is the well-known inventory that has been used very widely and gives measures of several personality traits. It has been successfully used with deaf college students and deaf adults with slight modifications in language made by the investigators (30).

Thurstone Personality Schedule. This gives a general measure of emotional stability. The language is probably within the comprehension only of deaf college students and educated deaf adults.

Vineland Social-Maturity Scale. This is a list of items to be checked by the observer and therefore can be used with any deaf child. Except for a few items depending upon hearing, it seems suitable for the deaf child.

Behavior Rating Scale by Haggerty, Olson and Wickman. This, like any other rating scale, can be freely used with the deaf, because it does not require any language response on the part of the subject being rated.

SPECIAL ABILITIES

The Stanford Motor-Skills Unit, devised by Seashore (37),

has been adapted by Long (21) for use with the deaf to give a measure of motor ability. As used by Long the series consists of seven tests: (1) spool packing; (2) serial discriminator; (3) pursuit rotor; (4) tapping; (5) motility rotor; (6) dynamometer; (7) balance board.

The Minnesota Mechanical-Ability Tests have been adapted by Stanton (38) for use with the deaf. These consist of (1) paper form-board tests; (2) four spatial-relations test boards; (3) three boxes of the assembly test. These tests seem well suited to test the mechanical ability of the deaf.

TESTS SUITABLE FOR THE HARD OF HEARING

So far no special tests or adaptations of standard tests have been prepared for the hard of hearing. There would seem to be no such need. The hard of hearing can use all of the tests constructed for the normal hearing child as well as those constructed for the deaf.

TESTS SUITABLE FOR THE BLIND

GENERAL REQUIREMENTS

Any test depending upon vision must, of course, be eliminated. That leaves at our disposal for use with the blind all oral tests and all tests that can be translated into braille. The blind, unlike the deaf, learn speech in a normal manner much as seeing individuals do, and so language is a medium through which we can measure their intelligence. Tests depending entirely upon the sense of touch are of course suitable for the blind, and several such have been used as intelligence tests to take the place of visual tests. No purely tactual tests, which exclude vision, are to be found among intelligence tests for the normal child, so that such tests are found only in scales constructed for the blind. On the whole, fewer changes or adaptations of our standard tests are required for use with the blind than is the case with the deaf. All tests requiring the reading of braille must of course make due allowance for the slowness of such reading, as compared with the speed of visual reading of ink print. Generally three to four times as much time should be allowed.

INTELLIGENCE

There are three individual scales for the measurement of the intelligence of the blind, but so far only the first one has been used extensively in actual testing in the schools for the blind.

The Hayes-Binet Scale, or the Stanford Revision of the Binet Scale, was adapted by Hayes (16). As its name implies, this is an adaptation of Terman's Stanford Revision of the Binet-Simon Scale. Twelve tests were substituted for tests which could not be given to blind children, but otherwise the tests and procedure follow very closely the Stanford Revision. This scale may be called at present the standard instrument for the measurement of the intelligence of the blind. Practically all of the data given in Chapter VII concerning the intelligence of the blind have been derived from the use of this scale.

The Yerkes-Bridges Point Scale was adapted for use with the blind by Haines (14); it is sometimes called the Columbus Point Scale for the Blind. Some early work in the measurement of the intelligence of the blind was done by Haines with this scale and this is described in Chapter VII. No recent work has appeared and this scale is of historic interest only.

The I.J.R. Intelligence Test for the Visually Handicapped was devised by Davidson and Brown (9). This is a new scale and few results of its use with the blind are as yet available, so that it is impossible to evaluate it at the present time. It consists of ten subtests which can be given orally and call for oral responses. Each subtest is given a score and the total weighted scores are turned into mental ages. The ten subtests are: (1) vocabulary; (2) comprehension of paragraphs read to the subject; (3) mental-arithmetic problems; (4) repetition of the thought of a passage read; (5) digits backwards; (6) opposites; (7) similarities; (8) disarranged sentences; (9) number sequences; (10) analogies.

Group intelligence tests for the blind are generally in braille and they are therefore expensive and unwieldy to handle. Furthermore the Hayes-Binet has proved well suited for the blind. This may account for the fact that up to the present time only a few group tests have appeared.

The Kuhlmann-Anderson Intelligence Test was adapted for use with the blind by Fortner (11). The tests suitable for grades VI to IX have been put into braille. These are tests 21 to 29 inclusive, with the exception of test 24 dealing with the drawing of parts of geometrical forms, omitted because it depends upon vision. The subjects write their answers in braille on separate slips of paper, so that the original test blanks may be used over and over again. The scorers must know braille or have the braille answers translated for them. The time limits of the ink-print test have been increased about three times to allow for the slower reading rate of braille. Slight adaptations have been made to make the tests more suitable for braille readers. The correlation between this test and the Hayes-Binet for 102 cases is reported as .57.

The Otis Classification Test was adapted by Sargent (35). Part of the original test is an intelligence test and part an educational-achievement test. The intelligence test part has been considerably abbreviated and adapted for the blind.

The Pressey Mental Survey or "cross-out" tests were adapted for the blind by Hayes (15). This is a short group test of the usual verbal type.

The C.E.B. Scholastic-Aptitude Test. Brigham (4) has described the adaptation of part of the College Entrance Board Scholastic-Aptitude Test for blind students seeking admission to some colleges. Three of the subtests, namely, opposites, analogies, and paragraph meaning, have been put into braille and also fifty items of the paragraph test have been recorded on "talking-book" records. The candidates write their answers on a typewriter or in braille and unlimited time is allowed. In 1938 six totally blind students were tested and presumably from now on these tests will be used with blind students who make application to the College Entrance Board. Naturally these tests are not published for general distribution.

EDUCATIONAL ACHIEVEMENT

The adaptation of standard educational tests for use with the blind is relatively simple. Many of them can be put into braille with only minor changes and the subjects can write their answers in braille on the writing slate or on the typewriter. Some of the tests can be given orally. All tests that require braille reading must have their time allowances considerably lengthened. In general the blind read braille only about one third as fast as the seeing read inkprint. Furthermore, when the blind subjects are expected to write their answers, we must remember that they write with a stylus only about half as fast as seeing children write with pen or pencil. A full discussion of these important points is given by Hayes (17).

To indicate to the reader the extent of standardized educational test material adapted for the blind, we give below a list of the various tests. At the end of this chapter a list of these tests is given, together with the names of the publishers from whom such material can be procured. The results of using these tests with the blind, together with the appropriate references to the workers who have so used them will be found in Chapter VII.

Comprehensive Educational-Achievement Tests.

Stanford Achievement Tests

New Stanford Achievement Tests. Forms V, W, X, Y, Z.

Standard Graduation Examination for Elementary Schools by Otis and Orleans

Unit Scales of Attainment

Sones-Harry High-School Achievement Test

Hayes' Self-Survey Tests for the Blind

Reading Tests.

Gray Oral-Reading Check Tests

Iowa Silent-Reading Tests

Monroe Silent-Reading Tests

Stone Narrative-Reading Tests

McCall-Crabbe Standard Test Lessons in Reading

English Tests.

Cross English Tests

Wilson Language-Error Test

Mathematics and Arithmetic Tests.

Wisconsin Inventory Tests in Arithmetic

Stevenson Arithmetic Reading Test

Co-operative Plane-Geometry Test

Latin Test.

Co-operative Latin Test

Spanish Test.

American Council Alpha Spanish Test

French Test.

Co-operative French Test

General-Information Tests.

Sangren Information Test for Young Children

Pressey Test of Practical Information

PERSONALITY TESTS

Very few personality tests have so far been used with the blind.

Neymann-Kohlstedt Introversion-Extraversion Test. This is a test by Neymann and Kohlstedt (24) and has been used by Brown (6) with the blind. The results are discussed in Chapter VII.

Thurstone Personality Inventory. A general test of emotional stability or neurotic tendency constructed by Thurstone (39) and used by Brown (7) with the blind. The results are discussed in Chapter VII.

SPECIAL-ABILITY TESTS

Only one of these seems to have been used and adapted to the blind.

Seashore Measures of Musical Talent. A series of phonograph tests constructed by Seashore (36) and used with the blind by Merry (23). The original tests are group tests. With the blind they were given as individual tests.

TESTS SUITABLE FOR THE PARTIALLY SIGHTED

Very little testing of the partially seeing has so far been done. The tests used have been the regular tests for the normal seeing, such as the Stanford-Binet and the like. The senior author is at present experimenting with enlargements of the standard picture and printed material of the New Stanford Revision. It is expected that the use of such enlarged material will prove to be better than the standard material for the visually handicapped child.

With reference to printed group educational and intelligence tests, it would seem probable that the only adaptations required for these children would be to reproduce the desired tests in some suitable large-size type, and to extend the usual time limits in order to allow for the slower rate of reading large-size type. Some tests have been so printed, but none seem so far to have been published for general distribution.

TESTS SUITABLE FOR THE CRIPPLED

Handicaps in this vast region are so varied, that it is impossible to generalize as to the requirements for a suitable test. Some children can be given the standard Binet tests. Some children can write well enough to be given the ordinary written group intelligence and achievement tests. But many cannot. Some are handicapped in speech, so that oral responses are difficult or impossible. Some are handicapped in muscular movement, so that all performance tests are ruled out, and sometimes also all written tests. So far no worker has made any special adaptations of standard tests for this large group of handicapped children.

SUMMARY

We have attempted in this chapter to give a description of tests especially adapted to the various handicapped groups. Elsewhere in this book the reader will find a full discussion of the results obtained by the use of these tests with the various handicapped groups. In general we may say that we now have fairly adequate tests for the measurement of some of the psychological characteristics of the deaf and the blind. We have very few tests especially adapted for the intermediate groups such as the hard of hearing and the partially seeing. Perhaps this is due to the fact that not much adaptation is required for these groups. But more research needs to be done here to make sure of this. And finally, no special tests have been constructed for the crippled child.

LIST OF TESTS AND PUBLISHERS *

FOR THE DEAF

Intelligence: Individual Tests.

1. Pintner-Paterson Short Performance Scale.
   Materials: C. H. Stoelting Co., Chicago, Illinois, and Marietta Apparatus Co., Marietta, Ohio.
   Manual: Teachers College Bureau of Publications, Teachers College, Columbia University, New York City.
2. Drever-Collins Performance Test. A. H. Baird, Scientific-Instrument Maker, Lothian Street, Edinburgh, Scotland.
3. Arthur Performance Scale.
   Materials: C. H. Stoelting Co., Chicago, Illinois.
   Manual: The Commonwealth Fund, New York.
4. Ontario School Ability Examination. Ryerson Press, Toronto, Ontario, Canada.
5. Porteus Maze Test. C. H. Stoelting Co., Chicago, Illinois.

Intelligence: Group Tests.

1. Pintner Nonlanguage Mental Test. College Book Company, Columbus, Ohio.
2. Pintner Nonlanguage Primary Mental Test. Teachers College Bureau of Publications, Teachers College, Columbia University, New York.

* Where a test, mentioned in the text, is not given here, it means that so far as we know the test has not yet been published for general use. The interested reader should then refer to the reference at the end of this chapter and communicate directly with the author of the article in which the test was described.

3. Chicago Nonverbal Examination. Psychological Corporation, New York City.
4. Goodenough Drawing Scale. World Book Co., Yonkers, New York.

Educational Achievement.

1. Pintner Educational Survey Test. College Book Co., Columbus, Ohio.
2. Stanford Achievement Test. World Book Co., Yonkers, New York.

Personality.

1. Brunschwig Personality Inventory. R. Pintner, Teachers College, Columbia University, New York.
2. Pupil Portraits. Teachers College Bureau of Publications, Teachers College, Columbia University, New York.
3. Aspects of Personality. World Book Co., Yonkers, New York.
4. Bernreuter Personality Inventory. Stanford University Press, Stanford, California.
5. Thurstone Personality Schedule. University of Chicago Press, Chicago, Illinois.
6. Vineland Social-Maturity Scale. The Training School, Vineland, New Jersey.
7. Behavior Rating Scale by Haggerty *et al.* World Book Co., Yonkers, New York.

Special Abilities.

1. Minnesota Mechanical Ability Test. C. H. Stoelting Co., Chicago, Illinois, and Marietta Apparatus Co., Marietta, Ohio.

FOR THE BLIND

A.P.H. means American Printing House for the Blind, 1839 Frankfort Ave., Louisville, Kentucky.

H.M.P. means Howe Memorial Press, 549 E. Fourth St., South Boston, Massachusetts.

Intelligence: Individual Tests.

1. Stanford Revision for the Blind. Perkins Institution for the Blind, Watertown, Massachusetts.
2. I.J.R. Intelligence Test. Dr. A. W. Brown, Institute for Juvenile Research, Chicago, Illinois.

Intelligence: Group Tests.

1. Kuhlmann-Anderson Intelligence Test. A.P.H.
2. Otis Classification Test. A.P.H.

Educational Achievement.

Comprehensive Educational Achievement.

1. New Stanford Achievement Tests, Forms V, W, X, Y, Z. A.P.H. and H.M.P.
2. Standard Graduation Examination (Otis-Orleans). A.P.H.
3. Unit Scales of Attainment. A.P.H.
4. Sones-Harry High-School Achievement Test. A.P.H.
5. Hayes Self-Survey Tests for the Blind. A.P.H.

Reading Tests.

1. Gray Oral-Reading Check Tests. A.P.H.
2. Iowa Silent-Reading Tests. H.M.P.
3. Monroe Silent-Reading Tests. A.P.H.
4. Stone Narrative-Reading Tests. H.M.P.
5. McCall-Crabbe Standard Test Lessons. A.P.H.

English.

1. Cross English Test. A.P.H.
2. Wilson Language-Error Test. World Book Co., Yonkers, New York.

Arithmetic and Mathematics.

1. Wisconsin Inventory Tests in Arithmetic. Public School Publishing Co., Bloomington, Illinois.
2. Stevenson Arithmetic Reading Test. Public School Publishing Co., Bloomington, Illinois.
3. Co-operative Plane-Geometry Test. A.P.H.

Latin.

1. Co-operative Latin Test. A.P.H.

Spanish.

1. American Council Alpha Spanish Test. A.P.H.

French.

1. Co-operative French Test. A.P.H.

General Information.

1. Sangren Information Test for Young Children. World Book Co., Yonkers, New York.
2. Pressey Test of Practical Information. A.P.H.

Personality Tests.

1. Neymann-Kohlstedt Introversion-Extraversion Test. C. H. Stoelting Co., Chicago, Illinois.

Thurstone Personality Inventory. University of Chicago Press, Chicago, Illinois.

Special-Abilities Tests.

1. Seashore Measures of Musical Talent. Columbia Phonograph Co., Boston, Massachusetts.

BIBLIOGRAPHY

1. Amoss, H., *Ontario School Ability Examination* (Ryerson Press, Toronto, 1936).
2. Arthur G., *A Point Scale of Performance Tests* (Vol. I, *Clinical Manual*) (Commonwealth Fund, N.Y., 1930).
3. Arthur, G., *A Point Scale of Performance Tests* (Vol. II, *The Process of Standardization*) (Commonwealth Fund, N.Y., 1933).
4. Brigham, C. C., "The Scholastic Aptitude Test for the Blind," *Sch. and Soc.*, LI (1940), 91–96.
5. Brown, A. W., "The Development and Standardization of the Chicago Non-Verbal Examination," *J. Appl. Psychol.*, XXIV (1940), 36–47, 122–9.
6. Brown, P. A., "Responses of Blind and Seeing Adolescents

to an Introversion-Extroversion Questionnaire," *J. Psychol.*, VI (1938), 137–47.

7. Brown, P. A., "Responses of Blind and Seeing Adolescents to a Neurotic Inventory," *J. Psychol.*, VII (1939), 211–21.
8. Brunschwig, L., *A Study of Some Personality Aspects of Deaf Children*, T.C. Contribs. to Educ., No. 687 (Bur. of Pubs., Teachers College, Columbia Univ., N.Y., 1936).
9. Davidson, M., and A. W. Brown, "The Development and Standardization of the I.J.R. Test for the Visually Handicapped," *J. Appl. Psychol.*, XXIII (1939), 229–39.
10. Drever, J., and M. Collins, *Performance Tests of Intelligence*, 2nd ed. (Oliver and Boyd, Edinburgh, 1936).
11. Fortner, E. N., "A Group Intelligence Test in Braille," *Teachers Forum (Blind)*,* XI (1939), 53–56.
12. Frampton, M. E., ed., *Education of the Blind* (World Book Co., Yonkers, N.Y., 1940), Ch. 27, "Tests and Measurements."
13. Goodenough, F. L., "A New Approach to the Measurement of the Intelligence of Young Children," *Ped. Sem.*, XXXIII (1926), 185–211.
14. Haines, T. H., "Mental Measurement of the Blind," *Psychol. Monogs.*, XXI (1916), No. 89.
15. Hayes, S. P., *Self-Surveys in Schools for the Blind*, Pubs. of Pa. Inst. for Instruct. of the Blind, No. 2 (Dec., 1921).
16. Hayes, S. P., *Terman's Condensed Guide for the Stanford Revision for the Blind* (Perkins Inst. for the Blind, Watertown, Mass., 1930).
17. Hayes, S. P., "Practical Hints for Testers," *Teachers Forum (Blind)*, XI (1938–39), 82–93.
18. Hayes, S. P., "Standard Graduation Examination for Elementary Schools: Adapted for Use in Schools for the Blind," *Teachers Forum (Blind)*, XII (1939–40), 22–32.
19. Hildreth, G. H., and R. Pintner, *Manual of Directions for*

* This abbreviation is used throughout the bibliographies for *Teachers Forum for Instructors of Blind Children.*

Pintner-Paterson Performance Tests, Short Scale (Bur. of Pubs., Teachers College, Columbia Univ., N.Y., 1937).

20. Keys, N., and L. Boulware, "Language Acquisition by Deaf Children as Related to Hearing Loss and Age of Onset," *J. Educ. Psychol.*, XXIX (1938), 401–12.
21. Long, J. A., *Motor Abilities of Deaf Children*, T.C. Contribs. to Educ., No. 514 (Bur. of Pubs., Teachers College, Columbia Univ., N.Y., 1932).
22. MacKane, K., *A Comparison of the Intelligence of Deaf and Hearing Children*, T.C. Contribs. to Educ., No. 585 (Bur. of Pubs., Teachers College, Columbia Univ., N.Y., 1933).
23. Merry, R. V., "Adapting the Seashore Musical Talent Tests for Use with Blind Pupils," *Teachers Forum (Blind)*, III (1930–31), 15–19.
24. Neymann, C. A., and K. D. Kohlstedt, "A New Diagnostic Test for Introversion-Extroversion," *J. Abn. and Soc. Psychol.*, XXIII (1929), 482–7.
25. Pintner, R., "A Nonlanguage Group Intelligence Test," *J. Appl. Psychol.*, III (1919), 199–214.
26. Pintner, R., "Results Obtained with the Nonlanguage Group Test," *J. Educ. Psychol.*, XV (1924), 473–83.
27. Pintner, R., *Intelligence Testing* (Holt, N.Y., 1931).
28. Pintner, R., "A Group Intelligence Test Suitable for Younger Deaf Children," *J. Educ. Psychol.*, XXII (1931), 360–3.
29. Pintner, R., and L. Brunschwig, "An Adjustment Inventory for Use in Schools for the Deaf," *Am. Annals of the Deaf*, LXXXII (1937), 152–67.
30. Pintner, R., I. S. Fusfeld, and L. Brunschwig, "Personality Tests of Deaf Adults," *J. Genet. Psychol.*, LI (1937), 305–27.
31. Pintner, R., and H. Marshall, "A Combined Mental-Educational Survey," *J. Educ. Psychol.*, XII (1921), 32–43, 82–91.
32. Pintner, R., and D. G. Paterson, *A Scale of Performance Tests* (Appleton, N.Y., 1917).
33. Porteus, S. D., *Guide to the Porteus Maze Test* (Pub. No. 25, Training School, Vineland, N.J., 1924).

34. Porteus, S. D., "The Validity of the Porteus Maze Test," *J. Educ. Psychol.*, XXX (1939), 172–8.
35. Sargent, R., "The Otis Classification Test," *Teachers Forum* (*Blind*), IV (1931), 30–33.
36. Seashore, C. E., *The Psychology of Musical Talent* (Silver Burdett, N.Y., 1919).
37. Seashore, R. H., "Stanford Motor Skills Unit," *Psychol. Monogs.*, XXXIX (1928), No. 178, 51–66.
38. Stanton, M. B., *Mechanical Ability of Deaf Children*, T.C. Contribs. to Educ., No. 751 (Bur. of Pubs., Teachers College, Columbia Univ., N.Y., 1938).
39. Thurstone, L. L., and T. G. Thurstone, "A Neurotic Inventory," *J. Soc. Psychol.*, I (1930), 3–30.

CHAPTER V

The Deaf

GENERAL

By "the deaf" we mean those individuals whose hearing is of no practical value for the purpose of communicating with others. Such individuals may range from the totally deaf to those with considerable sound perception, but in all cases their hearing is of little practical value in the ordinary affairs of life. Those whose hearing, although below normal, is sufficient to enable them to hear the speech of others are called "the hard of hearing." Another way of stating this distinction is as follows: The deaf are those in whom the sense of hearing is nonfunctional for the ordinary purposes of life; the hard of hearing are those in whom the sense of hearing, although defective, is functional with or without a hearing aid.* There is, of course, no sharp dividing line between these two groups of individuals. One cannot divide them into two groups by means of audiometer tests, because some of the deaf may have more sound perception than some of the hearing. Nevertheless, the difference between the two groups is psychologically clear and distinct. The

* These definitions were recommended by the Conference of Executives of American Schools for the Deaf.

deaf are those who have never learned language incidentally in the ordinary way—in the way the normal hearing child picks it up from his environment, casually, unconsciously. The hard of hearing are those who, in spite of their hearing handicap, did learn language in just this unconscious casual manner like the normal hearing child. This basic difference between the two groups means that they require quite different methods of education. For this reason we shall treat them separately. This chapter will be devoted to "the deaf," and the following chapter to the "hard of hearing."

Incidence. The United States Census since 1830 has enumerated the deaf in this country. The scope and method of enumeration has varied from decade to decade so much so that the number of deaf per million of the total population has varied from 321 to 675 per million. The definition of the deaf-mute to be enumerated in the 1920 census (83) is as follows: "The three following classes are considered as deaf-mutes in the census inquiries: (1) Totally deaf persons unable to use speech as a means of communication—those in the most literal sense 'deaf-mutes.' (2) All other totally deaf persons who have lost hearing before they were eight years old, including those able to use speech for communication. (3) All partially deaf persons whose deafness has occurred under eight years of age, and who can hear only with an ear trumpet or other mechanical appliance." And again (83), "The census of deaf-mutes covers all persons who by reason of defective hearing either have never acquired the faculty of articulate speech, or have required special instruction in order to acquire it." Similar definitions were used in the 1930 census (84).

The total number enumerated in 1920 was 44,885; in 1930, 57,084. In 1830, when the first enumeration of the deaf took place, there were approximately 6,000. The number per million of the total population was 425 in 1920 and 465 in 1930. In 1920 this meant one deaf to every 2,355 persons.

Because the scope and method of enumeration has varied greatly from 1830 to 1930, it is not profitable to discuss the question as to whether deafness is increasing or decreasing. There seems no evidence to indicate that it is increasing. If it is decreasing, the rate of decrease is very slow. As the total population has increased, the actual number of deaf in the country has increased during the past hundred years from approximately 6,000 to approximately 50,000. At present there is no indication of any major medical discovery or any special treatment that will wipe out deafness in the human race. Such a discovery may, of course, come at any moment, but in the meantime we are confronted with a large number of handicapped individuals (although a small percentage of the total population), who need special education, special study and special understanding on our part.

The Causes of Deafness. The 1920 census (83) received special schedules filled out by 35,026 of the deaf enumerated at that time. On the basis of these returns a tabulation of the causes of deafness was made. Congenital deafness, i. e., deafness occurring at birth whether due to hereditary causes or prenatal causes, accounted for 38.6 per cent of the cases. Acquired deafness amounted to 61.4 per cent.

Of the acquired cases the two most important causes were found to be scarlet fever, responsible for 17.6 per cent of acquired deafness, and meningitis, responsible for 17.0 per cent. Brain fever follows with 6.9 per cent. Brain fever means in most cases meningitis, so if we add it to meningitis, meningitis and brain fever are seen to cause 23.9 per cent of acquired deafness. Hence scarlet fever and meningitis together cause about 41.5 per cent or in all probability about half the cases of acquired deafness. Next in order of importance comes measles, causing 5.7 per cent of the cases. Then typhoid fever, whooping cough, disease of ear, abscess in head, each causing about 2 per cent. All these eight causes are equal to 58.6 per cent of acquired deafness. A great many deaf individuals do not know the cause, and many attribute deafness to a blow on the head or a fall, very improbable causes.

The great causes of deafness are therefore hereditary, prenatal, brain diseases, and the infectious and contagious diseases of childhood.

Pupils in School. The number of pupils in schools for the deaf were distributed as follows for 1939 (13):

Schools	*Male*	*Female*	*Total*
66 public residential schools	7,427	6,245	13,672
128 public day schools	2,456	2,146	4,602
19 denominational and private schools	452	435	887
Total–213 schools	10,335	8,826	19,161

This represents the load which educators have to face. How can we best educate these twenty thousand pupils so as to fit them for life? The more we know about the psychological traits of these individuals, the better will we be able to cope with their education.

EARLY PSYCHOLOGICAL STUDIES

Very little psychological work, as we understand the term today, appears in the early literature about the deaf and deafness. There is much speculation about the psychological characteristics of the deaf. There are a certain number of anecdotal accounts of particular incidents noted by various writers. There is much generalization without a factual or experimental basis.

As an example of this type of work we may mention Diderot's

"Letter on the Deaf and Dumb" (10), written about the middle of the eighteenth century. He relates certain anecdotes about deaf people. He tells how one deaf man came to the conclusion that musical instruments were a means of speech, because he had noticed that hearing people listened to them just as they would when other people were talking. But Diderot's real interest did not lie in the deaf themselves, but rather in philosophical speculation as to the function of the senses in relation to knowledge and thought. In all probability he had little contact with the deaf.

From men who devoted their lives to the education of the deaf in the nineteenth century we have many reports of observations and speculations of a psychological nature. Peet (47) investigated, by means of questions, the ideas of the deaf, before they had received formal education, especially as to their concepts of God and various natural phenomena. Much of his data was gathered from educated deaf adults who described the ideas they had had before receiving any formal education. He concluded that the uneducated deaf have "childlike ideas respecting the causes of certain natural phenomena, such as rain, thunder and the motions of the heavenly bodies." Other writers at this period were also interested in the idea of God and studied the deaf in relation to the problem of whether such an idea was innate or dependent upon education. This early work, therefore, may be described as speculative and philosophical. It is very far removed from the modern objective psychological approach.

The major interest of the educators of the deaf during the nineteenth century was concentrated upon the practical problems of education. In particular they were struggling with the problem of the best methods for educating the deaf, and their educational journals are filled with discussions as to the advantages and disadvantages of the oral, combined or manual methods of instruction. So bitter was this controversy as to methods of instruction that practically all other considerations were pushed into the background. However, in this background we notice an increasing concern over the fact that some deaf children seem to be extremely difficult to educate by any method. And so the problem of the feeble-minded deaf emerges. There is much discussion about how to detect the feeble-minded deaf and what to do with him. And it is in this connection that the first suggestion of a practical objective approach emerges. Greenberger (19) in 1889 seems to have stumbled on the idea of using something like a psychological test when confronted with the problem of weeding out the feeble-minded among the children applying for admission to an institution for the deaf. In addition to the ordinary tests for hearing, he says that there is a necessity for finding out something about their mental faculties. Attractive picture books should be shown to the child and the examiner should watch what the child does. If the child remains perfectly apathetic it is a bad sign. If, however, the child is attracted by the books and maintains an interest in them for a period of time, it is an indication of a fair mentality that can be improved by training. Greenberger also proposes a little number test, since "entire lack of an idea of numbers is, in my estimation, a sure sign of great weakness in a child's mind." He also shows the child forms and colors. Blocks are placed before the child and the examiner watches how well he can build with them. Modern mental tests for young children make use of all the material that Greenberger suggests—pictures, blocks, colors, and the like. Neither a standard method of procedure nor an evaluation of the child's responses in terms of the responses of other children was suggested by Greenberger, and so the essential elements of a standardized mental test were lacking. This is of course not surprising, because psychological tests were in their infancy when Greenberger wrote and he was probably totally unaware of what little there was to be known about them at that time.

There is no direct sequence to Greenberger's suggestions. Neither he nor any other worker seems to have developed the ideas implicit in his work. The practical need for tests was great, because during this period we find numerous articles referring to the problem of feeble-mindedness among the deaf. Love (32) in 1907 describes the procedure followed by educators of the deaf in Denmark. Jones (24) in 1909 estimates that 20 per cent of the pupils in one state school for the deaf are feeble-minded. McIlvaine, in 1909 (42) and again in 1912 (43), and other writers discuss this problem of the mentally retarded among the deaf, but none of them suggests any scientific methods for diagnosing the subnormal deaf child.

Testing was in the air during the last decade of the nineteenth and the first decade of the twentieth century. Both educational and psychological measurement were beginning. In 1897 Taylor (80) reported on a spelling test given to 148 deaf pupils and a group of hearing pupils. The test was a free-association test. The pupil was told to write as many words as possible in fifteen minutes. The average number of words written by the deaf was 151; by the hearing 153. The average percentage of spelling mistakes by the deaf was 2.7; by the hearing 4.3. Hence the deaf are superior in spelling ability.

Mott (45) during 1899 and 1900 published her comparison of eight-year-old deaf and hearing children. She chose eight-year-olds because this was, at that time, the age at which many deaf children entered residential schools. She wished to compare the deaf and hearing "in all respects in which data of normal children are available." She used physical as well as psychological tests. With reference to mental factors she says: "Memory and observation seemed the only mental powers capable of exact comparison between the two classes of children."

In physical measurements, in athletic tests, and manual dexterity, she finds the deaf to be as good as or even better than the hearing. Again, in memory and observation tests she finds the deaf markedly superior to the hearing. Some of these results are directly contrary to later work and it is of little value now to enter into a discussion of the shortcomings of this study. It is mentioned here because it shows the beginnings of the use of psychological tests for the comparison of the deaf and the hearing.

A little later, in 1903, Smith (72) published the results of memory tests with the deaf. Immediate and delayed memory were tested by means of a story. No comparison with hearing children was attempted.

In 1906 the results of psychological tests of deaf pupils were published by MacMillan and Bruner (36). This investigation, they say, "deals with deaf children attending the public day school whom this department considered of high enough grade of mentality to be educable by the special class methods of the public schools for the deaf." Evidently these are very selected cases and do not represent the general population of deaf children attending residential schools for the deaf nor even those attending public day schools for the deaf. This is shown by the fact that, among the 184 cases examined, none were found to be feeble-minded and only eleven slightly retarded or subnormal.

The importance of MacMillan and Bruner's work derives from its being the first study in which standard psychological tests were given to deaf children, so far as we have been able to discover. These tests were not the intelligence tests now in common use, but the tests of single separate abilities which preceded the general intelligence tests of the Binet type. The tests were both physical and mental. There were tests of hearing, visual acuity, height, weight, and head measurements. In lung capacity the deaf are on the average below the hearing. There is not much difference in strength of grip. In the tapping test, used as a measure of motor ability, only about 24 per cent reach or exceed the average for the hearing. In the cancellation of A's test the deaf were on the average "from two to three years less mature than hearing children of the same ages." In perception of size by sense of touch the deaf fall below the hearing, but in perception of differences in lifted weights the deaf are as good as the hearing. In visual memory span for numbers the deaf are definitely below the hearing. The authors, after summarizing their findings, conclude as follows: "This inferiority of the deaf on the mental side perhaps means no more than that the child is from three to four years less mature than the hearing child of his own age, and that his date of maturing will be correspondingly delayed. It does not necessarily mean that adult deaf individuals will be much inferior in mental comprehension and initiative to hearing adults. Indeed this mental retardation may be due to conditions in training, and were the deaf child's instruction begun in infancy instead of at six years, the difference might be reduced or even eliminated." These speculations as to the later maturing of the deaf child and the probability of his catching up with the hearing later on are not based upon anything in the work of the authors we have just quoted. It is very hazardous to venture such opinions, particularly if we keep in mind the fact that the group of deaf children tested by them was a highly selected group, from which the obviously feebleminded had already been eliminated. The results as to the retardation of three or four years have been repeatedly substantiated by later workers, but so far no investigation has shown that the deaf as a whole catch up in later life.

We have described this work of MacMillan and Bruner at

some length, because it seems to us to be the outstanding study on the mentality of the deaf prior to the introduction of Binet testing, and in it we note the three or four years' retardation on psychological tests, which is to appear so frequently in later studies.

INTELLIGENCE

The introduction of the Binet-Simon Scale for the measurement of intelligence started a new chapter in psychological measurement. An all-inclusive measure of general ability took the place of the single specific tests of very narrow psychological functions. The practical value of the Binet type of scale became immediately obvious, and in 1912 Kilpatrick (26) proposed applying the Binet-Simon Scale to all pupils "of two or three representative schools for the deaf" in order to find out the satisfactory tests and discover substitutes for the unsatisfactory ones. This proposal, however, was not carried out.

We shall now discuss the results of various types of intelligence tests given to deaf children under the four following headings: Binet tests, performance tests, group nonlanguage tests, learning tests.

BINET TESTS

The only thorough attempt to apply the Binet tests to the deaf was made by Pintner and Paterson (56), who published their results in 1915. It was the first attempt by these workers to apply a general intelligence test to the deaf. Before this time they had tried substitution tests with deaf children and these we shall discuss later under learning tests. They wished now to extend their investigations so as to obtain a better measure of the general ability of the deaf and so they turned to the Binet-Simon Scale, which at that time was relatively new and which was giving such good results with hearing children. They used the Goddard Revision of the Binet-Simon Scale, which was in general use at that time.

These investigators first attempted to apply the tests by the use of written language. The questions were typed and presented to the child, and the child answered, if possible, in writing. But this method was soon abandoned because it at once became apparent that many children did not understand the written questions, but did understand the same questions when asked by means of the manual alphabet or sign language. Therefore the workers used any method or any combination of methods, speech, writing, signs, or manual spelling, in order to put the question across. The tests did not work.

Twenty-two children were examined. Eighteen cases yielded enough tests to compute a tentative mental age. Only one child tested at age. All others were retarded. The average C.A. was 12.5 years; the average M.A. was 7.9 years. The average mental retardation was 4.58 years. Many tests were found to be totally unsuited for the deaf. The language of the questions was too difficult. Many children could not adjust to the question and answer situation. Lack of experience with certain things, e. g., money or stamps, handicapped the deaf child. The authors speak also of the peculiar psychology of the deaf child. They quote Binet himself as speaking of "the peculiar mentality of deaf-mutes." To the question "Were you alone?", Binet received from a deaf adult the answer, "Yes, I am alone and I have two deaf-mute comrades." Pintner and Paterson quote similar peculiar answers to questions of the Binet tests. For example to the question, "What would you do if you were going somewhere and you missed the train?" answers were received as follows: (1) Baltimore and Ohio; (2) Go home, get candy. Partial understanding due to language difficulty or lack of intelligence or both is in all probability the fundamental cause of these peculiar answers. A particular word such as "train" is understood but the whole significance of the sentence is not grasped. By mere association with "train" the response "Baltimore and Ohio" occurs.

Pintner and Paterson conclude this pioneer investigation of the Binet Scale with the deaf by stating that the Binet Scale as it stands is totally unsuited for the deaf. They suggest that performance tests might be more suitable. They took their own suggestion seriously and immediately started work with performance tests which led untimately to the construction of the Pintner-Paterson Performance Scale.

PERFORMANCE TESTS

Those performance scales which do not require the use of language in the directions to the subject are best fitted for the testing of the deaf. The one most commonly used in this country is the Pintner-Paterson Performance Scale; in Great Britain the Drever-Collins Performance Scale is used. MacKane (35) used these two scales and added a third, the Arthur Performance Scale, in which he made slight modifications in order to give it without verbal directions. He tested 130 deaf children, ages ten to twelve. Each deaf subject was paired with a hearing subject of the same age, sex, national background, and economic status. The mean differences between these hearing and deaf groups on these three tests, as well as on the group Pintner Nonlanguage Mental Test, are shown in Table I.

It will be noted that on all three of the performance scales the deaf fall below the hearing by about six or seven months and that the ratios of the differences to the standard errors of the differences are fairly large, the smallest one of 2.2 indicating that the chances are 98 in 100 that the true difference is greater than zero. The difference between the groups on the nonlanguage group test is still greater and we shall discuss this further in our next section dealing with group tests.

TABLE I

COMPARISON OF 130 DEAF AND HEARING MATCHED PAIRS ON THREE PERFORMANCE SCALES AND ONE GROUP TEST (FROM MAC KANE)

	Mean M.A. in Months			*D*
	hearing	*deaf*	*Diff.*	*S.D. Diff.*
Arthur Scale	126.6	119.6	7.0	2.9
Pintner-Paterson	126.8	121.2	5.6	2.2
Drever-Collins	146.9	140.0	6.9	2.4
Nonlanguage Group *	320.6	244.5	76.1	7.1

* Mean given in score points, not in M.A.

Table II compares these deaf and hearing groups in terms of M.A. and I.Q. for each of the three chronological ages involved. Again we see the deaf slightly below the hearing at each chronological age for each test. The Arthur and Pintner-Paterson scales show very similar M.A.'s and I.Q.'s, but the Drever-Collins shows M.A.'s and I.Q.'s much higher for both deaf and hearing groups. Evidently the standardization of the Drever-Collins Scale is very different from the other two scales. It gives much higher I.Q.'s. Nevertheless the deaf group does not equal the hearing group on this scale. In this respect the findings do not agree with those of Drever and Collins in Great Britain, who report no difference in the mental ability of the deaf and hearing tested by their scale.

Considering now the results from the other two scales, we note that the hearing I.Q.'s range from 91 to 95 for the various C.A. groups, and the deaf I.Q.'s from 86 to 92. The average for the hearing on both the Arthur and Pintner-Paterson is 93, and for the deaf 88 on the former and 89 on the latter scale. These matched deaf cases are therefore 4 or 5 points below the hearing in I.Q. If, however, we consider the deaf I.Q.'s themselves

TABLE II

MEAN MENTAL AGES AND I.Q.'S OF 130 MATCHED PAIRS OF DEAF AND HEARING SUBJECTS DIVIDED INTO C.A. GROUPS ON THREE PERFORMANCE SCALES (ADAPTED FROM MAC KANE)

Average C.A.	n pairs	Average Hearing M.A.			Average Deaf M.A.			Average Hearing I.Q.			Average Deaf I.Q.		
		A.	P.P.	D.C.	A.	P.P.	D.C.	A.	P.P.	D.C.	A.	P.P.	D.C.
10–6	46	10–0	10–0	11–9	9–6	9–8	10–9	95	95	111	90	92	102
11–6	57	10–6	10–6	12–2	9–10	10–0	12–6	91	91	106	86	87	109
12–5	27	11–6	11–6	13–5	11–0	11–0	13–1	93	93	108	89	89	105

A = Arthur Performance Scale P.P. = Pintner-Paterson Performance Scale D.C. = Drever-Collins Performance Scale

TABLE III

INTELLIGENCE TEST RESULTS FROM THE REAMER SURVEY

Age	8–6	9–6	10–6	11–6	12–6	13–6	14–6	15–6	16–6	17–6	18–6	19–6	20–6	21 +
n	22	63	96	151	219	260	313	312	227	171	112	91	20	82
Median N-L score	108	219	242	262	292	302	325	338	369	383	389	387	446	440
M.A.	8–10	9–9	10–4	10–10	11–6	11–8	12–2	12–5	13–6	14–2	14–6	14–5	15–9	15–7
I.Q.	104	103	98	94	92	88	87	85	90	94	97	96	105	104

and argue that according to the standardization of the scales an I.Q. of 100 is normal for each age, then we see that this deaf group is 11 or 12 points below normal. Whether this is true of deaf children in general we do not know, because this is a very small sampling of deaf children. By the same logic our hearing sample is also below normal by 7 points in I.Q.

In general, then, this study indicates a slightly lower intelligence of deaf children as compared with hearing children in regard to concrete intelligence as tested by the standard performance scales. The sample of deaf children used is very small, but they have been carefully matched with hearing controls.

Another report of deaf children tested by means of a performance scale is available. The deaf children in the South Dakota School for the Deaf (73) were tested by means of the Arthur Performance Scale. The distribution of I.Q.'s is as follows:

I.Q.	*n*
140–159	4
120–139	14
100–119	32
80–99	41
60–79	17
Total	108

The range of I.Q.'s is from 61 to 157 and the mean is 95.2. Seven cases or 6 per cent fall below an I.Q. of 70 and are called feebleminded in the report. The average I.Q. here is a little higher than that reported by MacKane.

Roth (65) reports the results of tests given by Bowers in the West Virginia School for the Deaf. Ten tests were used: six of the Pintner-Paterson series, the Kohs blocks, the Goodenough drawing, the Porteus maze, and one case was given the Kuhlmann-Anderson Test. An average I.Q. was calculated for each child on the tests he took. The range of I.Q.'s for 201 cases was 27 to 148, and the average was 89.2.

The I.Q.'s derived from the Ontario School-Ability Examination for 288 deaf children are reported by Amoss (1). These children ranged in age from five to twenty-two. The range of I.Q.'s was from 49 to 192, with a median I.Q. of 94.

This same test has been used by Morrison,* who reports the following distribution of I.Q.'s for 300 children in a school for the deaf during the year 1938–39:

I.Q.	*n*
140 and above	4
120–139	13
110–119	23
90–109	131
80–89	69
70–79	34
69 and below	26
Total	300

The range of I.Q.'s for these 300 cases is from 51 to 165 and the median I.Q. is 93. Morrison also gives the C.A.'s and I.Q.'s of 15 cases who were refused admission to the school. These 15 cases have I.Q.'s from 20 to 51. If these are added to the 300 cases in school, we obtain a total of 315 cases with a median I.Q. of 92.

Finally, Bridgman (5) gives the results for 90 deaf children tested by various individual tests. This was not a random sampling. Most of them were sent for examination because of difficulties in school. The median I.Q. is 90.

The means or medians of the I.Q.'s from these six studies of

* The results of the tests given here are from a private communication to the authors from W. J. Morrison, Superintendent of the Ontario School for the Deaf, Belleville, Ontario, and are reproduced with his permission.

the intelligence of deaf children by means of performance tests are:

MacKane	88.5
South Dakota	95.2
Roth	89.2
Amoss	94
Morrison	92.5
Bridgman	90

These findings are very similar, considering the differences in the samplings involved. The median of these six values gives an approximate I.Q. of 91 for deaf children on performance tests of intelligence. Let us now turn to the results of group tests of intelligence.

GROUP TESTS

The group intelligence test which has been used most frequently with deaf pupils is the Pintner Nonlanguage Mental Test. The Goodenough "Draw a Man" Test is the only other group intelligence test from which we have useful results.

Pintner Nonlanguage Mental Test. This test has been used in two large surveys. The Reamer (64) survey in 1921 covered 26 schools and reported results for 2,172 pupils in the age range from eight to twenty-one plus. The National Research Council Survey (9) in 1928 covered 41 schools and reported results for 4,432 pupils in the age range from twelve to twenty-one plus. Tables III and IV have been constructed to show the main findings of these two surveys. The median or mean scores on the Nonlanguage Test have been converted into mental ages based upon the standardization for hearing children. These M.A.'s have then been used to find I.Q.'s for each age group. The Terman-Merrill technique for the calculation of I.Q.'s for ages thirteen and above has been used.

TABLE IV

INTELLIGENCE TEST RESULTS FROM THE NATIONAL RESEARCH COUNCIL SURVEY

Age	12–6	13–6	14–6	15–6
Deaf				
n	547	608	678	590
mean score	258	276	300	320
Hearing				
n	1,361	1,295	1,120	700
mean score	321	348	362	364
Diff. / S.D. Diff.	12.1	13.6	11.6	7.2
M.A. of deaf	10–9	11–2	11–8	12–1
I.Q. of deaf	86	84	83	82

In general the Reamer Survey found higher I.Q.'s than the other survey. The Reamer I.Q.'s range from 85 to 105. The higher I.Q.'s are found at the lower and upper age levels, where the number of cases is smaller. The lower age groups are undoubtedly composed of more selected cases. They contained the more intelligent younger children who had reached the grades in which the tests were given. The upper age groups contained deaf college students at Gallaudet College and hence the higher scores at those ages. In all probability the most random sampling of deaf children is to be found in ages twelve to sixteen. Here the I.Q. range is from 85 to 92.

In the National Research Council Survey a very definite attempt was made to test all children in the age groups twelve to fifteen, and because of the wide geographical distribution of the schools examined, it is probable that these results give a true picture of the intelligence test scores of deaf children in the United States in the age range from twelve to fifteen. The differences in mean score between the deaf and the hearing are all large and statistically reliable. The I.Q.'s of the deaf range from 82 to 86.

Both of these surveys raised the question of the relationship between intelligence and age of onset of deafness and both of them found the age at which a child becomes deaf has no influence upon his score on the intelligence test. In the National Research Council Survey the median mental indices (an index is a kind of sigma score) of 2,423 deaf children between the ages of twelve to fifteen inclusive are given according to the age of onset of deafness as follows:

Age	*Unknown*	*Birth*	*0*	*1*	*2*	*3*	*4*	*5*
n	201	1,129	222	259	201	104	75	74
Index	48.4	50.0	49.7	50.5	49.6	51.2	52.7	51.1

Age	*6*	*7*	*8*	*9*	*10*	*11*	*12*	*13*
n	42	43	33	17	17	6	4	1
Index	51.6	51.5	53.1	56.0	56.0	53.0	53.0	50.0

These indices fluctuate around 50. There is no definite tendency to rise as the age of onset of deafness increases. Again we have Upshall's (82) correlations between age of onset of deafness and intelligence score on the Pintner Nonlanguage Test. For 311 day-school pupils it is – .02 and for 311 residential-school pupils + .09.

Again both surveys divided their cases according to the method of instruction, i. e., whether oral, manual, or combined. Both surveys found the intelligence of the manual pupils to be lowest. The Reamer Survey found the combined pupils to be highest, the other survey found the oral pupils highest. The results of the National Research Council Survey are as follows:

Method of Instruction	*Median Mental Index*	*n*
Oral	52.0	1845
Manual	41.2	186
Combined	46.9	392

The Reamer Survey finds no difference in intelligence between the congenital and the acquired deaf.

Deaf children are educated either in day or residential schools. The National Research Council Survey included 619 day-school pupils and 3,813 residential-school pupils. The median mental index of the day-school group was found to be 53.3, of the residential-school group, 47.6. The survey gives the following distribution for the two types of schools, dividing the cases into five intelligence categories according to their indices.

	Day		*Residential*	
Intelligence	*n*	*%*	*n*	*%*
Dull	7	1.1	126	3.3
Backward	88	14.2	1,034	27.1
Normal	327	52.8	1,858	48.7
Bright	185	29.9	730	19.1
Very bright	12	1.9	65	1.7
Total	619	99.9	3,813	99.9

Evidently the tendency of the day schools is to attract the brighter pupil. The residential schools have a much larger percentage of dull and backward children.

The average of the four I.Q.'s from the National Research Council Survey is 83.8; the average of the five I.Q.'s (ages twelve to sixteen) from the Reamer Survey is 88.4. An I.Q. of 86 might be considered as an approximate estimate of the intelligence of deaf children on group nonlanguage intelligence tests.

The Goodenough "Draw a Man" Test. This test has been

given to three small samples of deaf children and reported by the following workers:

Author	*Date*	*n*	*C.A.*	*I.Q.*
Peterson and Williams (48)	1930	330	4 to 13	80
Shirley and Goodenough (71)	1932	391	5 to 20	88
Springer (74)	1938	330	6 to 12	96

There is not much consistency in these reports, probably due to the differences in the methods of sampling. Shirley and Goodenough (71) tried to include all deaf children in the state of Minnesota. Springer (74) tested New York City children only. He had a control group of hearing children equated for C.A. and occupational status. His mean I.Q.'s for age-sex groups are very erratic. For the deaf they fluctuate from 73 to 108; for the hearing from 80 to 121. He finds a mean I.Q. for all his deaf group of 96.2 as compared with a mean I.Q. of 102.2 for his hearing group, and the difference of 6 points in I.Q. has a standard error of 3.3. The average I.Q. of these three reports is 88.

Shirley and Goodenough report a correlation of .33 between the Goodenough and the Pintner Nonlanguage Tests for 229 cases. Evidently the two tests have not very much in common. The Goodenough test is based solely on the child's drawing of a man. Although this performance is undoubtedly indicative of intelligence, it probably does not give such an all-around measure of intelligence as a group test composed of several subtests calling forth a variety of responses.

Tests of deaf college students have been reported by Fusfeld (14). These students are highly selected, but it is interesting to compare them with hearing college students. The median score of the freshmen class at Gallaudet College on the American Council Psychological Examination has been compared with the equivalent percentile for hearing students, and the college itself has been compared with the numerous hearing colleges taking the same test.

Year	*Hearing Percentile*								
1934	46	Gallaudet	surpasses	65	out	of	240	other	colleges.
1935	38	"	"	52	"	"	265	"	"
1936	55	"	"	217	"	"	304	"	"
1937	35	"	"	50	"	"	323	"	"
1938	32	"	"	88	"	"	356	"	"

Although in general the median for the deaf falls below that of the hearing, it is also pertinent to point out that many colleges for hearing students fall below this college for the deaf in so far as the intelligence of the student body is concerned.

LEARNING TESTS

Tests of learning ability may be considered as a type of intelligence test. Pintner and Paterson (58) worked with the well-known Digit-Symbol and Symbol-Digit Tests before the introduction of the modern type of group intelligence test. These tests are classified by Whipple (86) under the heading of "Substitution" and measure "the rapidity with which new associations are formed by repetition." In the digit-symbol test each digit from 1 to 9 has a special symbol under it in a circle. These digits and symbols are printed on top of the test blank and are always in view of the subject. The rest of the test blank consists of digits with empty spaces in which the subject writes the appropriate symbol. The symbol-digit test is similar in the sense that the subject writes the digits which go with each symbol. The more rapidly the subject learns the appropriate symbols or digits, the less frequently does he need to refer to the key at the top of the test blank and his speed of performance increases.

Pintner and Paterson tested 992 deaf children with the Digit-Symbol Test and 1,049 with the Symbol-Digit Test. Table V

TABLE V

RESULTS FOR THE DIGIT-SYMBOL AND SYMBOL-DIGIT TESTS

DIGIT-SYMBOL TEST

Age	8	9	10	11	12	13	14	15	16	17	18	Adult
n	15	44	79	84	95	116	91	85	113	108	67	95
Deaf median	0	3.6	8.9	7.5	14.0	17.5	18.4	20.9	21.1	22.1	22.6	23.2
Hearing age	-8	-8	-8	-8	9	11	11.5	12	12.5	12.5	12.5	13

SYMBOL-DIGIT TEST

n	25	53	90	92	103	109	103	95	103	106	72	98
Deaf median	0	5.0	9.7	11.2	16.0	19.6	18.4	21.8	22.4	23.0	23.7	23.5
Hearing age	-8	-8	-8	8.5	10	12	11.5	13.5	13.5	14	14	14

gives a summary of these results. The deaf median score for each age has been converted into an equivalent hearing age according to Pyle's (63) standardization for hearing children. For example, the table shows that on the Digit-Symbol Test 116 thirteen-year-old deaf children were tested and the median score was 17.5. This median score corresponds approximately to the norm for eleven-year-old hearing children as established by Pyle. No hearing norms are available for children below age eight and this accounts for the minus 8 in our table. A study of the table shows that at no age does the deaf child equal the norm for hearing children. The deaf are two to three years retarded at those ages where the best comparisons can be made. Pintner and Paterson found the average retardation on the Digit-Symbol Test to be 3.75 years and on the Symbol-Digit Test 2.9 years. They also compared the sexes and found no difference in score between the deaf boy and the deaf girl. Similarly their comparison between the adventitiously and congenitally deaf led to the conclusion that they were equal on this test. Taken as a whole the results on these two learning tests correspond very well to the later findings on the group intelligence tests which we have summarized above.

One other report on these tests was published by Newlee (46) after the work of Pintner and Paterson appeared. She gave the same tests to eighty-five deaf pupils in a day school for the deaf and found them to be about equal to the hearing norms. In all probability this small group of deaf represented a very select sampling of the deaf in general. Newlee had eighty-five cases in contrast to about one thousand tested by Pintner and Paterson. We cannot learn much about the intelligence of the deaf in general from such a small number of cases.

MISCELLANEOUS TESTS

Brown (6) gave the Pintner Nonlanguage Mental Test and

some of the Arthur Performance Tests to 333 deaf children. He does not give the results in terms of M.A. or I.Q. He merely reports a correlation between these two tests of .80, and, with C.A. partialed out, of .61. Goodlett and Greene (17) gave the Goodenough, the Pintner Nonlanguage Mental and a group of six performance tests to 29 negro deaf persons ranging in age from seven to thirty-three. There seemed to be great differences in ability on the different tests, but the sample is so small and heterogeneous in regard to age, that it is difficult to make any generalizations. Zeckel and van der Kolk (87) gave the Porteus Maze Test to one hundred deaf and one hundred hearing. The younger deaf are poorer than the older deaf, and they draw the conclusion that the deaf catch up as they grow older. But they also find that the younger hearing are poorer than the older hearing, so that it is difficult to understand what is meant by the improvement of the deaf as they grow older, because the hearing improve just as much. The average I.Q. for their deaf group is reported as 86.1; and for the hearing group as 99.4.

Another study deserves mention here, although it is difficult to interpret. In 1925 Lindner (30) in Germany published the results of a great number of tests of all kinds given to deaf children. They include tests of motor ability, dexterity, performance ability, drawing, memory, suggestibility, and the like. It is not possible to describe this extensive work in detail. We shall merely comment on some of his findings, especially with reference to those tests which resemble our so-called intelligence tests. The number of deaf children varies from test to test and the hearing group tested for comparison was not very carefully chosen. We have such results as these. In an easy block-building test, 29 per cent of the deaf were successful as compared with 36.5 per cent of the hearing. In a hard block-building test, 8 per cent of the deaf and 15 per cent of the hearing were successful. In picture arrangement, in suggestibility, in purposeful manipulation (similar to Köhler's tests for apes), the deaf were poorer than the hearing. In memory tests the deaf are equal and sometimes superior to the hearing. In some drawing tests Lindner found his deaf much superior to the hearing. It is difficult to summarize this study. One gets the impression that the more a test approximates an abstract intellectual task, the more likely are the deaf to fall below the hearing. The work of Lindner is important because of the wide range of tests employed and because of the suggestions it offers for further psychological work with the deaf.

SUMMARY OF INTELLIGENCE TEST RESULTS

Various types of intelligence tests have been used with the deaf. Our most extensive results are based on group nonlanguage tests. Scales of performance tests have been found suitable, but no large-scale investigation has been undertaken with them. The Goodenough "Draw a Man" Test can be easily administered and has been used in three small studies. The Binet Scale is definitely useless as a measure of mental ability. Only one type of learning test has been used extensively. At present, therfore, the number of standardized intelligence tests suitable for testing the intelligence of the deaf is very limited.

As to the findings themselves, we have the following results:

	Probable Deaf I.Q.
Performance scales	91
Nonlanguage group	86
Goodenough Test	88

These probable deaf I.Q.'s are averages from the various studies reported in this chapter. They are simply our best approximations at the present time. Most weight should be laid on the results of the nonlanguage tests, because these are obtained from a very wide sampling of deaf children. The performance-scale results are limited to rather small groups of deaf and the Goodenough is the average of three small groups. In spite of the great differences in the tests used and the samples of deaf children studied, there is a surprising degree of uniformity in our results. Our best estimate at present, therefore, is that the average I.Q. of the deaf does not quite reach 90.

The learning tests cannot be translated into I.Q.'s, but the general results corroborate very well the findings on the intelligence tests proper.

The age of onset of deafness seems to make no difference in the intelligence of the child.

There seems to be no difference on the average between the intelligence of the congenitally and the adventitiously deaf.

Both of the large surveys find the average intelligence of the manually taught pupils below the averages of the other two groups. The difference in intelligence between pupils taught by the oral and those taught by the combined method is not great. One survey finds the oral pupils slightly above and the other finds them slightly below the combined pupils. In all probability there is no difference. These slight differences found among pupils taught by different methods of instruction are due to selection and are not caused by the methods of instruction. There is a well-known tendency in those schools where the manual method is still employed to allow pupils who can make little progress in speech and lip-reading or in their studies generally to transfer to the manually taught classes. This tends in the long run to load such classes with pupils of inferior intelligence.

The average intelligence of deaf children taught in day schools is slightly higher than that of deaf children attending the residential schools. The residential school has more dull and backward pupils and fewer bright ones. In those parts of our country where no day schools exist there can, of course, be no selective factor at work. But where day schools are available it is likely that more of the competent intelligent families send their children to day schools, whereas more of the less intelligent families send their children to residential schools, so that they may not be burdened with the care of their deaf children.

This, then, is the general picture of the intelligence of the deaf child. As compared with the hearing child he is about 10 points below in I.Q. on nonlanguage and performance tests. These tests would seem to be as fair to him as to hearing children. This we must remember refers to the average child. The overlapping of the two groups, deaf and hearing, is very great. There are many bright and very bright deaf children. Many of them have higher intelligence than the average hearing child. Just because a child is deaf does not mean that he is therefore slow and dull. Fifty per cent of our deaf children probably have I.Q.'s of 90 and above. There is a large reservoir of fine native ability among the deaf. We must not let the small difference in intelligence between the deaf and the hearing warp our thinking as to the educational possibilities of the deaf. They are possessed of sound intelligence upon which education can build.

Two questions naturally arise with reference to this picture of the intelligence of the deaf. One is in regard to the type or kind of intelligence; the other as to the cause of this lowered intelligence. By the kind of intelligence we refer to the usual division of intelligence into three kinds: abstract, concrete, and social. Now all our results of testing the deaf are based upon tests which might be classed as tests of concrete rather than abstract intelligence. Certainly this is true of the performance scales. Probably it is true of some of the subtests of the Pintner Nonlanguage Mental Tests; it is not so obvious with some of the other subtests. But by and large it is concrete rather than abstract intelligence. Now, if there is a high correlation between these two kinds of intelligence, does this mean that the deaf are as good in abstract as in concrete intelligence? Or are the deaf fairly good in concrete intelligence but very weak in abstract intelligence? So far, all of our tests of abstract intelligence have been based upon language and are, therefore, useless with the deaf. Does the handicap of language carry with it the inability to develop abstract intelligence? Careful research is needed here. A nonlanguage test that correlates highly (much higher than the present Pintner Nonlanguage) with verbal intelligence is needed. Must abstract intelligence in its highest form always depend upon language or other symbols? Are the deaf, because of their lack of hearing, unable to develop a symbolic structure which seems to underlie abstract intelligence? These are unanswerable questions at present. In the meantime, we must be satisfied with our knowledge that the concrete intelligence of the deaf is not much below that of the hearing and is, therefore, an adequate foundation for an education leading toward the more concrete tasks of everyday life.

The other question as to why there should be this difference in concrete intelligence between the deaf and the hearing is difficult to answer. Our best hypothesis, suggested by Pintner and Paterson in 1918 (61), is somewhat as follows. Those who become deaf do so most frequently in early childhood because of such diseases as meningitis and scarlet fever or other diseases which frequently attack the central nervous system. Damage to the central nervous system, particularly in early childhood, frequently means a slowing up in mental development. The disease that caused the deafness may also impair the mentality of the child. The congenitally deaf child probably more frequently comes from families of inferior mental ability than from families of superior intelligence. We have no real evidence here and a careful study of the intelligence of the families from which our congenital cases come would be valuable. Only a slight tendency in the direction indicated would be necessary to account for the slight retardation in the intelligence of the average deaf child. This hypothesis, then, with reference to the congenitally and the adventitiously deaf, would account for the fact that we find no difference in intelligence between these two groups of deaf, and also for the fact that the deaf as a group are slightly below the hearing in general intelligence.

EDUCATIONAL ACHIEVEMENT

We shall divide this section on the educational achievement of the deaf into four parts. After a very brief glance at the early work before the advent of objective educational achievement tests, we shall discuss the findings of widespread surveys of educational achievement in general. Then we shall take up more detailed studies of particular subjects, such as language and reading, in which deaf and hearing children can be compared. Lastly we shall deal with the measurement of speech and lip reading.

Early Tests. Much discussion of the educational achievement of the deaf has always been found in the technical journals devoted to the education of the deaf. These discussions were undoubtedly of value to the early workers in this field, but it would not serve the purposes of this book to attempt any survey or summary of such reports. Most of them appeared before the time of the modern objective achievement test. No accurate comparisons as to the educational achievement of the deaf and hearing were possible.

Two of the early studies were of interest. Taylor (80) in 1897 compared the spelling ability of the deaf and hearing. He used a free-association technique, asking the child to write down as many words as he could in fifteen minutes. He concluded that the spelling ability of the deaf was better than that of the hearing. There is a suggestion here of the value of objective tests for comparing the educational achievement of the deaf and hearing.

Binet and Simon (3) in 1910 published their results of a follow-up of the graduates of a deaf school who had been taught by the oral method. They found that very few of them made use of speech. They questioned the value of teaching speech to the deaf, because of the fact that it seemed to be of little use to the deaf after they had left school. This report naturally created a great furore among educators of the deaf. They questioned both the findings and the conclusions drawn from them. But no one, since that time, has repeated Binet and Simon's study. It is something that needs to be done. It might or might not have an important influence on educational objectives in regard to the deaf. We do not know with any degree of accuracy how much use is made of speech or lip reading by those who have left our schools for the deaf.

GENERAL SURVEYS

In the two surveys previously mentioned, namely the Reamer Survey (64) and the National Research Council Survey (9), a short educational-achievement test was given. This test, the Pintner Educational Survey Test, consisted of subtests measuring reading, language, history, geography, arithmetic, and the like. It was too short a test to give an accurate measure of each of these subjects, but it did give a sufficiently accurate measure of the total educational attainment at the elementary school level. A comparison of deaf children in terms of what was at that time generally taught in elementary schools for the hearing was possible.

Table VI shows briefly the chief results. The number of cases tested at each age is approximately the same as the number

TABLE VI

EDUCATIONAL SURVEYS OF THE DEAF

REAMER SURVEY

Age of deaf	*9*	*10*	*11*	*12*	*13*	*14*	*15*	*16*	*17*	*18*	*19*	*20*	*21+*
Median score	7	8	10	15	19	24	28	31	34	36	43	66	68
Equivalent hearing grade	-3	-3	-3	3+	3+	3+	4+	4+	4+	4+	5+	6+	7+

NATIONAL RESEARCH COUNCIL SURVEY

Age of deaf	*12*	*13*	*14*	*15*
Average score	16	19	23	27
Equivalent hearing grade	3–3	3–5	3–9	4–1

tested with the intelligence test as shown before in Tables III and IV. The average score on the educational achievement test has been compared with the grade norms for hearing children. Thus the thirteen-year-old deaf on the Reamer Survey average a little more than third-grade hearing children (3+), and on the National Council Survey the thirteen-year-old deaf obtain an average score equal to a hearing grade of 3–5, i. e., the fifth month of the third grade. For the age groups common to the two surveys the results are practically identical. The scores for the nine-, ten-, and eleven-year-old deaf are below the third-grade norms for the hearing. There are no hearing norms below the third grade. The scores for the older deaf children rise steadily to the hearing norms for the seventh grade, but it must be remembered that these older deaf groups contained deaf students at Gallaudet College for the Deaf. These results show clearly the painfully slow progress in educational achievement made by the deaf in comparison with the hearing.

Another way of comparing the deaf and the hearing is by means of the educational quotient. We have computed the E.Q., using the Terman-Merrill technique, for the average score of the four age groups of the National Research Council Survey.

Deaf C.A.	*E.A.*	*E.Q.*
12–6	8–10	71
13–6	9–1	68
14–6	9–5	67
15–6	9–10	67

Here we see that the average score on the educational survey test for the deaf twelve-year-olds is equal to an educational age of 8–10 (8 years, 10 months) and this gives us an educational quotient of 71; and so on for the other ages. The average E.Q. for the four age groups is 68. If we remember that the average I.Q. for these same four age groups was 84, then the difference between 84 and 68 gives us some conception of the educational handicap of the deaf.

Still another way of comparing the two groups is by means of the percentage distribution of educational-achievement scores for the deaf and hearing shown in Table VII. This table shows the scores for 2,423 deaf between the ages of twelve to fifteen inclusive compared with the scores of 4,476 hearing children of the same ages. Note how the deaf scores pile up at the lower end of the distribution—57.5 per cent do not rise above a score of 19; 86.2 do not rise above a score of 39. The first two intervals contain almost all of the deaf, but only 14.8 per cent of the hearing. Only 13.8 per cent of the deaf make scores above 39, but 85.3 of the hearing do so. Again we note that loss of hearing involves an extraordinary handicap in acquiring the language necessary to respond to the questions of the educational-achievement test.

The influence of the age of onset of deafness on the educational scores was investigated by both of the surveys. This was done in both cases by means of the educational index (a

TABLE VII

DISTRIBUTION OF EDUCATIONAL SCORES

Scores	*Hearing* $n = 4{,}476$ *per cent*	*Deaf* $n = 2{,}423$ *per cent*
0–19	3.0	57.5
20–39	11.8	28.7
40–59	30.0	9.7
60–79	36.7	2.9
80–99	17.1	1.2
100–119	1.5	—
120 up	.03	

TABLE VIII

EDUCATIONAL ACHIEVEMENT AND AGE OF ONSET OF DEAFNESS

Age of onset of deafness	*Un-known*	*Birth*	*0–1*	*1*	*2*	*3*	*4*	*5*	*6*	*7*	*8*	*9*	*10*	*11*	*12*	*13*
Median Index: Reamer	52.5	47.5	51	52	52	54	53	53	65	62	71	71.5	70	71	68.5	69
Median Index: National Research Council	45.5	48.8	47.4	48.1	50.0	51.9	56.3	61.2	63.6	62.6	63.3	71	68	68	67	70

standard-deviation rating). These indices are shown in Table VIII. We notice that the median index begins to rise at six in the Reamer Survey and at four in the National Research Council Survey. Evidently those children who become deaf between the ages of four and six or later in life are able to achieve relatively more on educational tests than those children who are deaf at birth or become so shortly thereafter. To have learned and used language in the ordinary way as a hearing individual for the first four or six years of life or longer seems to give the deaf child an advantage thereafter in dealing with language. Something is acquired during those years of hearing before such a child becomes deaf which seems to leave a permanent effect upon his future language development. This "language sense" is only very painfully or perhaps never acquired by those born deaf or those who become deaf during the first few years of life. This effect of the age of onset of deafness on educational achievement is not reflected in intelligence as measured by our nonlanguage tests. There we found those born deaf or those deaf at an early age just as intelligent as those who become deaf later on. It would seem, therefore, to be the specific use of language for four to six years or more that leaves a permanent effect on later educational achievement. All of this serves further to emphasize that loss of hearing is a tremendous handicap to language development.

Does the residential or day school do the better job in the education of the deaf? This is a very broad and complex question. Upshall (82) compared these two types of schools on the basis of the National Research Council's survey tests, being fully cognizant of the fact that he was only taking into account one of the outcomes of the education of the deaf, namely, their achievement scores on a written test. He compared 311 day-school pupils with 1470 residential-school pupils between the ages of twelve and seventeen, and found their mean scores as follows:

	Day	*Residential*
Nonlanguage Mental Test	340.9	304.2
Educational Survey	35.4	23.3

Evidently the day school is somewhat selective from the point of view of intelligence. Its pupils are on the average brighter. Naturally, then, we should expect a higher average in educational attainment and we find this to be the case. Is this higher educational score merely due to the higher intelligence of the day-school pupils? To answer this question Upshall matched each one of these 311 day-school pupils with a residential school pupil of similar intelligence and similar age. Here are his findings:

	Day	*Residential*	*Diff.* / *S.D. Diff.*	*Day pupils have:*
Educational test score	35.4	25.3	6.2	Better educational scores
Audiometer rating	37.8	29.1	5.6	Better hearing
Years in deaf school	6.3	7.3	4.4	Fewer years in deaf school
Years in hearing school	1.9	0.7	8.7	More years in hearing school
Age of start to school	7.2	7.7	3.5	Begin school sooner
Age of becoming deaf	2.7	1.5	6.2	Become deaf later

Note first that when we match all the day pupils with residential pupils we select more of the brighter residential pupils in order to bring up the residential intelligence score to that of the day pupils, but even so we do not pull up the educational score to that of the day pupils. The residential score on the educational test moves up from 23.3 to 25.3 but it is still much below the day-school score of 35.4. Evidently the higher intelligence of the day-school pupils is not the only factor leading to their higher educational attainment. So Upshall looked for other factors, which we see above, namely, the day pupils have better hearing, become deaf later, spend more years in schools for the hearing, and so on. The question now is whether these other factors could account for the better educational attainment. So Upshall matched his cases again for age, intelligence score, age of becoming deaf, age of starting to school. When he did this he found he had 83 pairs of day and residential pupils and he also found that the groups were equal in amount of residual hearing. And now the average scores on the educational test were 30.5 for the day and 25.6 for the residential group. The difference between the means is now not quite statistically significant, the difference divided by the S.D. of the difference being 2.22. But the means are much closer than they were at first. The day school still has a slight advantage, but we can see that the main reason for the original superiority of the day school lies in the type of children attracted to that school. Whatever in addition remains may be due to greater emphasis placed on the type of material measured by the educational-survey test. Upshall reaches the conclusion that "the chances are very great that the day schools are superior to the institutions in the type of education which is measured by the Pintner Educational Survey Test."

This does not mean that the day school is superior to the residential school in general. We have only measured one narrow aspect of the school's work. There are many others. Upshall's study shows the method we must adopt to compare these two types of education of the deaf. We need objective measures of a great many more aspects of education, such as speech and lip reading, vocational training, personality traits, and attitudes in general.

Hall (22) reports the results of the New Stanford Achievement Test given to sixty-two freshmen and preparatory students at Gallaudet College. The average C.A. of these two classes was 20–6 and 21–2 respectively, and the average number of years in school 11–6 and 12–4. The preparatory class (about twelfth grade) reaches approximately ninth-grade hearing norms, and the freshman class rises a little above tenth-grade norms. Again we note the wide gap between the achievement of the deaf and the hearing, even with this very select sampling of deaf students.

More recent reports by Fusfeld (14) of testing at Gallaudet College show comparisons of the freshmen and sophomore classes with hearing students. In one such comparison the deaf median exceeded the hearing median in English usage, spelling, and current history, but fell below in reading, vocabulary, and mathematics.

Ewing and Ewing (12) in England have reported on educational and intelligence tests given to ten children, all, except one, born deaf. Most of them tested very high on performance intelligence tests. It seems that the Drever-Collins Performance Tests and norms were used in most cases. Many of the cases did extremely well on reading and arithmetic tests. The results are valuable as case studies, but give no help in regard to the general problem of the intelligence and educational achievement of the deaf.

SPECIAL SUBJECTS

Language. The deaf are, of course, extremely handicapped in understanding language. Progress in this area is very slow. Unless we make objective comparisons between the deaf and hearing, it is frequently difficult to realize how very retarded the deaf are, in spite of the emphasis placed upon language in schools for the deaf and in spite of the excellence and enthusiasm of the teachers of the deaf.

Pintner and Paterson (57) made one of the earliest of such objective comparisons by means of the Woodworth and Wells

Easy-Directions Tests. These tests each consist of twenty simple printed directions, such as: "Cross out the g in tiger." "What comes next after D in the alphabet?" "Draw a line around the three dots .. .." They demand very little actual knowledge. They test mainly the ability to comprehend simple language. Test A was given to 366 deaf pupils and Test B to 289 deaf pupils in a state school for deaf pupils ranging in age from nine to twenty. Hearing children to the number of 308 for Test A and 313 for Test B were also given the tests. The children were allowed to work at each test for as long as they wished. The median number of correct responses out of a possible total of 20 is shown below for Test A:

Age	*6*	*7*	*8*	*9*	*10*	*11*	*12*	*13*	*14*	*15*	*16*	*17*	*18*	*Adult*
Deaf	–	–	–	1	1	2	2	2	2	4	3	3	6	7
Hearing	1–2	4	9	18	18	18	19	19	19	19	20	–	–	–

Similar results were found for Test B. There were no six-, seven-, or eight-year-old deaf and no seventeen-year-old or older hearing. We can see readily that the test is very easy for the hearing child. From age nine on practically all the items were answered correctly by the average hearing child. The average deaf child never reaches this point of efficiency. For him, no matter at what age, the test is difficult. He rises by slow and painful steps from a median score of one at age nine to a score of 7 at about age twenty. He barely reaches the median of the eight-year-old hearing and never approximates the nine-year-old.

That age of becoming deaf has a decided influence on the understanding of language we have noted before and we see it again in the results of this test:

Age of deafness	*Cong.*	*Unknown*	*0*	*1*	*2*	*3*	*4*	*5*	*6*	*7*	*8*	*9*	*10*
Average score	2.2	2.8	3.1	3.8	3.5	3.6	3.7	7.8	11.6	5.0	8.0	10.0	10.0

Here a decided jump in average score takes place after age four. This agrees with our previous finding that children becoming deaf after age four to six have a decided advantage in objective educational achievement tests.

The authors of the study point out various differences between the deaf and the hearing. They note that the deaf child almost always makes some kind of a response regardless of whether he understands the meaning of the sentence or not; the hearing child is more likely to make no response if he does not understand. Frequently the deaf understands only one word and his response is in the nature of an association to that word. For example, the question, "Write any word of three letters," called forth the response "Post card" several times, evidently an association between "letter" and "post card." Again, in response to the direction, "Cross out the last word in this sentence," we find many deaf children writing out a sentence. Here the word "sentence" alone has been understood and the child has responded to this word alone and has done something he has frequently been called upon to do in his school work. These types of error and many others are all directly due to the partial understanding of the printed language.

Further studies of the language ability of the deaf were made by Pintner and Paterson (59) and by Pintner (49) by means of the Trabue Language-Completion Tests. These tests consist of sentences with one word omitted. The subject has to write in a suitable word. This type of exercise is familiar to many deaf children, because it is frequently used in language teaching in schools for the deaf. Scale B of the Trabue Tests was given to 1,098 pupils in four large state schools for the deaf. The deaf pupils were arranged according to the "year of instruction" in their schools. The median scores are as follows:

Year of instruction	3	4	5	6	7	8	9	10	11	12	13
n	173	178	176	159	134	88	85	41	29	23	12
Deaf median	2	3	4	5	6	7	7	7	8	8	9
Hearing grade median	8	10	11	12	13	13	14	—	—	—	—

The median grade scores for hearing children are shown in the bottom line. It is only in the eleventh year of instruction that the deaf reach the norm for hearing children in the third grade.

After an interval of six months another of the Trabue scales was given in two of the deaf schools in an attempt to measure the language progress of the children. The control group of hearing children were also retested with the same scale after the same interval of time. The scale for the second testing turned out to be more difficult than the scale first used and so we find the average gain for 1,016 hearing children to be only 0.46 points. There were 557 deaf children who took both tests and after six months they were found to have an average loss of 0.44 points. This does not mean that they really lost in language ability, since the second scale was more difficult. It means, however, that their progress was slower than that of hearing children, because on the same scales the hearing group gained slightly. The value of this study is not so much in the actual results but rather in its indication of the lack of any suitable instruments fine enough to measure the slow progress of the deaf in language ability. Such instruments would be of great help in assessing the value of different methods of instruction, of different teachers, and of different types of deaf children.

The language tests of Keys and Pedersen have been given by Keys and Boulware (25) to several groups of deaf children in a state school and in public schools. After one year the tests were repeated and the gains in score noted. The authors first raised the question as to whether gains in progress in language were influenced by the age at onset of deafness between birth and five years. Does the possession of hearing for different lengths of time during the first five years of life influence progress in language learning later on in life? To answer this question the children were divided into two groups: (1) those who became deaf before the age of two; and (2) those who became deaf at two to five years of age. No differences in language progress over a year were found in any of the tests for these two groups. These results seem to fit in with the previous findings of studies already mentioned, namely, that a child must have possessed hearing up to the age of from four to six in order to show better than average language development in later life.

Another comparison made by the same authors pertained to the gain in score as related to amount of hearing. Two groups were compared: (1) those children with only 0 to 20 per cent hearing; (2) those with 21 to 60 per cent hearing. Here there were marked differences in annual gains in language between the two groups. Those with more hearing made the greater gains. The authors believe that percentage of residual hearing is one of the best methods at present for the classification of deaf pupils entering upon language instruction. This study emphasizes once again the close interdependence of language development and hearing.

The most thorough comparison of the written language of the deaf and hearing so far made has been reported by F. and G. Heider (62). They analyzed 1,118 compositions of deaf and hearing children. These compositions were based upon a short motion picture shown to the children. It is impossible here to give a detailed account of this long study. We must be content to summarize briefly some of their conclusions:

1. The sentences of the deaf are shorter than those of the hearing.

2. The deaf use more simple sentences.

3. No significant differences in total length of compositions.

4. In general the compositions of the deaf resemble those of less mature hearing children.

5. If different forms of subordination in sentence structure are analyzed as to difficulty, it is found that the more difficult forms are used less by the deaf than by the hearing.

This gives merely an indication of some of the main findings. "The whole picture," say the authors, "indicates a simpler style, involving relatively rigid unrelated language units which follow each other with little overlapping of structure or meaning."

Reading. The language development of the deaf is slow. Their reading ability is poor. Reading is hard work and for the average deaf individual it remains hard work all his life long. This is one of the ironies of deafness, namely, that that great recreation which is dependent upon vision and not upon hearing should be difficult and laborious. Can we do anything to improve the reading ability of the deaf? Thompson's (81) work suggests that we might be able to accomplish more than at present. She dealt with young deaf children on entrance to school, about six and a half years old. She had ten pairs of children equated for chronological age, mental age, perception ability, school achievement, and length of time in school. The experimental group was given special instruction in reading for one hour every school day during the school year. At the end of the school year the two groups were tested with several reading tests and the experimental group showed decided superior gains as contrasted with the control group. It achieved in reading two and one half times as much as the control group. Furthermore, the experimental group "showed achievement equal to five sixths of the achievement of a normal hearing class in beginning reading." With reference to the other school subjects such as speech, lip reading, and writing, the experimental group showed only a very slight loss as compared with the control group.

This experiment raises the question as to whether more might not be accomplished in the teaching of reading to the deaf by more intensive work at the beginning of the child's school career, thereby overcoming some of the severe handicap in reading under which the deaf child suffers throughout his school life. The deaf as a group have no impairment of vision and hence we should make more use of this sense to compensate for their hearing deficiency. A long-time experiment in this field would be very profitable.

Speech and Lip Reading. These two subjects of instruction are of great importance in the education of the deaf. Much time and effort in all schools for the deaf are devoted to them. So far, however, no adequate means have been devised in order to measure achievement in these two fields. The difficulty of constructing objective measures of achievement is obvious. A standard objective test of lip reading must be one that can be presented to all children under exactly the same conditions. The same words or sentences spoken by different people vary too much to be considered objective. It would seem as if a standardized series of moving pictures of various faces speaking standardized sentences or paragraphs might form a possible scale for lip-reading ability. Again, the intelligibility of the speech of the deaf child is difficult to judge and at present we have no standard scale of intelligibility with which to compare the speech of any particular child. A standardized scale of speech samples on phonograph records, somewhat like our present drawing or composition scales, seems at present to be the best suggestion in this field.

Many workers have investigated these difficult problems. Kitson (28) sought for a means of prognosticating ability to learn lip reading. He sought to differentiate between synthetic and analytic types of perception, arguing that the synthetic type would make the better lip reader. Tachistoscopic reading and completion tests were used and he obtained correlations of .6 and .7 between these tests and lip-reading ability for fifteen subjects. Conklin (8) drew up lists of consonants, words and sentences, read these to deaf pupils who wrote down what they understood, and presented results for sixteen pupils. Göpfert (18) also worked with lists of vowels, consonants, words, and sentences, and gave them to many groups of hearing and deaf children and to recently deafened soldiers. He made many interesting and valuable observations and in particular stressed the advantages of the natural method of learning lip reading, i. e., by beginning with whole sentences, as opposed to the formal method of beginning with letters and syllables. Goldmann (16) used lists of words and sentences, and emphasized the importance for the lip reader of knowing the topic of conversation. Mason (39) has presented sentences and paragraphs for testing lip reading together with score sheets to be used by the examiner in an attempt to approach greater objectivity.

All of the work mentioned above has made use of the living human face as the stimulus for the lip reader, and thus no standard test for universal use has been achieved. Attempts to use photographs and motion pictures for the teaching or testing of lip reading are now beginning to appear. Beilinsson (2) has experimented with photographs of the lips in all sound positions, and Mason (38, 40) has reported preliminary experiments with motion pictures for teaching and for testing lip reading. F. and G. Heider (62) have published the most extended report up to the present time on the use of motion picture tests for lip reading. They used several lists of words, sentences, and two stories of about 150 words each. The scoring of the tests was as objective as possible and the intercorrelations of the different tests ranged from .77 to .95. Correlation between chronological age and lip reading was low, being .19 for one test. A comparison of lip-reading score and years of training for good and poor lip readers showed the following:

	n	*Average Score*	*Average Years of Training*
Good lip readers	29	30.8	4.77
Poor lip readers	28	22.8	4.95

All of these children had been in school for at least one and a half years. After this period, therefore, it would seem that additional years of training do not seem to differentiate between the good and poor lip readers, in so far, at least, as these tests can differentiate. The correlation between lip-reading score and educational age on the Stanford Achievement Test was .54. Ability to recognize vowels correlated higher with lip reading than ability to recognize consonants. There was also a positive correlation between lip reading and ability to follow a rhythm in dancing or gymnastics. All of these findings are important and suggestive for future research. It would also seem that a standard objective test for lip-reading ability by means of motion pictures is a possibility in the near future.

Up to the present time, the most extensive attempt to measure lip reading and intelligibility of speech was made by the National Research Council Survey (9). The lip-reading test consisted of carefully selected sentences embodying the entire range of sounds as they may be interpreted by the eye. Several sets of ten sentences each were constructed. These were read to the children, some by the classroom teacher and some by the survey examiner. The former represented the familiar element; the latter the new or stranger element. The survey examiner gave the tests in all the schools surveyed and thus allowed a comparison between schools.

Intelligibility of speech was measured by having the child read certain sentences. Several sets of sentences, chosen as similar in difficulty, were constructed. Each child tested was asked to read aloud two sets of sentences—one for the examiner and one for his teacher. The amount understood was the measure of intelligibility of speech.

It can be readily seen that these tests of speech and lip reading are far from objective and cannot be considered standardized tests; nevertheless they are the best that have been used up to the present time. Pintner (51) has reported on the results of these two tests given to 400 cases in the advanced classes of various schools included in the National Research Council Survey. The mean scores for the teacher and examiner were as follows:

	Mean: Teacher	*Mean: Examiner*	*r*
Speech test	60.3	49.3	.86
Lip-Reading test	51.7	40.0	.84

The mean scores for the teacher are considerably higher than for the examiner, because the teacher is familiar with the speech of her pupils and the pupils are familiar with the movements and expression of the teacher's face and lips. The correlations between the teacher's and examiner's scores show, nevertheless, that the ratings given to the pupils by both methods of rating are fairly consistent.

Correlations between scores on these two tests and scores on the Pintner Nonlanguage Mental Test were calculated. They are as follows:

Pintner Nonlanguage score with:		
Speech tested by examiner	= + .005	383 cases
Speech tested by teacher	= + .16	212 institution cases
Speech tested by teacher	= – .14	196 day-school cases

Lip reading tested by examiner	= +.02	212 institution cases
Lip reading tested by examiner	= +.13	196 day-school cases
Lip reading tested by teacher	= +.13	212 institution cases
Lip reading tested by teacher	= +.13	196 day-school cases

All of these correlations are practically zero. When deaf children reach the highest grades in their schools, there is no relation between speech or lip reading and intelligence as measured by nonlanguage tests. These deaf children form a highly selected group, both from the point of view of ability in speech and lip-reading as well as from the point of view of intelligence.

Correlations between the two tests and school achievement as measured by the Pintner Educational Survey Test were also calculated. These r's ranged from +.32 to +.65. Here we find a fair relationship, as we would expect. Even within a highly homogeneous group, differences in language ability will show themselves in written tests and in lip reading and speech.

For 214 residential-school children correlations between speech and amount of hearing are reported. These are +.26 (examiner's rating) and +.17 (teacher's rating). For the same group we have correlations between speech and age of onset of deafness: r = .34 (examiner's rating) and r = .30 (teacher's rating). Both these variables, amount of residual hearing and age of onset of deafness, are factors which influence the language ability and therefore the speech ability of the deaf child. All of the relationships as reported in this study are much lower than they would be if we possessed more reliable measures of speech and lip reading and if we had measured a wider range of ability, instead of a restricted range. Further studies in this field are urgently needed.

SUMMARY OF EDUCATIONAL ACHIEVEMENT

All comparisons of the deaf with the hearing child in educational achievement show the former to be greatly retarded. If we think in terms of years or grades, it would seem on the average to be about three or four years' retardation. If we think in terms of quotients, it would seem that their average E.Q. is about 70. We noted in the previous section a deficiency in intelligence denoted by an I.Q. of 90 or thereabout. If now we compare these two quotients, an E.Q. of 70 and an I.Q. of 90, we get some conception of the handicap in ability to learn and understand language from which the deaf suffer. Their general nonlanguage intelligence is not much below that of the hearing child, but their language ability certainly is.

That this deficiency in language is undoubtedly connected with the deficiency in hearing is borne out by the fact that educational achievement and age of onset of deafness are always correlated. Children who become deaf after age four to six do much better on all our educational-achievement tests than those who are born deaf or who become deaf during the first few years of life. To have acquired language normally through the ear during the first four or five years of life leaves a lasting impression on the individual which is reflected in better educational achievement in later life.

There is an appreciable difference in educational achievement in favor of the day as opposed to the residential school. But this difference is largely accounted for by the selective influence of the day school. The day school attracts pupils who, on the average, have higher intelligence, better hearing, who have become deaf later in life, and have begun their schooling sooner. Nevertheless, the one study which has attempted to equate for all these factors still found a slight advantage in educational achievement for the day school.

Experiments in reading have shown that young deaf children can be taught much more than is usually accomplished and have raised the question as to whether more use might not be made of the unimpaired visual abilities of the deaf.

In speech and lip reading we have found only the beginnings of objective standard measures. There is great need for such in order to assess these important subjects of instruction in schools for the deaf. The most notable attempt to measure these abilities in deaf children seems to point to little, if any, correlation with nonlanguage intelligence, but to a fair correlation with educational achievement. Furthermore age of onset of deafness and amount of residual hearing would seem to affect ability in speech and lip reading.

In general we may sum up by saying that much remains to be accomplished in the measurement of educational achievement of the deaf child and also in experimental search for the best means of teaching the various subjects of instruction.

PERSONALITY

A major handicap, such as deafness, would naturally be supposed to have a marked effect upon the personality structure of any individual. And many authorities in the field of deafness hold this to be the case. Until recently, however, we have had no carefully controlled studies making comparisons between the deaf and the hearing. There have been plenty of opinions, but few facts.

Brunschwig (7) has made the best survey of these opinions and beliefs, and we shall summarize briefly her findings.

1. Characteristics of the uneducated deaf. The uneducated deaf are supposed by various writers to be melancholy, suspicious, treacherous, cruel, narrow, unsympathetic, morbid, selfish, jealous, unreliable, vindictive, and the like. Early workers in this field expected these undesirable traits to be removed by education.

2. Is there a basic difference between the deaf and hearing? Brunschwig shows by quotations from various authorities that

opinions run all the way from a consideration of the deaf as belonging to a basically different psychological type to the view that the deaf are fundamentally exactly the same as hearing individuals. The deaf person is not normal; he belongs to a unique pathological type; the deaf are not integrated on the same biologic level as the hearing. The deaf have, mentally and morally, the same capability as the hearing; in no way different from other children; normal creatures, equally capable and human as all other men.

3. Environmental factors and personality. Before school their parents either spoil them or repress them. Hence we have selfishness, lack of self-control, despotic tendencies or frustration, bashfulness, hatred. During school life in a residential school the deaf child becomes too dependent, has no feeling of responsibility; there are a larger proportion of mental and emotional maladjustments; he is later on unable to make adequate social adjustments either to home or community. Or again, the deaf are happy and cheerful in school.

4. Personal adjustments. Delay in emotional maturation is supposed to occur among deaf children, and hence they are unsympathetic, cruel, and egoistic. The deaf have a feeling of inferiority and their personality make-up borders in many respects on the neurotic. They are subject to paroxysms of rage and emotional upsets. They are apathetic and listless. They are subject to a great number of fears. There are few psychoses among deaf adolescents; they achieve and maintain excellent mental equilibrium. They do not feel keenly their great misfortune. They are not unhappy but rather cheerful.

5. Social adjustments. They are deficient in manners, deportment, and tact. They have feelings of social inferiority. To offset this they become aggressive. They are shut out of much social life. They misunderstand much of what goes on around them. They experience feelings of resentment and helplessness in the

society of the hearing. Hence the tendency to clannishness, to restrict their social contacts to other deaf people. They become selfish, narrow-minded, and isolated. But again, we are told, the deaf are by no means an isolated class. They work extensively and associate freely with the hearing.

This is a very condensed summary of the survey of opinions made by Brunschwig (7). For the actual quotations and for the references to the various authorities cited, the reader must turn to Brunschwig's study. We have made this brief summary merely to show how great has been, and still is, the difference of opinion as to the personality of the deaf. Some believe that deafness per se has specific effects influencing personality development, but there seems no agreement as to the character or trend of this development. Others believe that the deafness has no specific influence, but that the deaf vary in personality make-up in the same way as do hearing individuals. It is fruitless to debate these different points of view. Let us rather turn to the recent attempts to use standard psychological tests or inventories in order to find out whether they may help us to a better knowledge of the personality of the deaf. We shall present the findings under three headings. First, we shall take up studies dealing with the general adjustment of the deaf; second, attempts to measure emotional stability; and, third, studies of other traits or characteristics.

General Adjustment. Brunschwig's Adjustment Inventory for deaf children (7) is the pioneer work in this field. After trying out inventories and rating scales constructed for hearing children, she decided that a special inventory for the deaf was desirable. Her inventory is couched in simple language well within the comprehension of pupils in the intermediate and advanced grades in schools for the deaf. Furthermore, the examiner is allowed to explain the meaning of words or phrases not thoroughly understood by the pupils, as the inventory is not a test of language comprehension. The items refer to school, teachers, friends, and home. They give a rough measure of the child's feelings or beliefs. Girls make better scores than boys, as is usually the case with similar inventories for hearing children. There are separate norms for boys and girls.

Brunschwig found low correlations between scores on this inventory (indicating good adjustment) and such variables as C.A., I.Q., maximum hearing, and age of onset of deafness. Correlations with C.A. range from −.09 to +.32 for various deaf groups. Only two small groups had usable I.Q.'s and these two correlations were +.20 and +.43. For amount of hearing we have two correlations of +.22 and +.37. Age of onset of deafness gives correlations for four groups ranging from +.01 to +.25. In all probability there is little, if any, relationship between these factors and feelings of adjustment.

A comparison of deaf and hearing children on this inventory gives the following results for groups of deaf and hearing roughly matched for C.A.:

		n	*Score*	$\frac{D}{S.D.\,Diff.}$
Boys	Deaf	171	105	3.46
	Hearing	191	109	
Girls	Deaf	150	110	2.64
	Hearing	156	113	

Another group of 80 deaf boys, matched carefully for age, intelligence, and racial background with 80 hearing boys, obtained a mean score of 99 as compared with 108 for the hearing boys, showing a statistically reliable difference between the two groups. Although these several comparisons between the deaf and the hearing show reliable differences, the size of the difference is small. For all practical purposes we may say that deaf school children feel almost as well adjusted as hearing school children, so far as this inventory can measure such adjustment.

Pintner and Brunschwig (53) have raised the question as to whether deaf children taught by different methods of instruction show differences in adjustment score. They have reported results for 714 children in four schools for the deaf which operate under the so-called combined method of instruction. In these four schools, 35 per cent of the children were being instructed by the oral method; 14 per cent by the manual method; and the remainder, or 51 per cent, by the combined method. The mean scores in general adjustment for the three different methods of instruction are as follows:

	Boys		*Girls*	
	n	*mean*	*n*	*mean*
Oral	132	106	143	112
Combined	182	106	147	110
Manual	80	101	30	106

The manually taught pupils score lowest. Comparing them with the orally taught pupils we find that the ratio of the difference to the standard error of the difference is 2.6 for the boys and 2.2 for the girls. There is no difference between the oral and combined pupils. The authors believe that this difference between the oral and manual pupils is due to the selection of pupils for the manual classes and has nothing to do with the effects of manual or oral instruction upon the adjustment of the pupils. They say, "In most schools having more than one method of instruction, pupils who are less intelligent, the least promising in the eyes of the teachers and the most difficult to handle, are relegated to manual classes."

In the same study we find a discussion as to the relationship between the adjustment score of the pupil and the amount of deafness in the pupil's family. The pupils were classified into four groups, as follows: (1) no deaf members of family and no deaf relatives; (2) one or more deaf relatives on either side of family; (3) deaf siblings but hearing parents; (4) deaf parents. The average adjustment scores for these groups are:

	Boys		Girls	
	n	*average*	*n*	*average*
(1) No deaf	533	103.2	346	109.0
(2) Deaf relatives	31	112.2	26	112.8
(3) Deaf siblings	128	106.7	112	110.7
(4) Deaf parents	42	110.4	45	112.2

The average scores for both sexes show the same trend, although the increase for the girls is very slight. There is a statistically reliable difference between the mean scores for groups 1 and 4 for the boys. Children from families where there are no other deaf members have the lowest average adjustment score. Children from families where there are other deaf people, particularly deaf adults, obtain higher average adjustment scores. The authors suggest that "it may be that the deaf child in a 'deaf' home is better understood during his preschool life. He is not handicapped by the absolute misunderstanding or by the misdirected sympathy which may be the lot of the deaf child in a home made up entirely of hearing individuals who have never had the experience of living with deaf individuals." If this suggestion of the authors is correct, nursery schools for the young deaf child would be indicated. In such schools, under the direction of skilled workers acquainted with the problems of the young deaf child, much might be done to help the child in his adjustments to the world at large.

Two investigators have reported the results of ratings by means of the Haggerty-Olson-Wickman Behavior-Rating Schedule. There are two parts: schedule A consists of items indicating undesirable behavior; schedule B consists of intellectual, physical, social, and emotional traits. Springer (75) obtained ratings on this scale from the teachers of 377 deaf and 415 hearing children with C.A.'s from 6 to 12, equated for C.A., intelligence score on the Goodenough Test, and social status on the Barr Scale. On schedule A the deaf and the hearing ratings were about equal, and corresponded to the 81st percentile of the norms. This means that the average rating of these two groups indicated a great many more behavior problems than is usual among hearing children. Assuming that the norms are representative of hearing children in general, then the hearing control group used in this study could not have been representative of hearing children in general. In this case the deaf are rated by their teachers as having more behavior problems. If, on the other hand, the author's control group of hearing is comparable to the deaf group, then there is no difference in problem behavior between the two groups as rated by their teachers. On schedule B the deaf boys are rated superior to hearing boys and the deaf girls are rated equal to hearing girls. Both deaf and hearing groups are rated inferior to the norms. Correlations between these ratings and age of onset of deafness ranged from .17 to .41, indicating poorer ratings going along with later deafness. The correlations with intelligence were low and negligible.

Kirk (27) used the same schedule to obtain teachers' ratings of 112 deaf and hard-of-hearing children in the Paul Binner School at Milwaukee. The scores for the deaf were compared with the norms for the schedules and in both cases the deaf rated markedly inferior to the hearing. Kirk does not consider schedule A suitable for deaf children.

It is difficult to know how to evaluate these two studies. They are loaded with all the unreliability that attaches to rating scales in general. At best we can say that most teachers of the deaf rate their pupils more severely than do teachers of the hearing as represented by the test norms. The teachers of Springer's control group of hearing children, however, did not do so. They rated their pupils as showing the same number of behavior problem tendencies as deaf children, and as being slightly inferior in the several traits of schedule B. Rating scales may be of some use in a school or class, but it is very doubtful whether we can uncover specific differences between the deaf and the hearing by means of them. Teachers of the deaf and teachers of the hearing are confronted with such different groups of pupils that they may unconsciously develop quite different bases for judgment.

Emotional Stability. Many psychoneurotic inventories have been constructed for use with hearing individuals. Some of these have been tried with the deaf. Springer (76) and Springer and Roslow (77) have made the most extensive comparison of deaf and hearing children. They gave the Brown Personality Inventory for Children to 397 deaf and 327 hearing children. The C.A. of the deaf was about 16 while that of the hearing was 12. In I.Q. on the Goodenough Test the deaf and hearing boys were equal but the deaf girls were 10 points lower. The mean Barr Scale ratings were about the same. The mean neurotic scores and the critical ratios are as follows:

	Deaf	*Hearing*	*C.R.*
Boys	37.4	21.0	8.9
Girls	35.9	24.2	5.5
Total	36.7	22.4	10.3

Obviously the deaf make much higher mean neurotic scores than the hearing control group, and their scores become alarmingly high when compared with the norms for the Brown Personality Inventory. The mean score for the deaf corresponds to the 10th decile score of the norms, indicating that about 50 per cent of the deaf are as neurotic as the most neurotic 10 per cent of the hearing. C.A. and neurotic score correlate + .27 for the deaf and + .13 for the hearing. I.Q. and neurotic score have practically no correlation, varying from .01 to .09 for deaf and hearing groups. Age of onset of deafness and neurotic score correlated + .14 for deaf boys and + .39 for deaf girls. Amount of residual hearing and neurotic score gave correlations of – .02 for boys and – .08 for girls. A further study of 59 pairs of deaf and hearing equated for C.A., I.Q., and Barr score showed the deaf group still markedly psychoneurotic. Seven questions of the inventory might have been influenced by the child's handicap of deafness. When these were dropped, the critical ratio between the means of the two groups increased rather than diminished.

Another study with a psychoneurotic inventory was made by Lyon (33), who gave the Thurstone Personality Schedule to 87 high-school boys and girls with an average C.A. of 19 in a residential school for the deaf. An attempt was made to explain any word or phrase not understood by the students. The results are given in terms of the classifications suggested by Thurstone:

Group	*Description*	*n*	*Per cent*
A	Very well adjusted	1	1
B	Well adjusted	18	21
C	Average	42	48
D	Emotionally maladjusted	11	13
E	Should have psychiatric advice	15	17

There are twice as many deaf pupils in the D and E groups as were found among university students. The author is careful in his interpretation of these results and points to the lack of understanding of words and situations among the deaf.

These two attempts to apply to deaf children psychoneurotic

inventories constructed for hearing children both make the deaf appear terribly emotionally unbalanced. To those who know the deaf, the results seem to be grossly exaggerated. We must be extremely cautious in accepting at their face value the results of inventories constructed for hearing children when applied to the deaf. We must make certain that the deaf pupil really understands the meanings of the various items.

A slightly different approach was made by Pintner, Fusfeld, and Brunschwig (55). They worked with deaf college students and deaf adults. They first of all tried out the original Bernreuter Personality Inventory with 50 college students. Then they revised the wording of those questions which might present language difficulties for deaf people. This first revised form was then given to hearing students who had previously taken the original Bernreuter to see whether the altered wording of some of the items caused any fundamental change in the inventory. As no fundamental change was discovered, this first revision of the inventory was given to 71 deaf people. These 71 subjects were given the test under the guidance of other deaf people who were specially trained to give it. On the basis of this experience further changes were made so as to adapt it more adequately for use with the deaf. The second or final revision was then given to 126 deaf adults (69 men and 57 women). We have noted briefly here the great amount of preliminary work done by the authors before they felt the inventory was suitable for deaf people. They stress the fact that even with the educated deaf adult the language handicap is such that great care must be taken in the use of inventories constructed for hearing individuals.

The results of these tests of 126 deaf individuals for the four traits are as follows:

		Mean Score of Deaf	*Equivalent Hearing Percentile*
Neurotic tendency	Men	– 46.9	61
	Women	– 8.3	60
Self-sufficiency	Men	+ 25.9	43
	Women	+ 6.8	54
Introversion	Men	– 21.2	57
	Women	– 0.6	63
Dominance	Men	+ 48.6	45
	Women	+ 12.1	48

Interpreting these figures, we might say that the deaf test slightly more neurotic and slightly more introverted, but slightly less dominant than the hearing. With reference to self-sufficiency the men seem slightly less, the women slightly more self-sufficient. These findings are based on a very small sampling of the deaf and so we must be careful about making broad generalizations, but we may note here the fact that they correspond very well with the findings of Welles and of Pintner with reference to hard-of-hearing adults (see Chapter VI).

The correlations of these personality scores with chronological age and amount of schooling were low for all traits. Some slight relationship was found with age of onset of deafness. We find positive correlations of +.49 (men) and +.32 (women) with self-sufficiency, which means the later in life one becomes deaf the more self-sufficient one may be. With dominance we find correlations of +.35 (men) and +.20 (women), which means those who become deaf later in life tend to show more dominance. Correlations with neurotic tendency and introversion are negative and rather low from –.06 to –.28, which only show a faint trend for those who became deaf earlier to be more neurotic and more introverted.

An attempt was made in this study to find out what relationships, if any, existed between personality scores and methods used by the deaf in communicating with the hearing. The detailed results cannot be given here. Certain statistically reliable differences were found between those who communicate with the hearing predominantly by means of speech and those who do so by means of writing. Those using speech test less neurotic, more extraverted, more self-sufficient, and more dominant than those using writing. The authors of the study carefully point out that this does not necessarily mean that training in speech and lip reading makes an individual less neurotic, more dominant and so on. It may equally well be that those who are more dominant, less neurotic, etc., are more likely to make use of speech and lip reading in communicating with their hearing companions. There are also other factors which play an important part in determining the speech efficiency of the individual, notably the age at becoming deaf. This is on the average nine years for the men and seven years for the women in the "speech" groups, whereas it is two for the men and three for the women in the "writing" groups. Those who use speech rarely, if at all, are those who were born deaf or became deaf very early in life so that they never learned language in a natural manner in childhood, and as adults they show themselves to be slightly more neurotic, less self-sufficient, more introverted, and less dominant, either because of their basic constitutional tendencies or because of their greater isolation from the hearing-speaking world.

The authors of this study have made a further analysis with reference to the way in which the hearing person communicates with the deaf person studied, and also as to whether the deaf person finds it hard or easy to make friends with hearing people. They also give a detailed analysis of six responses which referred to the subject's feelings in certain social situations when among hearing or among deaf people.

The authors conclude their study by saying that the deaf as a whole, in spite of their severe handicap, reach "almost the same levels of adjustment in daily life as are on the average attained by fully normal individuals." They are not separated from the hearing by a wide difference in their personality traits.

Other Traits. Fears, wishes, and social competence are the other traits about which we have some information. Pintner and Brunschwig (54) compared 159 deaf with 345 hearing children in similar school grades with reference to number of fears on a check list of thirty-nine items and with reference to seven pairs of wishes. The deaf children were on the average two or three years older in chronological age. The difference in number of fears reported by deaf and hearing boys is very small and not statistically reliable, whereas the difference between deaf and hearing girls is large enough to be statistically reliable. Sex differences as to number of fears reported were present in both the deaf and hearing groups. The six fears checked by over 50 per cent of the hearing boys are exactly the same as the six most frequently checked by the deaf boys. Similarly these six fears are the most frequently checked by both deaf and hearing girls. These six fears are "War," "Death," "Bad men," "Robbers," "Snakes," and "Fire." No other fears are checked by over 50 per cent of any of the groups, except the deaf girls who add to the above fears the following: "Lightning," "Mouse," "Thunder," and "Hospital." On the whole there is great similarity between the fears of these deaf and hearing children. Curiously enough "Thunder" is checked more often by both deaf boys and girls than by hearing boys and girls.

The seven wishes forced the child to make a choice between immediate and deferred gratification, as "Would you rather have (a) one cent now *or* (b) ten cents next week?" For both boys and girls there is a statistically reliable difference between the deaf and the hearing in the direction of greater preference for immediate gratification on the part of the deaf. It probably indicates a less mature attitude toward life on the part of the deaf, in spite of the fact that they are chronologically older.

Two studies report measurements of the social competence of deaf children by means of the Vineland Social-Maturity Scale. Bradway (4) obtained scores for 92 pupils in a residential school who were congenitally deaf or who had lost their hearing before age five. The mean social ages are below the chronological ages for all age groups from five to twenty. The mean social quotients or S.Q.'s range from 70 to 89 for various age groups with a mean S.Q. of 80.7 for the 92 cases. She assumes that her deaf children were average in potential intelligence and concludes "that deafness handicaps a person's social intelligence by about 20 per cent." She further compares her main group of 92 pupils who had lost their hearing before the age of five with another group of 52 deaf children who lost their hearing after the age of five. The mean S.Q. of this second group is 84.6 and this does not show a statistically reliable difference from the S.Q. of the first group, and hence the author concludes that "the age at loss of hearing had no significant effect on social competence."

The other study with the same scale by Streng and Kirk (79) reports results for 97 deaf and hard-of-hearing children in a public day school. The mean S.Q. for this group is 96.2. The mean I.Q. on the Arthur Performance Scale is 100.9 and on the Chicago Nonverbal Test 95.5. The correlation between S.Q. and I.Q. is +.29 for both intelligence tests. These authors divided their cases into 51 deaf and 46 hard of hearing, and found a mean S.Q. of 96.5 for the former and 95.5 for the latter. They compare their findings with those of Bradway and suggest as an explanation of the difference that either Bradway's cases were inferior in intelligence or that deaf children in day schools are higher in social competence than deaf children in residential schools. It seems probable that both of these suggestions might be true. We generally find a higher I.Q. among children in day schools for the deaf. They are usually a selected group. Although in this study the correlation between I.Q. and S.Q. was only + .29, we would expect to find it to be much higher in a more random sample of deaf children. Furthermore, deaf children living at home are more likely than institution children to have more opportunities to try many of the tasks found in the Vineland Social-Maturity Scale.

Summary. The scientific study of the personality of the deaf has only just begun. It is to be hoped that such research will free us from the vague generalizations and preconceived notions as to the personality of the deaf which have been and still are common. Our findings so far would seem to indicate that the deaf child in his own school does not feel quite as well adjusted as the hearing child does in his, but this difference is probably very small. We must beware of using inventories constructed for the hearing. All such inventories are too difficult in language construction and vocabulary to be applied without modification to the deaf. If we do use them, they will make the average deaf child appear very emotionally maladjusted and this is probably false. Wherever the research worker has modified the language to bring it within the comprehension of the deaf the differences between the deaf and the hearing have turned out to be small. Nevertheless, there are differences. Other things being equal, it would seem that the deaf find it just a little more difficult to adjust to their environment. They are probably just a little more emotionally unstable. They seem to be slightly more introverted and a little less dominant. They may have on the average more fears and they probably are a little less mature in judgment and social competence.

Deafness per se does not cause a certain type of personality. The deaf belong to all types. But deafness does necessitate a kind of adaptation to the world about us which is different from the adaptation required by the hearing. How this difference influences the development of the personality of the deaf child is the goal of our research in this area. So far we know very little about it. We have one or two hints. Children who come from homes where there are other deaf people seem better adjusted than those from homes where there are no deaf. Furthermore, in many studies we had suggestions that orally taught pupils or adults making much use of speech or lip reading were more like hearing persons in their reactions to our inventories. We must be careful here not to jump to hasty conclusions as to the influence of methods of teaching upon the personality of the deaf child. We know so little at present. That problem must be more thoroughly investigated. Does speech and lip reading help to develop a more wholesome personality? Or rather under what circumstances is this true? What effects upon the personality does the continual emphasis upon speech and lip reading have upon a totally and congenitally deaf child with an I.Q. in the eighties or nineties? What happens to the personality of the deaf adolescent when he finds, as he often does, that the speech he has so laboriously acquired at school is unintelligible to almost all strangers and practically useless in his vocational contacts? We must phrase our questions in this manner if we hope for adequate answers. And as these studies develop we will obtain a better understanding of deafness and be better able to guide the education of the deaf.

SPECIAL ABILITIES

This section will take up the research that has been done with reference to certain special abilities and aptitudes. We have a few studies in three fields: (1) Motor ability; (2) Mechanical ability; (3) Memory.

Motor Ability. This refers to the physical ability of the individual to carry out certain motor activities. It has nothing to do with mechanical ability or aptitude and should not be confused with the latter. The question we are particularly interested in is whether the deaf have any handicap in general motor ability.

Long (31) has investigated this problem most thoroughly. He used seven tests briefly described below. The first five were taken from the Stanford Motor Skills Unit organized by Seashore (70). The seven tests were as follows:

1. Spool packing: to measure speed in an activity involving bimanual co-ordination: spools packed into a frame in pairs, one spool in each hand.
2. Serial discriminator: to measure speed of finger movements in reaction to visual stimuli: four numbered keys to be pressed according to the visual stimulus which may appear.
3. Pursuit rotor: to measure the ability to follow, with the hand, a small target moving in a circular path; a measure of eye-hand co-ordination.
4. Tapping: to measure the speed of finger and forearm movement.
5. Motility rotor: to measure the speed in turning the crank of a small hand drill.
6. Dynamometer: to measure strength of grip.
7. Balance board: to measure ability to balance the body while walking along a board one inch wide.

Long tested 37 deaf girls and 51 deaf boys each equated with a hearing child of the same age, sex, and race. He gives the detailed results for each pair for each test. On only one test did he find a statistically reliable difference between the deaf and the hearing and that was on the Balance Board. Here the deaf are definitely inferior to the hearing and this is to be expected because of the nature of their defect, which frequently involves the adequate functioning of the semicircular canals. Apart from this test, however, we find the deaf boys slightly superior to hearing boys on five out of the other six tests, but the deaf girls are slightly superior to hearing girls on only two of the other six tests. All these differences are very small as we can see from the following table, in which the superiorities on the tests are expressed as ratios of the differences of the means to the standard deviations of the differences.

	Boys		*Girls*	
Test	*Deaf*	*Hearing*	*Deaf*	*Hearing*
Spool packing	2.06		1.04	
Serial discriminator		1.09		1.47
Pursuit rotor–slow	0.56			1.26
Pursuit rotor–fast	0.15			1.81
Tapping	1.93		0.05	
Motility rotor	2.43		0.83	
Grip	2.02			1.59
Balance		5.20		6.91

Long rightly concludes that so far as his tests go he can find no difference in motor ability between deaf and hearing children, with the obvious exception of the sense of balance. One other finding, which Long believes important, is the rather striking inferiority of the deaf girl as contrasted with the deaf boy. The deaf boy is much like his hearing comrade in motor activity, but the deaf girl is inferior to the hearing girl. Long speculates as to whether this may not be due to the fact that the home and school "protect" the deaf girl too much because of her physical handicap, and thus she fails to get as much opportunity as the deaf boy to develop her motor ability.

One other study of motor ability was made by Morsh (44), who tested deaf children between the ages of eleven and twenty, and made certain comparisons with hearing children. In tapping he found no difference between the deaf and the hearing. In hand steadiness the deaf seemed slightly superior. On the balancing board the results were ambiguous because of the many disturbing factors. In speed of eye movement the hearing were superior.

So far as these two studies go, therefore, we may conclude that the deaf are under no handicap in general motor ability, unless it be in body balance.

Mechanical Ability. How does the mechanical ability of the deaf child compare with that of hearing children? Stanton (78) has given us the best study of this problem. She worked with 157 deaf children. Each deaf child was paired with a hearing child of the same age, sex, nationality of parents, and occupational level of the father. These children ranged in age from 12–0 to 14–11 and the deaf children represented 95 to 97 per cent of the enrollment of children of those ages in the two schools for the deaf concerned, so that we may consider them an unselected sampling of deaf children of that specific age range. Battery A of the Minnesota Mechanical-Ability Tests was used. This battery is a very thorough test, consisting of the Paper Form-Board Tests, Forms A and B; the Spatial Relations Test, Boards A, B, C, and D; and the long form of the Assembly Test, Boxes A, B, and C.

Stanton gives all the possible comparisons between the deaf and hearing groups of both sexes on each of the several tests. These results may be summarized as follows in terms of the superiority of the various groups, expressed as the ratio of the difference of the means to the standard deviation of the difference:

Test	*Boys* *Deaf*	*Hearing*	*Girls* *Deaf*	*Hearing*	*Deaf* *Boys*	*Deaf* *Girls*
Form Boards	1.61			1.58	1.78	
Assembly	2.30			2.16	7.71	
Spatial Relations —time	2.01			0.34	2.32	
Spatial Relations —errors	3.68		2.97			0.08
Battery A	2.81		0.15		2.67	
Battery B	2.66			1.08	4.83	

In all comparisons the deaf boys are superior to hearing boys, and in one case the ratio is above 3. The hearing girls are superior to the deaf girls in four out of six comparisons, but in no case does the ratio reach 3. Deaf boys are superior to deaf girls in five out of six comparisons, and two of the five are well above 3. Stanton concludes that deaf boys are at least equal to hearing boys of the same age, nationality, and occupational level of parent, while deaf girls are probably inferior. We may note here the general similarity of these results with Long's results for motor ability. In both cases the deaf and hearing boys are about equal, whereas the deaf girls are inferior to hearing girls. And again the deaf boys are distinctly superior to the deaf girls.

Stanton goes on to compare her deaf and hearing groups with the published norms of the Minnesota test and finds that both deaf and hearing groups fall far below these norms. On Battery A only 19 per cent of the deaf and 16 per cent of the hearing boys reach or exceed the median score for their age; none of the deaf girls and only 3 per cent of the hearing girls reach or exceed their respective medians. This would seem to indicate either that the Minnesota norms are too high for the population in general or that Stanton's sampling of hearing children was not a random sampling of hearing children with respect to mechanical ability. For the time being, therefore, we cannot generalize about the mechanical ability of the deaf as compared with the hearing. When paired carefully with the hearing, the boys are by no means inferior. However, larger groups of deaf and hearing should be compared.

One smaller study by Lyon (34) used the Minnesota Mechanical-Ability Tests with fifty-nine boys aged thirteen to twenty-two. Comparing the scores with the norms, it was found that 36 per cent of the deaf reached or exceeded the median of the hearing.

Memory. Pintner and Paterson (60) report the most extensive study of immediate visual memory. They tested 481 deaf, aged seven to twenty-six, for visual memory span for digits, exposing each digit for about one second. They compare their results with Smedley's norms for hearing children, and find that the memory span for the deaf is much below that of the hearing at each age from seven to adult. Smedley shows a progressive increase from 5 at age seven to 8 at age nineteen, whereas Pintner and Paterson find that the deaf show an increase from 1.5 at age seven to only 4 at adult. The authors find no sex differences but orally taught pupils do better than manually taught pupils at each age. There is an irregular increase in memory span with increasing age of onset of deafness.

Morsh (44) says the deaf seem superior to the hearing in "location memory." In his test, the subject observes objects on a board for one minute; then the objects are mixed with others and the subject has to replace them in proper position.

Finally Lindner (30) on several unstandardized memory tests compares very small groups of deaf and hearing children and finds the deaf superior or at least equal in many comparisons.

From these few and rather restricted studies we cannot generalize about the memory ability of the deaf. Many other studies with different types of memory tests are greatly needed.

Summary. This survey of our knowledge about the special abilities or aptitudes of the deaf is notable for showing our ignorance in this field. We know a little about motor and mechanical ability and perhaps about memory. We need to know much more about all these areas and the many other areas not even mentioned, such as artistic ability, artistic appreciation, different kinds of memory and observation, suggestibility, constructive ability, athletic ability, and so on. At present all that we can say is that the deaf do not appear to be handicapped in motor ability and probably not in mechanical ability. If these findings are verified by more extensive research, they should influence the aims and methods of the education of the deaf. If, in these areas of motor and mechanical ability, the deaf are not inferior to the hearing, then we have discovered valuable potential assets which should be developed to the utmost. The education of the deaf should center around their assets not their liabilities.

VOCATIONAL TRAINING

One important aspect of the education of the deaf has always been their vocational training. Various courses of a vocational type are offered in almost all schools. Residential schools in particular have for a long time paid much attention to such courses. Much criticism, however, has been leveled at the vocational training in schools for the deaf. It is claimed that it does not function in the afterschool life of the pupil; it does not fit him for a specific job; it is too general and often old-fashioned; there is not enough of it; and so on.

A recent survey throws some light on some of these questions. Martens (37) made a nationwide survey of the deaf and the hard-of-hearing with regard to their status in the occupational world. Information was gathered from 19,580 deaf and hard-of-hearing individuals, of which 13,251 were men and 6,329 women, ranging in age from sixteen to sixty and over. The author estimates that about 43.6 per cent were deaf and 56.4 per cent hard of hearing. An attempt was made to find out how effective their occupational or trade training, received while at school, had been in later life. It was found that 10,145 had received some occupational training while at school. With regard to their later career we note that such occupation was:

	Per Cent
Followed exclusively in later life	30.2
Followed to a large extent	16.3
Followed to a small extent	16.1
Not followed at all	37.4

Whether this is a good record or not, it is hard to say. That 62.6 per cent made some use of the training they received in school is by no means a bad record when we consider the difficulties of vocational guidance while in school, the fact that many older people are included in these data, and the rapid changes and modifications that have taken place in trade and industry during the last thirty or forty years. On the other hand, when we note that 37.4 per cent made no use whatever in later life of the vocational training received in school, we must recognize that there is room for great improvement in educational and vocational guidance while the pupil is in school, for the psychological measurement of each pupil's abilities, for better integration between the school and industry, for more vocational training for modern jobs, for help in placement when the pupil leaves school. The wastage represented by the 37.4 per cent who made no use of their school training is too great to go unchallenged.

The same report gives us other items of information that are provocative. It was found that a greater percentage of the deaf men (60.7 per cent) were employed at the time of the survey than of the hard-of-hearing men (51.1 per cent). Again, those who lost their hearing early in life are represented among the employed in greater proportion than are those who became deaf in later life. Perhaps both of these findings mean that those who are deaf (as opposed to merely hard of hearing) and those who become deaf early in life are generally educated in schools for the deaf, where they receive more thorough vocational training, and are therefore more able to find and hold their positions than those who are merely hard of hearing and those who become deaf later in life. The latter have probably received their education or part of it in ordinary schools. They have looked forward to entering occupations as hearing individuals and, therefore, when loss of hearing arises they find it very difficult to readjust. Most of them have not been trained for occupations especially adapted to the deaf. In line with these results, the Martens report also finds that those who use signs, gestures, or the manual alphabet as the chief means of communication are represented among those employed in greater proportion than those who use the spoken language. A great number of those who use the spoken language are of course the hard of hearing. When the deaf alone are considered the difference is still there although greatly diminished. The percentage employed of those using signs, gestures, or manual alphabet was 63.2; of those using spoken language, 58.3; of those using writing, 56.1. The report suggests that some of this difference may be caused by the employment of deaf people in residential schools for the deaf. It may also be partially due to the fact that the deaf person who makes no pretense to speak is content to accept simpler and less well-paid jobs. He competes less with the hearing. He stays within his own niche.

The types of occupations held by the deaf can be seen from the percentage distribution of 3,786 men and 1,151 women who "could not understand speech at all." This is as follows:

	Men	*Women*
Agriculture, fishing, and forestry	5.0	0.3
Manufacturing and mechanical trades	29.8	7.1
Transportation and communication	0.7	0
Trade	2.4	2.6
Public service	0.3	0.1
Professional and semiprofessional service	7.1	12.9
Domestic and personal service	5.2	19.7
Clerical occupations	3.2	6.1
Managers, foremen, inspectors	0.7	0.5
Operatives, laborers, and porters	45.6	50.7

From this it is clear that the chief occupations for the deaf are semiskilled and unskilled jobs.

Another interesting table in the Martens report gives the number of students who were prepared for certain occupations in schools for the deaf and the number employed in those occupations at the time of the survey. To quote from the report: "On the one hand, an excess of training appears in certain time-honored crafts of mechanical nature, and on the other hand there is very extensive employment in certain fields for which no training is now offered."

What do the employers think of these deaf people employed by them? Again the Martens report gives us some light on this. Considering the deaf only (those who cannot hear at all) we find that there were ratings by employers on 2,864 men and 1,009 women, and that 55.7 per cent of the men and 56.4 per cent of the women were rated as succeeding very well. At the other end of the scale only 2 per cent and 3 per cent respectively were rated as failing. Evidently those deaf people who can get and hold jobs are on the whole rated highly by their employers. But when inquiry was made of the employers as to the prospects of promotion, the picture looks very black. Only 6.5 per cent of the men and 9.4 per cent of the women had excellent prospects, whereas 72.1 per cent of the men and 68.6 per cent of the women had no prospects. The deaf must stay within their own niche. There is little chance of getting out of it.

SUMMARY

The deaf person, that is the individual born deaf or deaf at an early age, looks exactly like a normal hearing person. There is no outward sign of his deficiency. And yet in some respects he is more severely handicapped in his relations with the people around him than are the other physically handicapped types, for he lacks the ordinary language by means of which most thoughts and feelings are rapidly conveyed from individual to individual. He is, therefore, shut off more completely than is the blind person or the crippled. Left to himself, he quickly develops a language of signs and gestures, a language that is quick, direct, and accurate, yet it is doubtful whether this language can ever be developed to express the abstractions and finer relationships which the written and spoken language can attain, and at any rate this sign and gesture language is restricted to a few people, for the hearing world does not understand it. Hence it becomes a necessity for the deaf person in a hearing world to learn a second language. He becomes a bilingual individual. His first or "mother tongue" is the language of signs and gestures. His second or learned language is the spoken-written language of the hearing world. Now the learning of this second language is evidently a slow and painful process, as the whole history of the education of the deaf bears witness. It is a much more difficult process than is the case with the hearing bilingual individual. In this latter instance the child has learned quickly and unconsciously his mother tongue at home, and then he learns at school and on the playground almost as quickly the second language. This second language surrounds him for a part of the day at least and he assimilates it in the same manner, through the ear, as he did his first language. But not so the deaf child. His second language is totally different from his natural language of signs and gestures. It is a language of fine lip and face movements, of delicate throat and mouth movements, of little black marks on paper. There is little in common between it and his natural language. It requires close observation and strict attention on his part. It does not surround him, press upon him, pervade him whether he will or not, as the sounds of a spoken language do the hearing child. Hence for most deaf individuals for most of their lives this "second" language always appears to be a little "foreign." It may be something like the second language to a bilingual individual, who has not yet reached that degree of familiarity so that he "thinks" entirely in the second language.

Now it is maintained by certain educators of the deaf that the thing to do is to prohibit as far as possible all use of the "natural" language of the deaf, the language of signs and gestures, so that the child will be forced to use more frequently the "second" language. We should, they maintain, try to duplicate as far as possible the conditions under which a hearing child grows up and learns unconsciously his mother tongue. Surround the deaf child with nothing but the English language in the form of lip-reading and speech and written words. Make this the only avenue of communication, so that he will not be distracted by his "natural" language of signs and gestures. The analogy is to the best method of quickly inducting a foreign child into a second language. A little German boy comes to this country. Send him to school where he hears nothing but English, surround him with English-speaking playmates, talk to him in English at home, and lo and behold in a year or so he will be speaking fluent English and all the initial strangeness of the "foreign" language will have vanished. The analogy seems a good one. But somehow it does not seem to work so well with the deaf child. The strangeness of the second language does not vanish in a year or two—no, not even in ten or fifteen years. The second language does not come so easily to the deaf child. The analogy is probably a false one, mainly because the language media in the two cases are different. The hearing child hears and sees the one who is speaking, and also, and most important, he hears as well as feels the muscles of his throat and mouth when he himself speaks. The deaf child does not see his own lips and face when he speaks. But further than that, there is an insistence in sounds—they penetrate the ear whether we will or not. We can never duplicate this insistence with vision.

That the acquisition of the English language is slow and difficult for the deaf child is attested by all the results of our measurement of educational attainment among the deaf. This is the outstanding result of all the work with standardized achievement tests up to the present time. A consequence of this is that all tests employing language are ruled out as measures of general intelligence for deaf children. Hence the use of performance and nonlanguage group tests for this purpose. The results of these tests seem to indicate a slightly lower general intelligence for the deaf as a group when compared with the hearing. The difference is not great and many deaf exceed the average intelligence of the hearing. Why there should be this difference in intelligence on tests which seem equally fair to both deaf and hearing is not clear. The hypothesis advanced here is that, in the first place, the congenitally deaf may come from families which on the average are somewhat lower in intelligence than the average family, and, in the second place, the adventitiously deaf may suffer on the average a slight arrest of mental development due to the same diseases that caused the deafness.

Another important finding of the research so far accomplished is that every year of hearing after the age of four to six is a tremendous asset for the deaf child for his future language development. If he learns language naturally and unconsciously in early life he gains something that seems to remain afterwards.

With regard to the personality traits of the deaf, research has only just begun. The indications at present seem to be that there is no peculiar "deaf" personality. Deaf people seem to differ little from hearing people. There are suggestions of slight differences. On the average they may be a little less well adjusted, a little less emotionally stable, a little less dominant, a little more fearful. There is also the important suggestion that needs to be followed up carefully, namely, that deaf children from homes where there are no other deaf people are somewhat less well adjusted than those from homes where there are other deaf relatives. Perhaps the chief stresses and strains come from attempts of the deaf to adjust to the hearing world. The deaf among the deaf are more normal than the deaf among the hearing.

Is there any area in which the deaf are specially competent? So far none has been discovered. But there are indications that the deaf are practically on a par with the hearing with reference to motor ability and perhaps with reference to mechanical ability. And there are many other areas about which we have no information.

In the vocational world at present the deaf as a whole take a lowly place. They find it hard to get jobs and hard to keep them.

This is a general picture of what we know about the deaf at the present time. We need to know a lot more. But certain things seem to be fairly well established. The motor and mechanical ability and the concrete intelligence of the deaf are their great assets. Their abstract verbal intelligence, their academic achievement, are their great liabilities. This being so, is not the time ripe to reorient the whole education of the deaf? For most deaf children the emphasis should be upon the motor, the mechanical, the concrete. Make the core of their education center around the concrete and the mechanical. Make the learning of language subsidiary and ancillary to making and building and doing. Only for a few should the academic curriculum be followed. Shopwork, home economics, trade training of all kinds, dramatics, gardening, and the like, these would be the main "subjects," and reading and writing and arithmetic would be subsidiary and incidental aspects of the main "course." Some bold and wise educator of the deaf has a great opportunity here.

Furthermore, it seems to follow from this whole discussion that experiments are needed in early preschool work with deaf children. More than the hearing child does the deaf child need early guidance by experts who understand him. And here it seems to me could be initiated crucial experiments on teaching methods of communication. What I have called the "natural" language of signs and gestures might be given free play and intensive cultivation in the early life of the deaf child, so that he will build up a rich store of reactions to the things and persons of his environment. He will be led to "tell" about and share his experiences in his own language before we try to teach him another more difficult mode of expression and communication (speech and lip reading). For it has often seemed to me that we have been trying to teach the young deaf child words and phrases before he has had enough experience with the underlying reality, and furthermore we use too much valuable time in early schooling on drill in speech and lip reading, time which might more profitably be spent in real living.

There are now enough suitable tests and scales for the deaf school child to warrant their systematic and periodic use in every school for the deaf. Every residential school should have a school psychologist and counselor. Every deaf child should have a cumulative record card showing his development from the time he enters to the time he leaves school. Deaf children vary as much as hearing children. Each child has his own particular strengths and weaknesses, and these should be discovered as early as possible so as to strengthen his desirable qualities and weaken his undesirable ones.

The aim of the education of the deaf child should be to make him a well-integrated, happy deaf individual, and not a pale imitation of a hearing person. Let us aim to produce happy well-adjusted deaf *individuals,* each different from the other, each with his own personality. If a child cannot learn to read lips well or cannot speak well, far better let him develop other modes of expression and communication, writing and gesturing, than make him feel ashamed and frustrated because he cannot acquire the very difficult art of speech and lip reading. Our aim must be a well-balanced, happy *deaf* person and not an imitation of a hearing one.

BIBLIOGRAPHY

1. Amoss, H., *Ontario School Ability Examination* (Ryerson Press, Toronto, 1936).
2. Beilinsson, A., "Eine Methode zur Untersuchung optischer Artikulations-Wahrnehmungen," *Zeitschr. f. Kinderforsch.,* XXXVII (1930), 93–101.
3. Binet, A., and T. Simon, "Peut-on enseigner la parole aux sourds-muets?" *L'année psychol.,* XV (1909), 373–96.
4. Bradway, K. P., "The Social Competence of Deaf Children," *Am. Annals of the Deaf,* LXXXII (1937), 122–40.
5. Bridgman, O., "The Estimation of Mental Ability in Deaf Children," *Am. Annals of the Deaf,* LXXXIV (1939), 337–49.
6. Brown, A. W., "The Correlations of Non-Language Tests

with Each Other in a School for the Deaf," *J. Appl. Psychol.*, XIV (1930), 371–5.

7. Brunschwig, L., *A Study of Some Personality Aspects of Deaf Children*, T.C. Contribs. to Educ., No. 687 (Bur. of Pubs., Teachers College, Columbia Univ., N.Y., 1936).
8. Conklin, E. S., "A Method for the Determination of Relative Skill in Lip Reading," *Volta Rev.*, XIX (1917), 216–19.
9. Day, H. E., I. S. Fusfeld, and R. Pintner, *A Survey of American Schools for the Deaf* (Natl. Research Council, Wash., 1928).
10. Diderot, D., "Lettre sur les sourds et les muets," *Oeuvres complètes, editées par J. Assezat*, Vol. I (Paris, 1875), 343–428.
11. Drever, J., "Intelligence Tests for the Deaf," *Teacher of the Deaf*, XXVII (1929), 163–7.
12. Ewing, I. R., and A. W. G. Ewing, *The Handicap of Deafness* (Longmans, Green, London, 1938).
13. Fusfeld, I. S., "Tabular Statement of American Schools for the Deaf," *Am. Annals of the Deaf*, LXXXV (1940), 8–35.
14. Fusfeld, I. S., "Research and Testing at Gallaudet College," *Am. Annals of the Deaf*, LXXXV (1940), 170–83.
15. Glau, W., "Vergleichende Betrachtungen über die Vitalkapazität Taubstummer," *Päd.-psychol. Arbeiten, Instit. Leipziger Lehrervereins*, XIV (Leipzig, 1925), 56–66.
16. Goldmann, P., "Untersuchungen über das Ablesen vom Munde bei Taubstummen und Spätertaubten," *Arch. gesamte Psychol.*, LXVII (1929), 441–504.
17. Goodlett, C. B., and V. R. Greene, "The Mental Abilities of Twenty-Nine Deaf and Partially Deaf Negro Children," *West Va. State Coll. Bull.* (June, 1940).
18. Göpfert, H., "Psychologische Untersuchungen über das Ablesen vom Munde bei Ertaubten und Hörenden," *Z. Kinderforsch.*, XXVIII (1923), 315–67.
19. Greenberger, D., "Doubtful Cases," *Am. Annals of the Deaf*, XXXIV (1889), 93 ff.

20. Gregory, I., "A Comparison of Certain Personality Traits and Interests in Deaf and Hearing Children," *Child Develop.*, IX (1938), 277–80.
21. Groff, M. L., "An Analysis of the First-Year Vocabularies of the Public Residential Schools for the Deaf in the United States," *Am. Annals of the Deaf*, LXXVII: 4 (1932); LXXVIII: 2, 3, 5 (1933); LXXIX: 2 (1934).
22. Hall, P., "Results of Recent Tests at Gallaudet College," *Am. Annals of the Deaf*, LXXIV (1929), 389–95.
23. Holland, B. F., "A Study of the Reactions of Physically Normal, Blind and Deaf Children to Questions in a Verbal Intelligence Test," *Teachers Forum (Blind)*, IX (1936), 1–10.
24. Jones, J. W., *Report of the Ohio School for the Deaf* (1909), 17.
25. Keys, N., and L. Boulware, "Language Acquisition by Deaf Children as Related to Hearing Loss and Age of Onset," *J. Educ. Psychol.*, XXIX (1938), 401–12.
26. Kilpatrick, W. M., "Comparative Tests," *Am. Annals of the Deaf*, LVII (1912), 427.
27. Kirk, S. A., "Behavior Problem Tendencies in Deaf and Hard-of-Hearing Children," *Am. Annals of the Deaf*, LXXXIII (1938), 131–7.
28. Kitson, H. D., "Psychological Tests for Lip-Reading Ability," *Volta Rev.*, XVII (1915), 471–6.
29. Lindner, R., "Das Seelenbild des Taubstummen in der Literatur und Abgrenzung des Begriffes 'taubstumm,'" *Päd.-psychol. Arbeiten, Instit. Leipziger Lehrervereins*, XIV (Leipzig, 1925), 7–20.
30. Lindner, R., "Vergleichende Intelligenzprüfungen," *Päd.-psychol. Arbeiten, Instit. Leipziger Lehrervereins*, XIV (Leipzig, 1925), 67–208.
31. Long, J. A., *Motor Abilities of Deaf Children*, T.C. Contribs. to Educ., No. 514 (Bur. of Pubs., Teachers College, Columbia Univ., N.Y., 1932).

32. Love, J. K., "Classification of Deaf Pupils in Denmark," *Am. Annals of the Deaf,* LII (1907), 114–16.
33. Lyon, V. W., "The Use of Vocational and Personality Tests with the Deaf," *J. Appl. Psychol.,* XVIII (1934), 224–30.
34. Lyon, V. W., "A Study of Vocational Abilities of Students Who Have Attended the Illinois School for the Deaf," *J. Appl. Psychol.,* XVIII (1934), 443–53.
35. MacKane, K., *A Comparison of the Intelligence of Deaf and Hearing Children,* T.C. Contribs. to Educ., No. 585 (Bur. of Pubs., Teachers College, Columbia Univ., N.Y., 1933).
36. MacMillan, D. P., and F. G. Bruner, *Children Attending the Public Day Schools for the Deaf in Chicago,* Special Report of the Department of Child Study and Pedagogic Investigation (Chicago Public Schools, May, 1906).
37. Martens, E. H., *The Deaf and the Hard of Hearing in the Occupational World,* U.S. Dept. of Interior, Bull. No. 13, 1936 (Govt. Printing Office, Wash., 1937).
38. Mason, M. K., "A Laboratory Method of Measuring Visual Hearing Ability," *Volta Rev.,* XXXIV (1932), 510–14.
39. Mason, M. K., "Objective Scoring in Tests of Visual Hearing," *Volta Rev.,* XXXIX (1937), 576–93.
40. Mason, M. K., "Individual Deviations in the Visual Reproduction of the Speech of Two Speakers," *Am. Annals of the Deaf,* LXXXIV (1939), 408–24.
41. Max, L. W., "Experimental Study of the Motor Theory of Consciousness," *J. Comp. Psychol.,* XXIV (1937), 301–44.
42. McIlvaine, J. A., "A Plea for the Feebleminded Deaf," *Am. Annals of the Deaf,* LIV (1909), 444–50.
43. McIlvaine, J. A., "The Disposal of the Feebleminded," *Am. Annals of the Deaf,* LVII (1912), 128 ff.
44. Morsh, J. E., "Motor Performance of the Deaf," *Comp. Psychol. Monogs.,* XIII (Nov., 1936), No. 66.
45. Mott, A. J., "The Ninth Year of a Deaf Child's Life," *Am. Annals of the Deaf,* XLIV (1899), 401–12; XLV (1900), 33–39, 93–109.

46. Newlee, C. E., "A Report of Learning Tests with Deaf Children," *Volta Rev.,* XXI (1919), 216–23.
47. Peet, P., "Notions of the Deaf and Dumb before Instruction, Especially in Regard to Religious Subjects," *Am. Annals of the Deaf and Dumb,* VIII (1855), 1–44.
48. Peterson, E. G., and J. M. Williams, "Intelligence of Deaf Children as Measured by Drawings," *Am. Annals of the Deaf,* LXXV (1930), 274–90.
49. Pintner, R., "A Measurement of Language Ability and Language Progress of Deaf Children," *Volta Rev.,* XX (1918), 755–64.
50. Pintner, R., "A Mental Survey of the Deaf," *J. Educ. Psychol.,* XIX (1928), 145–51.
51. Pintner, R., "Speech and Speech-Reading Tests for the Deaf.," *J. Appl. Psychol.,* XII (1929), 220–5; also in *Am. Annals of the Deaf,* LXXIV (1929), 480–6.
52. Pintner, R., "Contributions of Psychological Testing to the Problems of the Deaf," *Internatl. Conf. on Educ. of Deaf* (June, 1933), 213–20.
53. Pintner, R., and L. Brunschwig, "Some Personality Adjustments of Deaf Children in Relation to Two Different Factors," *J. Genet. Psychol.,* XLIX (1936), 377–88.
54. Pintner, R., and L. Brunschwig, "A Study of Certain Fears and Wishes among Deaf and Hearing Children," *J. Educ. Psychol.,* XXVIII (1937), 259–70.
55. Pintner, R., I. S. Fusfeld, and L. Brunschwig, "Personality Tests of Deaf Adults," *J. Genet. Psychol.,* LI (1937), 305–27.
56. Pintner, R., and D. G. Paterson, "The Binet Scale and the Deaf Child," *J. Educ. Psychol.,* VI (1915), 201–10.
57. Pintner, R., and D. G. Paterson, "The Ability of Deaf and Hearing Children to Follow Printed Directions," *Ped. Sem.,* XXIII (1916), 477–97.
58. Pintner, R., and D. G. Paterson, "Learning Tests with Deaf Children," *Psychol. Monogs.,* XX (1916), No. 88.
59. Pintner, R., and D. G. Paterson, "A Measurement of the

Language Ability of Deaf Children," *Psychol. Rev.*, XXIII (1916), 413–36.

60. Pintner, R., and D. G. Paterson, "A Comparison of Deaf and Hearing Children in Visual Memory for Digits," *J. Exper. Psychol.*, II (1917), 76–88.
61. Pintner, R., and D. G. Paterson, "Some Conclusions from Psychological Tests of the Deaf," *Volta Rev.*, XX (1918), 10–14.
62. Psychological Division, Clarke School for the Deaf, "Studies in the Psychology of the Deaf, No. 1," *Psychol. Monogs.*, LII (1940), No. 232.
63. Pyle, W. H., *The Examination of School Children* (Macmillan, N.Y., 1913).
64. Reamer, J. C., "Mental and Educational Measurements of the Deaf," *Psychol. Monogs.*, XXIX (1921), No. 132.
65. Roth, S. D., "Survey of the Psychological Examination Given by Dr. Stella M. Bowers, May, 1937," *West Va. Tablet*, LXI:7 (1938), 1–6.
66. Schick, H. F., "A Performance Test for Deaf Children of School Age," *Volta Rev.*, XXXVI (1934), 657–8.
67. Schick, H. F., and M. F. Meyer, "The Use of the Lectometer in the Testing of the Hearing and the Deaf," *Am. Annals of the Deaf*, LXXVII (1932), 292–304.
68. Schlenkrich, J., "Köperlänge und Körpergewicht taubstummer Kinder," *Päd.-Psychol. Arbeiten, Instit. Leipziger Lehrervereins*, XIV (Leipzig, 1925), 21–55.
69. Schmähl, O., "Optische Anschauungsbilder bei Taubstummen," *Zeitschr. f. Kinderforsch.*, XXXVIII (1931), 67–133.
70. Seashore, R. H., "Stanford Motor Skills Unit," *Psychol. Monogs.*, XXXIX (1928), No. 178, 51–66.
71. Shirley, M., and F. L. Goodenough, "A Survey of Intelligence of Deaf Children in Minnesota Schools," *Am. Annals of the Deaf*, LXXVII (1932), 238–47.
72. Smith, J. L., "Mental Characteristics of Pupils," *Am. Annals of the Deaf*, XLVIII (1903), 248 ff.

73. South Dakota, State of, *Seventh Biennial Report of the State Commission for the Control of the Feebleminded, for Period Ending June 30, 1938.*
74. Springer, N. N., "A Comparative Study of the Intelligence of a Group of Deaf and Hearing Children," *Am. Annals of the Deaf,* LXXXIII (1938), 138–52.
75. Springer, N. N., "A Comparative Study of the Behavior Traits of Deaf and Hearing Children of New York City," *Am. Annals of the Deaf,* LXXXIII (1938), 255–73.
76. Springer, N. N., "A Comparative Study of the Psychoneurotic Responses of Deaf and Hearing Children," *J. Educ. Psychol.,* XXIX (1938), 459–66.
77. Springer, N. N., and S. Roslow, "A Further Study of the Psychoneurotic Responses of Deaf and Hearing Children," *J. Educ. Psychol.,* XXIX (1938), 590–6.
78. Stanton, M. B., *Mechanical Ability of Deaf Children,* T.C. Contribs. to Educ., No. 751 (Bur. of Pubs., Teachers College, Columbia Univ., N.Y., 1938).
79. Streng, A., and S. A. Kirk, "The Social Competence of Deaf and Hard-of-Hearing Children in a Public Day School," *Am. Annals of the Deaf,* LXXXIII (1938), 244–54.
80. Taylor, H., "A Spelling Test," *Am. Annals of the Deaf,* XLII (1897), 364–9.
81. Thompson, H., *An Experimental Study of the Beginning Reading of Deaf-Mutes,* T.C. Contribs. to Educ., No. 254 (Bur. of Pubs., Teachers College, Columbia Univ., N.Y., 1927).
82. Upshall, C. C., *Day Schools vs. Institutions for the Deaf,* T.C. Contribs. to Educ., No. 389 (Bur. of Pubs., Teachers College, Columbia Univ., N.Y., 1929).
83. U.S. Census, *The Deaf-Mute Population of the United States, 1920* (Dept. of Commerce, Bur. of the Census, Govt. Printing Office, Wash., 1928).
84. U.S. Census, *The Blind and Deaf-Mutes in the United States, 1930* (Dept. of Commerce, Bur. of the Census, Govt. Printing Office, Wash., 1931).

85. Vertes, J. O., "Das Gedächtnis taubstummer Kinder," *Zeitschr. f. päd. Psychol.*, XXXII (1931), 136–42.
86. Whipple, G. M., *Manual of Mental and Physical Tests, Part II* (Warwick and York, Baltimore, 1915).
87. Zeckel, A., and J. J. van der Kolk, "A Comparative Intelligence Test of Groups of Children Born Deaf and of Good Hearing by Means of the Porteus Test," *Am. Annals of the Deaf*, LXXXIV (1939), 114–23.

CHAPTER VI

The Hard of Hearing

GENERAL

The hard-of-hearing individual is one who established language in the normal way, either because his loss of hearing developed after the natural establishment of language, or because his loss of hearing has never been severe enough to prevent him from learning language in the ordinary way. The fundamental difference between the deaf and the hard of hearing depends upon the way in which they develop their language. There can be no sharp dividing line between the two groups. Both of them suffer from loss of hearing in various amounts. There is, however, a crucial difference in their needs. The deaf need to be taught the English language from the ground up. The hard of hearing learn it normally just as a hearing child does, except that the learning may be slower and more difficult. The term "deafened" is sometimes used for those who once had good hearing, and who in youth or later life lost all useful hearing.

How many hard-of-hearing individuals there are is not known. If any slight deviation from normal hearing is considered, there are probably millions in the United States. From audiometric surveys of school children, it has been estimated that perhaps 15 per cent of such children have hearing defects and this would mean about three million school children in the United States, according to Phillips and Rowell (10). Peck and Samuelson (9) estimate that 11 per cent of school children are hard of hearing. Conway's (3) careful study of 962 children in grades 6, 7, and 8 found 10.6 per cent to be hard of hearing. Another careful estimate of 6.8 per cent has been given by the English Committee Report (4). One of the most conservative estimates is about 1½ per cent or 342,000 school children in this country (19).

The differences in these and other estimates of the percentage of the hard of hearing are due to different methods of measurement employed and also to various definitions of what constitutes a hard-of-hearing individual. It makes a great difference in our percentages as to where we draw the dividing line in terms of decibel loss on the audiometer. The precise percentage, however, is not important for our purposes. We know that there are enough cases to present an educational and psychological problem of great importance.

INTELLIGENCE

It has generally been assumed that hard-of-hearing children find school work more difficult than do normal-hearing children. Sometimes this is supposed to be due to lower intelligence among the hard of hearing. Let us then examine the results of standard intelligence tests given to hard-of-hearing children. There are three important studies, and we shall deal with them in the order of their publication.

Waldman, Wade, and Aretz (16) report results for 1,079 children in grades IV to VIII tested by means of the N.I.T. and the 4A audiometer. The mean I.Q. for the total group is 95 and the correlation between hearing and I.Q. is +.05. For a subgroup of 552 cases the authors find the mean I.Q. to be 98.5

with a correlation of + .23 between hearing and intelligence. Again, dividing their 552 cases into two groups of good and poor hearers, they find a mean I.Q. of 99.6 for 466 good hearers and a mean I.Q. of 92.1 for 86 poor hearers. They also divide this same group according to loss in the better ear. For those having less than 9 S.U. loss the mean I.Q. is 99.4 and for those having more than 9 S.U. loss the mean I.Q. is 92.1. In general, therefore, these authors find the hard-of-hearing child to be slightly handicapped in intelligence as measured by a verbal general-intelligence test.

Madden (8) tested various groups of children by means of several different audiometers and several different intelligence tests. His results may be briefly summarized as follows:

		n	*n*	*Mean I.Q.*		
School	*Test*	*H. of H.*	*Normal H.*	*H. of H.*	*Normal H.*	*Diff.*
X	Binet	46	46	77.04	83.46	6.42
X	Rapid Survey	46	537	77.09	84.85	7.76
Y	Otis Group	13	170	93.38	101.55	8.17

The forty-six Binet pairs were matched for age, sex, and race. Madden also reports correlations between intelligence and hearing loss of – .137 for 183 cases and – .124 for 537 cases.

Pintner and Lev (14) report the results of intelligence tests given to 1,186 hard-of-hearing children in grades V and VI and 218 cases in grades VII and VIII. Control groups of normal-hearing children in the same classes were also tested at the same time. The Pintner Intelligence Test was the main test used. This is a group intelligence test of the usual verbal type. In addition a smaller sample was tested by means of the Pintner Nonlanguage Mental Test. This is a group test which does not require the use of any language in the giving or taking of the test. The directions are given by the examiner by means of pantomime and examples on the blackboard. The content of the test is entirely nonverbal.

The authors of the study give many comparisons of various normal-hearing and hard-of-hearing groups for boys and girls separately and in general they find the hard of hearing slightly below the normal in I.Q. on the verbal-intelligence test. Their final comparison of all the cases in grades V and VI is as follows:

Group	*n*	*Mean I.Q.*	*Sigma*	*Mean Diff.*	*Sigma Diff.*	*Diff. / Sigma Diff.*
Normal hearing	1,286	99.75	24.55			
All hard of hearing	1,186	94.67	24.12	5.08	0.98	5.2
Extremely hard of hearing	461	92.47	24.57	7.28	1.33	5.5

The last group, called extreme hard of hearing, is made up of all those cases in the main group of hard-of-hearing children whose hearing loss is 15 decibels or more in both ears. It can be seen from the above comparison that hard-of-hearing children in the public schools differ from normal-hearing children in the same grades only slightly as far as verbal intelligence is concerned. There is a difference, and it is a statistically significant difference as the table indicates, but it is not a very large difference. However, if we study the more extreme cases of hearing loss, we note that the difference increases sharply. The average I.Q. for these more extreme cases is 92 as compared with about 100 I.Q. for their normal-hearing comrades.

When, however, we turn to the comparison of hard-of-hearing and normal-hearing children on a nonlanguage test, we find that all differences between the two groups disappear. Here are the comparisons on the nonlanguage test:

Group	*n*	*Mean I.Q.*	*Sigma*	*Mean Diff.*	*Sigma Diff.*	*Diff. / Sigma Diff.*
Normal hearing	372	102.16	21.5			
All hard of hearing	315	99.29	20.5	2.86	1.60	1.8
Extremely hard of hearing	140	99.26	21.0	2.89	2.09	1.4

Further analysis of these results shows that with children who took both tests we obtain an increase in I.Q. on the nonlanguage test for hard-of-hearing children, but not for normal-hearing children.

The authors interpret these results to mean that loss of hearing in amounts such as we encounter among hard-of-hearing children in the public schools, tends to impair the language development of the child to a slight extent. Hence we find that on the average the hard-of-hearing child is slightly retarded in educational achievement. This slight language handicap is probably also the cause of the lower I.Q. on the usual verbal group test of intelligence or on individual tests of the Binet type. In concrete or nonverbal intelligence the hard-of-hearing child is in no way different from the normal hearing child.

If these conclusions of Pintner and Lev should be supported by other and more extensive studies of normal-hearing and hard-of-hearing school children, we might then conclude that the best instruments for the measurement of the intelligence of hard-of-hearing children are intelligence tests that do not require the use of language.

EDUCATIONAL ACHIEVEMENT

The hard-of-hearing child is commonly supposed to be handicapped in his school work. The evidence for this assumption is derived from studies of retardation, grade repetition, and standard educational-achievement tests.

Warwick (17) tested the hearing of 18,864 school children. He found that 3,830 of these cases had defective hearing and that 648 or 17 per cent of them were grade repeaters. Bock (1) surveyed the hearing of public-school children in Rochester, New York, and found an average of 1.27 grade repetitions for the hard of hearing as contrasted with an average of 0.37 repetitions for the normal-hearing child. Waldman *et al.* (16) found an average grade repetition of 0.55 for their group of 466 good hearers as contrasted with an average of 0.99 for their group of 86 poor hearers. These same groups are contrasted for grade age in months. The poor hearers show a mean retardation of 3.65 months; the good hearers a mean acceleration of 2.55 months; that is a difference of 6.2 months between the two groups. Other studies show much the same picture. Unpublished data collected by the author show the per cent of normal-hearing and hard-of-hearing children in the same grades in the same schools repeating one grade or more.

Group	*n*	*Per Cent*
Normal hearing	477	31.0
All hard of hearing	329	34.3
Extremely hard of hearing	78	47.4

Caplin (2) reports on the amount of retardation among hard-of-hearing children. Among 4,566 hard-of-hearing children who had been taking special lip-reading instruction for an average length of time of one year, he found 41.9 per cent who showed retardation before lip reading and only 5.6 per cent after lip reading. Among a control group of 5,310 normal-hearing children in the same schools and classes, 28 per cent showed retardation. Of 21,617 children showing a hearing loss of 9 S.U. in one or both ears on the 4A audiometer, Caplin found 46.8 per cent showing some grade retardation. Of 5,000 children diagnosed as hard of hearing after adequate otological examinations, 37.8 per cent had repeated grades in school. Evidently the hard-of-hearing child finds it a little more difficult than the normal-hearing child to move along through the grades at the normal rate. As the hearing loss increases, the difficulty of keeping up with the normal-hearing child becomes greater.

Further evidence of educational retardation is supplied by

studies using standardized educational-achievement tests. Madden (8) used the Stanford Achievement Test. He used his results for comparisons of normal hearing and hard-of-hearing groups equated or paired for intelligence on the Binet or verbal group intelligence test. Such equated groups showed no differences in educational-achievement scores. Given the same amount of verbal intelligence as the hearing child, the hard-of-hearing child can achieve as much as the hearing child on standard educational-achievement tests. Waldman *et al.* (16) also gave the Stanford Achievement Test and found correlations varying from + .18 to + .26 between amount of hearing and E.Q. Furthermore, their group of 466 good hearers obtained a mean E.Q. of 101.97 as contrasted with a mean E.Q. of 93.76 for their group of 86 poor hearers. This difference of 8.21 points of E.Q. is interpreted as equivalent to a whole year of grade achievement. A further analysis of the separate subtests of the Stanford Achievement Test shows lower mean E.Q.'s for all subtests for the hard of hearing. When these hard-of-hearing children are equated for I.Q. with hearing children, very little difference remains between the two groups.

A comparison of hard-of-hearing and normal-hearing children in grades V and VI on the Pintner Educational-Achievement Test made by the writer shows the following results:

Group	*n*	*Mean Score*
Normal hearing	536	35.4
Hard of hearing	402	34.4
Extremely hard of hearing	78	33.1

Again we note the same trend for the hard-of-hearing children to score slightly below the normal hearing and for the extreme cases to fall still lower. The differences between the mean scores are very small and are not statistically reliable.

All of these reports on the educational status of the hard-of-hearing child are consistent. They all indicate a slight educational retardation.

PERSONALITY

Several attempts have been made to study the personality traits of the hard-of-hearing individual. Does loss of hearing cause any deviations from normal personality development? Are there particular aspects of personality in which the hard-of-hearing individual differs from the hearing individual? Granted that hard-of-hearing individuals are subjected to all the influences that cause personality differences among normal hearing individuals and, therefore, like the latter differ among themselves enormously, are there in addition special influences due to hearing defect that cause the hard of hearing as a group to deviate from the normal hearing?

The studies can be grouped into those dealing with children in school and those concerned with hard-of-hearing adults.

School Children. Madden (8) provided a rating scale to be used by the teachers. The teachers rated both the hearing and hard-of-hearing children in their classes. The traits chosen were attentiveness, obedience, leadership, social attitude, aggressive-withdrawal behavior. Madden matched normal-hearing and hard-of-hearing groups for intelligence, sex, age, and race. He found no difference between the groups in ratings of attentiveness, obedience, and social attitude. The hard of hearing were rated lower in leadership and very definitely as less aggressive or more shy.

Pintner (12) used a general adjustment test, the Pupil Portraits Test, to compare 1,397 hard-of-hearing children with 1,604 normal-hearing controls in grades V to VIII. The mean scores for various groups were as follows:

Group	Boys		Girls	
	n	*mean*	*n*	*mean*
Normal hearing	832	79.5	772	84.0
All hard of hearing	698	76.7	699	83.4
Slightly hard of hearing	445	77.4	375	84.6
Extremely hard of hearing	253	75.4	324	81.9

The scores for the two sexes are given separately because of the usual sex difference found on this test. The hard-of-hearing groups have been divided into two groups, namely, slightly hard of hearing with the better ear showing a loss of less than 15 decibels, and the extreme hard of hearing, having a better ear with a loss of 15 or more decibels. The higher the score on the test, the better the adjustment. The mean scores for the total hard-of-hearing groups for both sexes are lower than those of the respective normal-hearing groups. The differences are small. The difference for the boys is statistically significant, but this is not true for the girls. When the total hard-of-hearing group is divided into two groups according to amount of hearing loss, we note that adjustment scores decrease as hearing loss increases. For both extreme hard-of-hearing groups the mean scores are lower than those of the normal-hearing groups by an amount that is statistically significant. The actual differences in score are, however, not great, and we must not exaggerate them. Extremely hard-of-hearing children feel themselves slightly less well adjusted than their normal hearing companions. But, in general, most hard-of-hearing children indicate on tests of this type that they feel as well adjusted as normal-hearing children. Auditory deficiency is a real handicap, but so far as the hard-of-hearing child in school is concerned, we may conclude from the results of this study that he is almost as successful in his adjustments as his normal-hearing fellows. The variation in adjustment scores for the normal and hard of hearing is practically the same. When loss of hearing amounts to 15 decibels or more, then normal adjustment would seem to become somewhat more difficult, but on the average only slightly so.

With reference to specific personality traits, we have the study of Pintner (13), who used the Aspects of Personality Test in a comparison of 1,171 hard-of-hearing children with 1,208 hearing controls. This test attempts to measure three traits, namely, ascendance-submission, extraversion-introversion and emotional stability. The two sexes must always be considered separately because of known differences in score between them. The author gives many comparisons for various samples of children. For our purpose it will be sufficient to give the mean scores for the total groups. Here are the results for ascendance-submission:

	Boys		*Girls*	
Group	*n*	*mean*	*n*	*mean*
Normal hearing	657	18.31	551	16.37
All hard of hearing	582	18.37	589	16.37
Hard of hearing (15 or more decibel loss)	223	18.64	293	16.65
Hard of hearing (30 or more decibel loss)	17	18.71	31	17.45

We see no difference in mean score between the normal hearing and hard of hearing. As hearing loss increases the scores tend to become slightly higher, but none of the differences between the means is statistically significant. The correlations with hearing loss are for boys +.05 and for girls +.08. The author comes to the conclusion that as far as this test goes there is no difference in ascendant-submissive behavior between normal-hearing and hard-of-hearing children in general. There may be a very slight tendency for the more extreme cases of hearing loss to show more aggressive behavior as a compensation for their physical handicap, but this is a tentative finding that should be subjected to more extensive and detailed study.

Coming now to the second trait, extraversion-introversion, we may summarize the author's results as follows:

Group	*Boys*		*Girls*	
	n	*mean*	*n*	*mean*
Normal hearing	657	21.79	551	20.82
All hard of hearing	582	21.16	589	20.61
Hard of hearing (15 or more decibel loss)	223	21.13	293	20.54
Hard of hearing (30 or more decibel loss)	17	21.71	31	19.36

Here, again, there is no difference between the various groups of hearing cases. The normal hearing, both boys and girls, have the highest mean, are the most extraverted. As hearing loss increases the mean for the girls drops regularly, but not so for the boys. The correlations between hearing loss and score on the test are +.004 for the boys and –.08 for the girls.

The third trait is emotional stability and we may again summarize the author's results as follows:

Group	*Boys*		*Girls*	
	n	*mean*	*n*	*mean*
Normal hearing	657	25.34	551	26.35
All hard of hearing	582	24.36	589	25.88
Hard of hearing (15 or more decibel loss)	223	23.87	293	25.37
Hard of hearing (30 or more decibel loss)	17	22.24	31	21.03

Here the differences are not great, but the trend is regular and obvious. For both sexes we note the drop in score from normal to severe loss of hearing. Many of the differences between the hard-of-hearing and normal-hearing groups are statistically significant. The correlations between hearing loss and emotional stability are – .07 for the boys and – .14 for the girls. The sharp drop in score for the most extreme cases of hearing loss is present both for boys and girls. Here, then, in this trait of emotional stability we seem to have discovered a real difference between hard-of-hearing and normal-hearing children. The difference is very small, but it seems to be a real one. The hard-of-hearing child is on the average not quite so emotionally stable as is the hearing child. In all probability his slight hearing impairment acts as an irritation in some of the situations he has to face.

We have one study dealing with hard-of-hearing children at the high-school level. Habbe (5) made an intensive study of forty-eight hard-of-hearing boys each matched with a normal-hearing boy in the same grade and school, with the same chronological age, intelligence, nationality, and socioeconomic background. The hard-of-hearing group all had more than 15 decibels loss in both ears. The mean loss for the group was 27 and 29 decibels for the right and left ears respectively. They were, thus, very definitely a hard-of-hearing group. The mean C.A. of the groups was fourteen years. The mean I.Q. of the hard-of-hearing group was 90.8 with a range from 75 to 123. The mean I.Q. of the normal hearing group was 92.5, with a similar range in I.Q.

The measures of personality used in this study were numerous. They included the Symonds Adjustment Questionnaire, the Aspects of Personality Test, and the Haggerty-Olson-Wickman Behavior-Rating Schedules. In addition the author constructed an autobiographical outline which allowed the child to express himself with some freedom about matters relating to his personal life. On the basis of a composite score derived from all these tests, the hard-of-hearing boys were ranked in order of adjustment. The ten best adjusted and the ten poorest adjusted boys were given a lengthy interview by the author.

The results of this very thorough comparison of these two

groups of normal-hearing and hard-of-hearing adolescent boys showed that the two groups were very much alike on the personality tests and rating scales, although five comparisons out of six favored the normal-hearing group. The hard-of-hearing group was slightly more submissive and introverted than the normal-hearing group. Again there was little difference between the two groups on items from the autobiography, although seven items favored the normal-hearing group, four the hard-of-hearing group and three were identical. On the whole, therefore, there was no fundamental difference in personality characteristics of these two groups of boys. To quote the author, "Personality maladjustments do not necessarily accompany real or imagined organ deficiencies. . . . If a boy's total adjustment to life is good, then it is quite possible for him to resolve minor difficulties."

Adults. A great deal has been written about the personality problems of the hard-of-hearing adult, both by authorities in this field and by the hard of hearing themselves. Welles (18) has covered the literature very well and given numerous quotations from many writers. He shows the great divergence in existing views, ranging from the belief in a peculiar or unique psychology of the hard of hearing to the belief that there is little or no difference in personality between the hard of hearing and the normal hearing. Welles groups the supposed personality handicaps into three categories: (1) social inadequacies; (2) depressive tendencies such as despondency, hopelessness, introversion, inferiority feelings, and the like; (3) paranoid tendencies, such as brooding, suspicion, anger, and delusions of persecution. Furthermore, the factors which are supposed to cause such changes in personality are numerous: the influence of fatigue poisons in the body because of the enormous expenditure of energy needed by the hard-of-hearing person to keep up with the hearing; tinnitus or internal head noises, which may be continuous, day and night, year after year; isolation and loneliness; economic factors involving special difficulties in getting or holding a job; finally, the deprivation of sound itself, leading to a diminution of feeling tone and emotional intensity.

It can be readily seen that the psychological problems as briefly summarized are numerous. Up to the present, however, very few attempts to measure actual personality differences between the hard of hearing and the normal hearing have been made. Welles (18) made the first notable contribution in this area. He used the Bernreuter Personality Inventory with hard-of-hearing adults who were members of various leagues for the hard of hearing. Pintner (11) followed this up by using the same personality inventory with hard-of-hearing individuals living in rather isolated rural regions, individuals who had little opportunity of meeting other hard-of-hearing people. Because these two studies followed similar methods, we shall present their findings together.

Welles found that his various hard-of-hearing groups differed significantly from their hearing controls in three of the four measures of personality. They were on the average more emotional, more introverted, and less dominant. A "special group" of thirty-one hard-of-hearing women, chosen because they had surmounted their handicap exceedingly well, were found not to differ at all in any of the traits from their control group.

If, now, we take the average scores obtained on the four personality traits and turn them into equivalent percentiles for hearing women (there were too few men in these studies), we get the following results:

	Emotionality	*Self-Sufficiency*	*Introversion*	*Dominance*
Urban hard of hearing	57	60	66	47
Total hard of hearing	66	61	68	41
Rural hard of hearing	69	62	74	30

On the first scale of the Bernreuter, that which measures emotional instability, the average score for the hard-of-hearing women (n = 196) tested by Welles was equivalent to a percentile rating of 57 for normal-hearing women. This means that the hard-of-hearing woman tends to be more emotionally unstable than the norm. Pintner found that the rural hard-of-hearing women (n = 94) had a still higher score, equivalent to a hearing percentile of 69. The second row of the table shows the result of combining the two groups tested by Welles and by Pintner. As we study this table we note that the rural group always emphasizes what may be thought of as the less desirable traits. They are a little more emotional, more self-sufficient, more introverted, and less dominant than the urban hard-of-hearing group, just as this group itself is a little more emotional, more self-sufficient, more introverted, and less dominant than the hearing group. The two studies are consistent in the picture they present of these personality traits of the adult hard of hearing, and the picture seems to agree with common observation. Deficiency in hearing seems in general to be accompanied by more nervousness or emotional instability, a greater tendency toward introversion, and a less dominant attitude toward life. There are, of course, the usual individual differences among the hard of hearing just as among the normal hearing, and a given hard-of-hearing individual may be better balanced emotionally and more dominant than the average normal-hearing person. All these results apply to women. We have no adequate study of hard-of-hearing men, but from the few cases reported by Welles, there is no reason to suppose that the results would be vitally different.

Pintner gathered information from his cases as to their feelings at the time they became aware of their hearing loss. From this he concluded that the shock was greatest if loss of hearing occurred in adolescence or early maturity and much less so if in childhood. Feelings of despair and resentment were most common, then came feelings of humiliation and shame. Both Welles and Pintner noted that those suffering from tinnitus had a higher average score for emotionality or nervousness than the hard of hearing in general. This again seems to fit logically into the general picture.

Summary of Personality Studies. Do these various studies render a consistent picture of the personality of the hard-of-hearing individual? In some respects they do. They all point very definitely to the fact that in regard to all the traits so far studied, the differences between normal-hearing and hard-of-hearing groups are very slight. All of the studies agree in finding the hard of hearing somewhat more introverted than the normal hearing. Most of the studies find the hard of hearing less well emotionally balanced (more neurotic) than the normal hearing. With reference to these two traits the evidence is consistent all the way from fifth- and sixth-grade children to various groups of adults. With reference, however, to the trait of dominance-submission, we find a slight tendency for the younger hard of hearing to be more dominant, while the adolescents and adults are more submissive. Whether future more extensive studies will verify this or not, remains to be seen. A tentative hypothesis might be that the young hard of hearing individual unconsciously compensates for his handicap by taking a dominant attitude where possible. As he becomes older, he becomes more conscious of his handicap, and finds less satisfaction in adopting a dominant attitude. Furthermore, the adult groups contain a number of individuals who have become hard of hearing in adolescence or early maturity. These cases may reduce the amount of dominance in the adult groups.

Finally, our measure of feelings of happiness or general adjustment in school point to the fact that hard-of-hearing children do not feel so well adjusted as do normal-hearing children.

We have no similar study for adults. It is probable that they would also show themselves as feeling less well adjusted than normal-hearing adults. Difficulty in hearing is something added to all the other possible causes for feeling maladjusted which the hard of hearing share with their hearing comrades.

SUMMARY

Whereas we found decided differences in many respects between the deaf and comparable hearing individuals, we note in this survey of the psychology of the hard of hearing only minor differences. The hard of hearing as a group are hardly distinguishable from the normal hearing. In school they test slightly lower on Binet and verbal-type intelligence tests, but perhaps not on nonlanguage tests. If they are somewhat mentally retarded, the retardation is slight. Yet they find it not so easy to keep up in their school work. They repeat more grades. Lip-reading instruction would seem to be of great help here. As a rule they do not feel quite so happy or well adjusted in school. They are in general inclined to be more introverted and less well balanced emotionally than comparable normal-hearing individuals.

None of these differences must be pushed too far. They are all small group differences. Each hard-of-hearing individual will have his own problems to face—the usual host of problems common to humanity, and his particular hearing defect is only one among many others. Nevertheless, in some cases this defect may become the focus around which all other personal problems gather. Relatively sudden loss of hearing during adolescence or early maturity would seem to be particularly dangerous for the integrity of the personality. Children who grow up with the defect have had time to come to terms with it.

Because the hard-of-hearing individual can hear and speak

normally, or nearly so, the most obvious treatment is the increase of hearing by hearing aids and training in lip reading. We need studies on the influence of hearing aids and lip reading at various age levels on all kinds of abilities and personality characteristics.

BIBLIOGRAPHY

1. Bock, F. W., *Deafness Prevention* (Rochester League for the Hard of Hearing, Rochester, N.Y.).
2. Caplin, D., "A Special Report of Retardation of Children with Impaired Hearing in New York City Schools," *Am. Annals of the Deaf,* LXXXII (1937), 234–43.
3. Conway, C. B., *The Hearing Abilities of Children in Toronto Public Schools,* Dept. of Educ. Research, Bull. No. 9 (Ontario Coll. of Educ., Toronto, 1937).
4. Great Britain, Board of Educ., *Report of the Committee of Inquiry into Problems Relating to Children with Defective Hearing* (His Majesty's Stationery Office, London, 1938).
5. Habbe, S., *Personality Adjustments of Adolescent Boys with Impaired Hearing,* T.C. Contribs. to Educ., No. 697 (Bur. of Pubs., Teachers College, Columbia Univ., N.Y., 1936).
6. Hofsommer, A. J., "Lip Reading and the Intelligence Quotient of the Hard of Hearing Child," *J. Am. Med. Assoc.,* CVII (1936), 648–50.
7. Lorenz, J., *Consistency of Auditory Acuity or Variability of Individuals among Four Tests with the 2A Audiometer* (Privately printed, N.Y., 1936).
8. Madden, R., *The School Status of the Hard of Hearing Child,* T.C. Contribs. to Educ., No. 499 (Bur. of Pubs., Teachers College, Columbia Univ., N.Y., 1931).
9. Peck, A. W., and E. E. Samuelson, "Twenty-five Years for the Hard of Hearing Child," *J. Except. Child.,* II (1936), 116–19.
10. Phillips, W. C., and H. G. Rowell, *Your Hearing, How to Preserve and Aid It* (Appleton, N.Y., 1932).

11. Pintner, R., "Emotional Stability of the Hard of Hearing," *J. Genet. Psychol.*, XLIII (1933), 293–311.
12. Pintner, R., "An Adjustment Test with Normal and Hard of Hearing Children," *J. Genet. Psychol.*, LVI (1940), 367–81.
13. Pintner, R., *Some Personality Traits of Hard of Hearing Children* (To appear shortly in *J. Genet. Psychol.*).
14. Pintner, R., and J. Lev, "The Intelligence of the Hard of Hearing School Child," *J. Genet. Psychol.*, LV (1939), 31–48.
15. Sterling, E. B., and E. Bell, "Hearing of School Children as Measured by the Audiometer and as Related to School Work," *U.S. Pub. Health Rep.*, XLV (1930), 1117–30.
16. Waldman, J. L., F. A. Wade, and C. W. Aretz, *Hearing and the School Child* (Volta Bur., Phil., 1930).
17. Warwick, H. L., "Hearing Tests in Public Schools of Fort Worth," *Volta Rev.*, XXX (1928), 641–6.
18. Welles, H. H., *The Measurement of Certain Aspects of Personality among Hard of Hearing Adults*, T.C. Contribs. to Educ., No. 545 (Bur. of Pubs., Teachers College, Columbia Univ., N.Y., 1932).
19. White House Conference, *Preliminary Committee Reports* (Century, N.Y., 1930).

CHAPTER VII

The Blind

GENERAL

By "the blind" we mean those individuals whose vision is of no practical value to them for the purposes of education or in the general business of living. Among this group we have individuals who are totally blind as well as those who have considerable light perception, but in all cases their vision is not enough to play the part that vision plays in the lives of the sighted. Loss of vision ranges all the way from a slight loss to a total loss. There is no definite sharp dividing line between the blind and the sighted. It is usual to consider children who have a visual acuity of less than 20/200 as educationally blind. They do not possess enough vision to be able to make use of the ordinary tools of education used by sighted children. Children with a visual acuity between 20/70 and 20/200 in the better eye after correction are usually considered partially sighted cases, and form a group intermediate between the blind and the sighted. These are rough lines of demarcation. The individual case must always be considered on its own merits.

The United States Census Bureau (73) says, "Include as blind any person who cannot see well enough to read a book or other printed matter even with the aid of glasses." Using this practical definition of blindness, the 1930 census reported a total of 63,489 blind persons in the United States. This is a ratio of 517 blind per million of the total population. The blind have been enumerated in every census since 1830. The total number has varied from a low point of 5,444 in 1830 to a high point of 64,763 in 1900. The ratio per million of the general population has varied from a low of 403 in 1860 to a high of 976 in 1880. The ratio has dropped irregularly from the high point of 976 in 1880 to 517 in 1930. Because the scope and method of enumeration has varied greatly from 1830 to 1930, it is difficult to tell whether blindness is increasing or decreasing.

Best (3) believes that the census has generally underestimated the total number of the blind. He gives 100,000 as the probable number, that is, one blind person for every 1,227 people in the United States. Irwin (48) estimates the number of blind as 130,000, or from 1 to 1.5 per 1,000 of the population of the United States.

With reference to children of school age, the White House Conference on Child Health and Protection (77) estimated that there are about 15,000 blind and 50,000 partially sighted children of school age in this country. In terms of percentages it is estimated that 80 per cent of the total school population has normal vision, 19.75 per cent has correctible eye defects, 0.2 per cent is partially sighted, and 0.05 per cent blind.

Causes. Blindness may be due to heredity, disease, or accident. The chief causes of blindness which seem to be influenced by heredity are cataract, retinitis pigmentosa, and atrophy of the optic nerve. Infectious diseases, such as scarlet fever, measles, mumps, and meningitis, are frequent causes of blindness. Syphilis and gonorrhea are responsible for much blindness. Ophthalmia neonatorum, frequently caused by infection of the mother, is now easily preventible and has showed a steady decline as a cause of blindness during the past forty years. Berens (2) says that in 1904 about 28.2 per cent of the pupils entering schools for the blind were cases of ophthalmia neonatorum and that this percentage gradually decreased to 9.1 in 1935–36. Accidents to the eye, caused by sharp instruments, firearms, and the like, are still numerous.

The United States Census (1920) groups the causes of blindness into five large categories as follows:

I. Disease	54.4 per cent
II. Accident	16.5 per cent
III. Other definite causes	2.6 per cent
IV. Indefinite causes	25.5 per cent
V. Combination of different causes	0.9 per cent

Best (3) indicates that the proportion due to disease is undoubtedly greater than the percentage given above, possibly as much as three fourths. For a more detailed analysis of these categories, the reader should consult Best, who estimates that 72 per cent of the blindness in the United States is of a preventable character. In addition, his discussion of the increase or decrease of blindness during the past one hundred years is of interest. He believes that "blindness has within a measurable time shown on the whole a decrease, although this decrease cannot as yet be called a very material one." (3, p. 155.)

Early Studies of the Blind. Until the eighteenth century there was little scientific interest in the blind. What interest had arisen up to that time was mainly humanitarian, and there was very little of that. It was Diderot's "Letter on the Blind" in 1745 that marked the first philosophical or psychological interest in the condition of blindness, just as his "Letter on the Deaf and Dumb" had aroused interest in deafness. The interest was purely abstract and theoretical, but it was at least a beginning.

At the end of the eighteenth century came the beginnings of the education of the blind under the stimulus of Haüy. The nineteenth century is notable for the rapid extension of educational institutions for the blind all over the civilized world. It was a period of intense activity in educational methods and procedures. It saw the invention of the braille system of reading, introduced by Braille about 1829 and now used universally. This important aid to reading was not invented by a psychologist or scientist, but was arrived at empirically by a blind man. Much later the work of Wundt showed that the limit of the span of attention was six separate simultaneous impressions. Braille arrived at this psychological principle empirically, for he made a field of six points the base for all his letters.

The latter half of the nineteenth century saw the establishment of modern psychology, and from the very beginning interest in the blind was manifested. It is not, however, so much an interest in the blind for their own sakes, as rather an interest in two or three aspects of the psychology of the blind in order to see what light may be thrown upon certain universal problems of general psychology. Most of these early studies cluster around the problems of space perception, touch sensitivity, and the sense of obstacles. Congenitally blind individuals who later regain their sight were studied to throw light upon the development of visual space perception. Stanley Hall (24) studied the touch sensitivity of Laura Bridgman, the famous blind-deaf woman, and found her to be about three times as sensitive as sighted individuals. Jastrow (44) studied another famous blind-deaf individual, Helen Keller. He made tests at the World's Fair, Chicago, when Helen Keller was about fourteen years old. He found her to be equal to the average individual in "muscle sense," tested by arranging weights in order. In rapidity of movement and accuracy of movement Jastrow found "nothing beyond the ordinary." In three tests, however, he diagnosed his subject as above average. In touch sensitivity on forefinger and palm of the hand she was "decidedly more acute than the average individual." This was also true of tests of sensitivity to roughness or coarseness. And in memory for letters and words she was "decidedly above the normal."

Binet (4) included the blind as well as the deaf in a series of cephalometric studies of children. He compared various head measures of blind and seeing children. He tested eighty children between the ages of nine to nineteen, as well as a smaller sample of younger children between the ages of five to eight. He found in general that the blind had smaller heads than the sighted. The heads of those becoming blind after birth differed less from the seeing than did the heads of the born blind. He found no relation between the size of the head and degree of blindness. He drew no inferences as to intellectual development as a result of this study.

References to the blind and the blind-deaf are found in almost all the early books on general psychology, and always with reference to the help that a study of these individuals may give in the problems of space perception and sensory sensitivity. The psychology of blindness or of the blind was not studied for its own sake, but only as an adjunct to general psychology. Heller's (40) book is the best example of this early work in the psychology of blindness. It deals with the problem of synthetic and analytic touch, of touch sensitivity, of auditory localization, and of the sense of obstacles. In reference to this so-called "sixth" sense, Heller conducted some experiments (not very rigidly controlled) and came to the conclusion that it is made up of a fusion of auditory sensations and sensations of air pressures on the skin. The auditory sensations give the first cues or signals and then the attention is directed to the very delicate pressure sensations on the skin. Heller comes closer than any of these early workers to problems of a practical nature in his rough experiments comparing the speed of reading in braille as contrasted with the speed of reading raised line print. He found, of course, that braille was read much more rapidly.

INTELLIGENCE

Interest in the measurement of the intelligence of the blind by means of the Binet Scale seems to have begun with R. B. Irwin, who went to Vineland in 1914 and collaborated with H. H. Goddard on an adaptation of the Goddard-Binet Scale for use with blind children. Tests requiring vision were dropped from the scale and other tests were shifted from one year level to another. No final calibration or standardization of this adaptation was made, but it served as a stimulus to other workers in this field.

The next attempt was made by Haines (21, 22). He took the Yerkes-Bridges adaptation of the Binet Scale as his point of departure. He dropped seven tests requiring vision, for some of which he found substitutes, and added other new tests. He then proceeded to a tentative standardization, and arrived at his Point Scale for the Blind. He attempted a comparison of the mentality of the blind and the sighted by comparing the performance of his blind subjects with the norms for the sighted on those tests which were common to the scales for the sighted and for the blind. He found his group of seventy-eight totally blind to be very slightly below the sighted in intelligence, but his eighty-two partially blind cases were on the average very much below the sighted. The latter finding, he believed, was due to the fact that their subnormality of vision had been made the excuse for constituting the school an asylum for some feeble-minded persons. He stresses the point that in the state school in which he was working he found an unusually large percentage of subnormal and feeble-minded children. This, he argued, was probably due to the fact that some causes of blindness were also causes of mental defect, e. g., hydrocephalus, encephalitis, syphilitic degeneration.

The next definite step in the mental measurement of the blind was due to the work of Hayes, which resulted in 1923 in the Stanford Revision of the Binet-Simon Scale Adapted for Use with the Blind by Hayes and Irwin, and culminated in 1930 with the publication of Terman's Condensed Guide for the Stanford Revision of the Binet-Simon Intelligence Tests Adapted for Use with the Blind by S. P. Hayes (28, 29, 30). Hayes writes: "The intelligence quotients obtained by the use of the 1923 Revision for the Blind give approximately a normal distribution curve, and retests at two-year intervals showed about the expected constancy of the I.Q. . . . The median attainment of the blind stands somewhat below that for the seeing. . . . A curve of the I.Q.'s obtained when only those tests were included which could be given in the same way to the blind and to the seeing, took the normal form with its median about ten points below Terman's curve of one thousand seeing children."

Hayes * gives the results of the Hayes-Binet Test given in a great many schools for the blind from 1930 to 1939. In all, there are 4,735 I.Q.'s (some pupils were tested twice). The median I.Q. for the different schools ranges from 92 to 108. The median for these various school medians is about 99. In another distribution of 4,508 cases, Hayes shows the frequency of very low and very high I.Q.'s in the various schools. The percentage of low I.Q.'s, i. e., 70 and below, ranges from 3.4 per cent to 19 per cent, with an average percentage for the various schools of 8.8 per cent. The percentage of high I.Q.'s, i. e., 120 and above, ranges from 4 per cent to 23 per cent, with an average percentage for the various schools of 10.5 per cent. This would

* Hayes, S. P. Private communication from Dr. Hayes to the writer. Permission to reproduce these data has been kindly granted by Dr. Hayes.

seem to indicate about a normal percentage of high I.Q.'s. With reference to the percentage of low I.Q.'s, namely 8.8 per cent, there seems to be no doubt that this is much greater than would be found in the population at large. A maximum of 3 or 4 per cent is indicated by the best survey so far made (70). It would therefore seem that the percentage of slow or dull children among the blind is more than twice that among the seeing.

Group intelligence tests have also been adapted for and used with the blind. Hayes (26) has reported on several tests, such as the Trabue Completion Test, Terman Vocabulary Test, various Pressey tests, Opposites, Analogies, and the like. In all cases where adequate comparisons between the blind and the sighted have been made, the blind are usually inferior at every age.

Although we have now at least two standard group intelligence tests adapted for the blind, namely the Otis Classification Test, Form A, by Sargent (69) and the Kuhlmann-Anderson in braille adapted by Fortner (19), we do not yet seem to have any extensive comparison of the intelligence of the blind and sighted by means of these tests.

One of the earliest problems encountered in the measurement of the intelligence of the blind is the seemingly better intelligence of the totally blind as compared with children in schools for the blind who possess some vision. The data here are not very extensive and further work on this problem needs to be done.

The age at which vision has been lost seems not to affect the I.Q., according to Hayes (27). His curve for the average I.Q. according to age of loss of vision is practically a straight line, and hence he concludes that early loss of vision does not cause permanent mental retardation.

That the percentage of feeble-mindedness among the blind is greater than among the seeing seems to be recognized by most educators of the blind. Percentages ranging from 5 to

20 have been suggested by various authorities. This wide range in the estimates is due to different conceptions of feeble-mindedness and also to a lack of thoroughgoing surveys by means of standard intelligence tests. Hayes in 1920 made a distribution of 670 blind children tested by means of the Irwin-Binet tests according to the seven categories suggested at that time by Terman and compared his percentages with those of Terman established on one thousand unselected children.

	Blind (%)	*Seeing* (%)
Genius	0.3	0.5
Very superior	1	2
Superior	5	9
Average	68	76
Dull	12	8
Borderline	7	2
Feeble-minded	5	0.3

If this comparison is valid, it will be noted that the feebleminded are much more numerous among the blind than among the sighted. Furthermore, the percentages in the dull and borderline categories are also much larger for the blind population.

More recent percentages published by Merry (62) are interesting. They are not directly comparable to those above. The categories are different. They refer to one large institution for the blind over a period of years. (The table is reprinted by permission of the President and Fellows of Harvard College.)

Group	*I.Q. Range*	*1924–25*	*1925–26*	*1926–27*	*1927–28*	*1928–29*	*1929–30*
Probably feeble-minded	below 70	7.2	11.6	10.1	10.8	12.2	10.7
Dull and borderline	70–89	26.4	29.6	34.7	32.4	31.2	34.3
Average	90–109	37.5	43.1	39.7	39.0	37.1	37.7
Superior	110–140	26.0	14.8	14.6	11.2	13.2	14.4
Not tested	——	2.9	0.9	0.9	6.6	6.3	2.9

Here the percentage of children with low I.Q.'s is very large, even if all of those with I.Q.'s below 70 are not technically feeble-minded. In addition we note the large percentages in the dull and borderline category. Merry points to what seems to be an increase in the percentages of the low I.Q. groups over the period of years in question. Both the "feeble-minded" and the "dull" groups seem to show an irregular tendency to increase from 1924 to 1930. Merry suggests that this may be due to the greater reduction of specific eye diseases (such as ophthalmia neonatorum) as contrasted with the lesser reduction of blindness caused by systemic diseases and general constitutional defects.

In a brief article by Cairns (12) we are given a graph showing the distribution of I.Q.'s for students at Perkins Institution. There were 266 pupils and 73 per cent had I.Q.'s of 90 or above. The remaining 27 per cent had I.Q.'s below 90 and "may be considered dull, borderline, or feeble-minded." Only 9 had I.Q.'s below 65. The results of 36 new pupils just entering show that this new group had only 52 per cent with average intelligence or above.

In a report of a survey of the California State School for the Blind, Muhl (64) states that the I.Q.'s range from 43 to 161 with a larger percentage in the superior group than is usually found, but no distribution of the specific I.Q.'s is given.

The problem of the feeble-minded blind is a much debated one among educators of the blind. Institutions for the blind have increasingly stressed the function of education as opposed to custodial care. Most of them during the past one hundred years have changed their names from "asylum" or "institution" to "school" in order to emphasize what they regard as their most important and perhaps sole function. If education is the sole purpose of these institutions, it follows that the noneducable blind do not belong there. This is simple logic, but in practice the problem is to draw the line between the noneducable and educable blind. In a sense, no child, however feeble-minded, is noneducable. He can always be taught or trained to some extent. However, those children who have I.Q.'s below 50 will probably never be able to learn to read and will never develop far enough to be at all self-supporting. Like most of the sighted with I.Q.'s below 50, they will remain custodial cases for the rest of their lives. This type of child, argues the educator of the blind, does not belong in a school, but in an institution for the feeble-minded. If this policy is adopted, then institutions for the feeble-minded will find themselves in charge of a small number of blind inmates ranging all the way from young children up to grown men and women. If these blind individuals are to receive any training worthy of the name, they will require the special attention of a teacher who is at least partially trained in the problems of the blind. The chances are that in most institutions this will not be provided and hence the feeble-minded blind are likely to suffer from neglect. Some educators of the blind, therefore, suggest that residential schools for the blind set aside a special cottage for feeble-minded cases, that these be trained as long as possible, and then be dismissed or sent to an institution for the feeble-minded when it becomes apparent that further training would not be profitable. In this way the child would be under the care of experts in the training of blind children during the most educable period of his life.

Learning Ability. Tests of ability to learn may also throw some light on the intelligence of individuals. Ability to find the way out of a maze has been used for a long time in the psychological laboratory as a test of learning for both animal and human subjects. At least three studies using blind subjects have been published. Koch and Ufkess (46) used a stylus maze and matched nineteen blind adolescents with seeing subjects very roughly as regards intelligence. In general the blind were somewhat inferior to the seeing. Knotts and Miles (45) used two different types of mazes: the stylus maze and the high relief maze where direct finger contact is possible. Forty blind children were matched with seeing children with respect to sex, chronological age, and mental age. All children were blindfolded. In general the blind did somewhat better than the sighted on both mazes. Ability to learn the maze correlated higher with mental age than with chronological age.

These studies led Merry and Merry (63) to consider the possible use of the high-relief maze as a test of intelligence for blind children to supplement intelligence tests of the Binet type. They therefore tested thirty blind children ranging in age from eight to sixteen. The mental age range of these cases was from 7–4 to 18–0, with a median M.A. at 13–5. The I.Q. range was from 81 to 146 with a median at 111. The experience of these two workers with this maze led them to conclude that it would form a valuable supplementary test for blind children, particularly between the ages of ten to fourteen. Norms of accomplishment would have to be established on a large sampling of blind children. They found that M.A. correlated higher than C.A. with maze learning. They did not find any correlation between age at which vision was lost and maze learning among their small sample of subjects.

From these three studies we can draw no definite conclusions as to the superiority or inferiority of the blind to the sighted in maze learning. They have, however, opened up a profitable field for further psychological research. They suggest the possibility of a nonverbal type of intelligence test to supplement the predominantly verbal type of test now in use.

Summary of Intelligence Testing. We may summarize this section on the intelligence of the blind by noting that adequate individual and group intelligence tests now exist and that sufficient work has been done with them to give a fair picture of the distribution of intelligence among the children in our schools for the blind. The median I.Q. is probably a little below 100. The percentage of high I.Q.'s probably differs but little from that found among the seeing. The greatest difference would seem to lie in the excessive number of low I.Q.'s among the blind. The percentage of slow, dull, and feeble-minded cases among the blind seems to be at least twice that found among the sighted. Some causes of blindness also cause arrested mental development. Congenital blindness and feeble-mindedness seem occasionally both to derive from a poor family stock.

EDUCATIONAL ACHIEVEMENT

The first attempt at the measurement of the educational achievement of the blind was made by Hayes. He began about 1916 to adapt for use with the blind existing standardized achievement tests constructed for seeing children. Some of the early tests adapted by Hayes (25, 26) and put into braille were the Trabue Sentence Completion Tests, Ayres Spelling Scale, Courtis Arithmetic, Hahn-Lackey Geography, Harlan American History, and the like. Tentative results on these early tests showed the blind below the norms for seeing pupils. He found the reading speed of the blind to be very slow, and estimated that, at the end of their elementary school training, the rate of reading for the blind was about one third of that of the sighted at the end of the fifth grade. Hayes (27) also raised the question as to the influence upon school achievement of the age at loss of vision. He did not find any significant effect of this upon such school subjects as reading, composition, vocabulary, general information, and so on.

Reading Ability. Maxfield (54) describes some results of reading tests given to blind children. The Gray Oral-Reading Check Tests put into braille have been effectively used in grades

I through VIII. The average number of errors made by the blind is the same as for seeing children of the same grade, but the reading rate is about one and a half to three times slower. Although by grade standards there is little difference between the blind and the sighted, we must remember that blind pupils are much older than seeing children of the same grade, so that the blind are considerably retarded according to age standards.

The three reading tests of the Stanford Achievement Test have also been put into braille and are described by Maxfield (54). Time limits have been considerably lengthened to make allowance for the slowness of reading braille. A time limit of fifteen minutes for the seeing is extended to fifty minutes for the blind; a time limit of five minutes is extended to twenty. As to the results on this test with blind pupils, Maxfield says that they are "somewhat superior to seeing children in the second and third grades, and approximately on a par with them in the higher grades." However, she calls attention to the higher chronological age of the blind and gives a table showing the percentage of pupils retarded by various amounts when comparison is made by age rather than by grade standards. From this table we note that from 15 to 29 per cent of the blind test at age or above on the various tests. This means that 71 to 85 per cent are retarded two months or more. More serious retardation of two years or more is found in from 60 to 71 per cent of the pupils.

Caldwell (13) used the Stanford Achievement Test described above with thirty-four blind children and a comparable seeing group. He found it necessary to lengthen slightly the time limits proposed by Maxfield. Again he found no difference between the blind and the seeing when compared on grade norms, but the average chronological age of the blind was 17–9 as compared with an average of 12–6 for the seeing.

This same phenomenon appears again in a report by Abel

(1). She used the Van Wagenen Unit Scales of Attainment in braille with eighty fifth- and eighty-three sixth-grade blind pupils. The blind exceed somewhat the grade norms for the sighted, but again she points out that the median C.A. of the fifth-grade pupils is 13–4 and of the sixth-grade pupils 14–8.

Vocabulary Ability. An extensive study of the vocabulary ability of the blind has been reported by Hayes (37), who used two measures of this ability. Using the fifty-word vocabulary list of the Stanford-Binet as a group test, he arrived at an approximate vocabulary rating for 443 blind children, ten years of age and up. Comparing the blind and the seeing, he finds the 11-year seeing standard reached by the blind at 12 years, the 12-year seeing standard reached by the blind at 15 years, the 13-year seeing standard nearly reached by the blind at 16 years, and so on, the gap becoming wider as age increases. Hayes also presents the results of the vocabulary test when given as a part of the regular Binet test for the blind for over two thousand cases, and these results also show the increasing retardation of the blind as they grow older. This same study presents the results of the Word-Meaning Test of the New Stanford Achievement Test given in grades IV to IX in two schools for the blind for two successive years. The average scores by grade cluster around the grade norms for the seeing, being sometimes a little below and sometimes a little above. When, however, our author presents the results in terms of mental age, the picture is decidedly different. Instead of attaining about 100 per cent of the norm, we find one school having a median at 90 per cent and the other at 84 per cent. In comparison with mental age standards, we find that "at 9 and 10 M.A. the blind do decidedly better than the seeing; from 12 to 15 M.A. they show a retardation of about one year; and from 16 M.A. on they are retarded two or three years." To explain this progressive retardation Hayes points to the "slowness and laboriousness" of the blind child's reading and to his restricted experience because of his life in a residential school.

The Psychology of Touch Reading. All of these reports agree more or less in showing that the blind child is considerably retarded in reading ability and in word knowledge as compared with the seeing child. Reading braille is slow and difficult. In spite of all the best schools can do, it would seem that the blind child is handicapped in acquiring information and in fluent reading, and that he does not catch up with the seeing child as he grows older. This raises the question as to whether braille reading can be made more efficient, and opens up the whole problem of the psychology of touch reading. A good deal of experimental work has been done in this field, notably in Germany and much of this has been summarized by Bürklen (11). We shall briefly mention his main conclusions. The arrangement of the dots in braille in a horizontal upright field is psychologically the best type of arrangement. The legibility of the various characters is not dependent upon the number of dots making up a character. Characters having a few dots are not necessarily the most readable. It is the characteristic shape of each character that determines its legibility. The usual size of the characters seems to be satisfactory. The best spacing of the dots has not yet been determined, and a reduction of the braille type below the present measurements seems possible. In reading, the index fingers of both hands seem better than all others. The touch movement of good readers is a straight running movement. Less capable readers show more irregularities. The pressure of the fingers with good readers is slight and uniform. Poor readers show a stronger and less steady pressure. On the average, blind readers read three to four times more slowly than the seeing. Reading with both hands is the fastest. In general the left hand reads better than the right hand in one-handed reading.

Maxfield (54) has studied the whole reading process from

the point of view of the teacher. She stresses the importance of relaxation of the whole body while reading, especially if the child is later to enjoy reading for long periods at a time. The child should be taught not to press down too heavily on the words. Too much and constant pressure induces nervous strain in the child. The reading fingers should be held at a slant which makes them form an acute angle with the line of braille being read. In general children should be taught to use both hands rather than one, but Maxfield would not insist upon this if a child shows a decided preference for using only one. She, furthermore, is skeptical of the German evidence cited by Bürklen as to the superiority of the left hand, and, therefore, she would teach children to use their right hand, except in the case of children who are definitely left-handed in most of the things they do. But two-handed reading is preferable and children should be taught this at first. Later most children can read with either hand and this should be encouraged. Excessive up-and-down motion of the finger tips retards the reading process, is probably an indication of letter-reading rather than word-reading and should be discouraged. Maxfield calls attention to the value of reading ahead on a lower line with the left hand before the right hand has finished the preceding line. Just how many blind readers do this or how much of their reading is done this way seems uncertain. It is evidently not very common. Maxfield says that only fifteen out of 1,200 readers used this procedure, but 12 of these 15 were in the faster group of readers. In another experiment "it was found that nine of the twenty fastest readers went ahead on the next line and that none of the slowest readers did so." Maxfield believes that children should be encouraged to read ahead, but doubts the value of specific training in this procedure, particularly with children below the average in intelligence. She also finds the word method of teaching braille reading to be much better than the letter method, although there may be some blind children who need to learn by the letter method. Evidently there is still room for much useful experimentation in the reading of braille.

A laboratory experiment on the question of the best hand for reading braille has been reported by Smith (72), using one seeing subject wearing dark glasses. Braille material was read with the left, the right, and with two hands, and it was also read in two directions from left to right and from right to left. She found the left hand to be superior to two-handed reading and the right hand to be poorest of all. She explains this result by calling the left hand a sensory organ and the right a motor organ in right-handed people. Furthermore, she found slightly better results for right to left reading across the page than for the conventional left to right. If right to left braille reading were to be adopted, then braille writers could be made to type braille on one side and ink print on the other at the same time. These findings of Smith contradict the findings of Bürklen, Maxfield, and others with reference to the best way of reading braille. They stand unsupported, but they indicate the need for further experimentation in this field.

Holland's (41, 42) studies on good and poor braille readers showed differences in their habits and techniques of reading. He took photographs at constant intervals of the fingers of twenty-eight children while reading braille. Half of the readers were selected as "good," and half as "poor" readers. He found the "good" readers moved the fingers more quickly and at a more uniform speed along the line. The "good" readers read more with the right hand, made fewer regressive movements, and spent less time at the beginning and at the end of the lines. Furthermore, these "good" readers spent less time in making return sweeps from the end of one line to the beginning of the next. Objective measures of the pressure of the fingers showed that "fast" readers tended to use less pressure than "slow" readers, and they registered fewer variations of pressure as they proceeded along a line. This suggests that further intensive study of the techniques of reading braille and the methods of teaching braille reading may in the future lead to better reading ability on the part of the blind child.

From all of this it is evident that reading for the blind is no easy accomplishment. It is a slow and tedious process as compared with the reading of inkprint by the seeing child. It is no wonder, therefore, that the blind child is retarded in reading ability, particularly when we remember that he is on the average somewhat retarded also in general intelligence.

Achievement in Geography. With reference to special subjects, Hayes (36) has reported on the results of geography tests given to blind children. He used the Hahn-Lackey Geography Scale, the Courtis Map Test, and the Stanford Achievement Geography Test. On the whole, the blind seem to make satisfactory scores. On the Stanford Geography Test he reports that for one school the scores obtained by the children from nine to fifteen inclusive were practically equal to the seeing norms, but after age fifteen the attainment suddenly dropped. When compared with their M.A., the 177 blind children tested fell only slightly below expectation; the median percentage of the norm for eleven age groups is 95. When grade comparisons are made, we find four out of six grades exceeding the grade norms for the seeing.

Achievement in Arithmetic. The blind child's ability in arithmetic has been reported in two studies by Merry (58, 59). She gave the Wisconsin Inventory Tests in Arithmetic to 348 children in grades III to VI and made a detailed analysis of the errors. In general, the types and frequencies of errors were very much like those made by seeing children, except that the blind made more errors in items where zero occurred, and also in short division. The total scores on the tests were similar to the corresponding grade norms for seeing children, but of course the blind children were older. In the second study, she found similar results with the Stevenson Arithmetic Reading Test given to 170 children in grades IV to VI.

Tests of general information have been reported by Hayes (39). He used the Sangren Information Tests for Young Children with thirty-five blind children in the kindergarten, first and second grades. He found that the kindergarten children tested practically equal to the seeing norms in the tests of numbers, vocabulary, social information, household knowledge, language and literature, but that they were distinctly inferior in nature study. The first-grade children tested above the seeing in language and literature, about equal to the seeing in social information, and below the seeing in the other tests. The number of children tested is too small to permit of conclusions about blind children in general. The experiment, however, shows the practicability of using this type of test with the blind. In the same article Hayes also reports on the results of the Pressey Test of Practical Information with 567 blind children, ages nine to twenty inclusive. This test is available in braille. The results show "an apparent retardation of four years in each age group from ten to sixteen and of five years in the seventeen- and eighteen-year groups." The age of becoming blind seems to have only a slight influence on the test results. Those blinded at birth or during the first three years score 55 per cent correct; those blinded during the fourth, fifth, or sixth years score 60 per cent correct; and those blinded after the sixth year score 65 per cent correct.

Spoken language is important for the blind. It is their chief method of keeping in contact with the people round about them. Yet their language development in infancy seems to be slow and to be retarded as compared with seeing children. Maxfield (55) has made an initial attack upon this problem in her preliminary study of the spoken language of the blind preschool child. Because of the inherent difficulties involved in this observational type of research, she considered her work as a study of method, laying the foundations for more extensive work in the future. She studied eight young blind children and no extensive generalizations can be obtained from such a small number. Nevertheless, certain findings are interesting. Among the older children, 40 to 50 per cent of the responses were concerned with things. This is about twice the percentage reported for seeing children, and therefore might be important. Again, the blind asked more questions and gave fewer commands. A very large number of the responses of the blind children studied were emotionally toned. There were many more incomplete responses among the blind than among the seeing. An important feature was the naming of children and adults. This tendency to use proper names frequently as well as the habit of asking many questions may, according to Maxfield, be closely connected with the need for a feeling of security on the part of the young blind child.

School Success. Hayes (32) raises the general question as to what factors influence the school success of the blind child. He finds that the cause of blindness, whether congenital or accidental, has no influence. The age of becoming blind seems to play no part. In 500 cases, with 289 born blind, he finds the median score of the born blind on a standard reading test to be the same as that for the total group. Those blinded early (at birth and up to twenty-three months) are on the average superior on some tests, such as the Binet, the Pressey Memory, etc., but they are also inferior on others, such as the Pressey Practical-Information Test, etc. In general, therefore, the age of becoming blind seems to have no clear-cut influence upon educational achievement as measured by standard tests. Age at entrance to school does seem to have some influence, according to Hayes. Those who enter earlier do somewhat better on later educational tests. The factor of sex is also studied by Hayes on numerous tests, but so far he has failed to find any reliable differences between boys and girls.

Excessive Verbal Education. The present-day education of the blind is in general too verbal, according to Cutsforth (15, 16). The blind make use of words that can have little real meaning for them. This he demonstrates by means of a simple association test consisting of forty stimulus words given to thirty-nine totally blind, twenty-six of whom were born blind. These children were in grades II to XII with C.A.'s ranging from 9 to 21, and I.Q.'s ranging from 60 to 134. An analysis of the 1,560 response words obtained showed that 54 per cent could be classified as visual. Slightly more visual responses (65 per cent) were given by the adventitious cases as contrasted with 48 per cent visual responses given by the congenital cases. The next most frequent sensory category was tactual, with 24 per cent for the adventitious and 36 per cent for the congenital. Taste and smell together accounted for 6 per cent for the adventitious and 7 per cent for the congenital. The auditory category contained the smallest percentages of all the sense modalities, namely about 3 per cent for both groups. From these results Cutsforth argues that the blind tend to use words that are "unreal" to them, that their excessive verbal education makes them underestimate the value of their own experiences.

Summary. This survey of the educational achievements of the blind by means of standard tests seems to show that in general the blind start out in their school work more or less on a par with the seeing. Their scores on the various tests are more nearly equal to those of the seeing at the younger ages. As the blind progress through the grades, retardation sets in to a much greater extent than among the seeing. Grade norms for the blind and the seeing are pretty much the same. This means that the grade standards in schools for the blind are kept fairly similar to those in seeing schools. To keep up these standards, blind children progress more slowly through the grades, i. e., they are older chronologically, so that they show educational retardation when compared with the age norms for the seeing. This discrepancy between the two groups seems to increase as age increases. There may be at least two causative factors at work here, namely, the slightly lower general intelligence of the blind as a group and also the greater difficulty involved in reading braille as compared with reading inkprint. This difficulty would seem to slow down slightly the academic accomplishment of the blind, but it does not prevent those of high intelligence from ultimately reaching the highest levels of academic attainment, as witnessed by the presence of numerous blind students in our colleges and universities.

PERSONALITY

Preconceptions as to the personality characteristics of the blind exist probably to the same extent as with respect to the deaf. Nobody seems to have made a thorough search of the literature to the same extent as Brunschwig has done for the deaf.

The use of modern tools for the study of the personality characteristics of the blind seems only to have begun. We have found only three studies. Muhl (64) used the individual interview technique. She inquired into the fears, worries, and dreams of her blind subjects. For example, she reports that "of 105 only 9 or 8.5 per cent said they had no fears"; the rest expressed themselves as having definite fears. Four children said they would rather be deaf than blind, while 101 preferred blindness to deafness. She also watched the child while giving the Binet test and noted personality characteristics. She suggests that the chief characteristics that need attention in the personality education of the blind child are the marked suggestibility, the lack of initiative, the tendency to discouragement and to undue sensitiveness. The suggestions of this author would seem to provide a good point of departure for more objective studies of specific personality characteristics.

The other two reports are both by Brown (7, 8). In one study he used the Kohlstedt Test of Introversion-Extraversion with 218 blind, ages sixteen to twenty-two, and 359 seeing high-school seniors. The mean I.Q. of the blind on the Hayes-Binet was 97.6, and that of the seeing on the Otis Test was 98.7. There was no reliable difference in score on the introversion-extraversion test between the blind and the seeing. There was, however, a reliable difference between the blind males and the blind females, the blind females being more introverted. The seeing males were slightly, but not significantly, more introverted than the blind males, and Brown suggests a "compensation" mechanism at work among the blind males. No relation between I.Q. and amount of introversion was found, the r's being, for the sighted + .02, for the blind + .06. In the other study Brown used the Clark Revision of the Thurstone Personality Schedule with the same subjects noted above. The blind as a group tested reliably more maladjusted than the sighted. When sex differences are studied, it is to be noted that the blind females score much more maladjusted than the blind males, and it is the high maladjustment scores of the blind females that are responsible for the statistically reliable difference which was found between the means for the total blind and total seeing groups. Again no relation between intelligence and adjustment was found, the r's being, for the sighted + .04, for the blind + .06. These two studies point to a greater maladjustment and a greater tendency to introversion on the part of blind girls, whereas blind boys seem to test about the same as seeing boys. Whether this is a real sex difference or a condition resulting from educational experience in the lives of the children cannot be determined. At any rate, Brown's work has raised interesting questions that call for answers. Indeed the whole field of the personality of the blind is a fertile one for research. At present our knowledge in this area is practically zero.

SPECIAL ABILITIES

Facial Vision or the Sense of Obstacles. One special ability of the blind, about which much has been written, is the ability of some of them to sense obstacles in their path and thus avoid collision with them. This ability has been given various names, such as distance sense, warning sense, or sense of obstacles; or again sensation of approach; and very frequently it is called the sixth sense, often with a more or less mysterious connotation, as if the blind in general were endowed with an extra sense which the seeing do not possess. This ability was noted early by workers among the blind and discussion and experimentation in regard to it have been going on for more than a hundred years. It would be impossible in this book, and certainly not profitable for the reader, to attempt a summary of the voluminous literature of this subject. We shall merely describe some of the outstanding theories and refer those interested in a more detailed discussion to the admirable summary prepared by Hayes (34).

Heller (40) was one of the earlier workers who attacked the problem in a scientific manner. He made numerous experiments with blind subjects. He found that, if auditory sensations were cut off, his subjects made many mistakes. This was also true if pressure sensations were excluded. The blind pay attention to the slight changes in pitch which occur in the sounds made by their footsteps when approaching obstacles. Heller called this ability "Fernsinn" or sense of distance. He concluded that both auditory sensations and pressure sensations of the air on the face were necessary. They work together. The auditory sensations give the first signal and then the attention is directed to the pressure sensations on the skin.

James (43) stressed the importance of the pressure sensations on the tympanic membrane rather than on the skin. MacDougall (51) called attention to the importance of temperature differences. In Germany some investigators stressed the importance of the auditory sensations, while others believed this sense to be entirely dependent upon pressure. The individual pushes ahead of him a mass of air which rebounds from the obstacle as he approaches near to it and this causes a slight pressure sensation on the forehead and temples. The skin of the blind was believed to be peculiarly sensitive, made so by the same diseases that caused the blindness, and hence those blinded by accidents did not possess this ability. But Villey (75) threw doubt on this theory by stating that 42 out of 63 blinded French soldiers claimed to possess this sense of obstacles. One investigator stressed the importance of temperature sensations, showing that the blind could perceive differences in the temperature of objects at a much greater distance than seeing subjects could.

Lamarque (47) believed that there are great individual differences among the blind; that some depend mainly upon auditory cues, some upon pressure sensations, and some upon both. More recently Dolanski (17), himself a blind man, conducted a series of very carefully controlled experiments by means of discs of various sizes moving towards the face. With the ears covered and auditory sensations thus excluded, his blind subjects could not judge whether an obstacle was before them or not. With masks covering the face, thus excluding pressure sensations, his blind subjects judged the presence or absence of obstacles just as accurately as when their faces were not masked. But in these masked experiments his blind subjects had no confidence in their judgments; they felt that they could not judge at all; whereas, they really were judging as accurately as without masks. This is the novel finding in Dolanski's experiments, which leads him to conclude that it is audition alone that accounts for the sense of obstacles. The auditory sensations give the blind man the cue for an approaching danger. A skin response is then aroused, perhaps analogous to "goose flesh," and it is the sensations aroused by these skin responses that the blind man perceives and recognizes as a danger signal. The feelings on the skin, attributed to pressure sensations of the air, are ruled out as causes by this theory. They are not caused by air pressure. They are an effect, due to a reflex action caused by a knowledge that an obstacle is near. Auditory sensations give the signal which sets off this reflex action.

From this brief discussion of various theories, it can be seen that a complete understanding of this ability has not yet been reached. Hayes (34) suggests future work along four lines: (1) a genetic study of the development of this ability from birth onwards; (2) extended laboratory experiments with numerous blind and seeing subjects equated for general ability; (3) careful standardization of procedure and control of all variable factors; (4) physical measurements of the stimuli assumed to arouse sensory responses in the subjects. To which the present writer would add experiments with the deaf-blind, since according to Dolanski's theory they should not possess this ability at all.

Sensory Compensation. The theory of sensory compensation held that the loss of any one sense automatically increased the acuity of the remaining senses. It is a theory that has been and still is frequently applied to the blind, much less so to the deaf. It is not now upheld by any modern authority on the blind. It arose as a facile explanation of the seemingly marvelous sensitivity of some blind people in the realms of touch, hearing, and in some cases of smell and taste. A great deal of psychological work has been done to test this hypothesis of sensory compensation. Bürklen (10) summarizes the numerous studies done in Germany in both the fields of hearing and touch. Although he finds differences among the various research results, he concludes that no one has satisfactorily proved that the blind possess greater auditory sensitivity than the seeing. Neither do they possess greater ability in sound localization. With reference to touch sensitivity, active and passive, and the two-point threshold of the skin, there is no difference between the blind and the seeing. Their ability to differentiate in certain areas better than the seeing is due to practice.

Seashore and Ling (71) tested the pressure sensitivity of blind and seeing subjects by means of a fine copper wire under numerous sheets of paper. The sheets were removed one by one until the wire was located by active pressure of the fingers. The seeing subjects were slightly better than the blind. The average number of sheets of paper through which the seeing could locate the wire was 30, whereas the average for the blind was only 26. The best performance of any blind subject was 38, but four seeing subjects made better scores than this. The lowest score for the seeing was 18, and the lowest for the blind was 10.

Hayes (31) gave audiometer tests for hearing to ninety-two blind boys, eighty-four blind girls, and nineteen seeing college students. The seeing subjects were on the average superior to the blind. He also devised a touch and hearing test consisting of ten small cardboard boxes containing different materials. The subjects had to shake the boxes and identify the materials in the boxes. In this test also the seeing subjects were superior. He concludes from these results that there is no evidence for the heightened sensitivity of the blind in performances where they have had no practice. Again Hayes (33) has experimented with sound localization, using as subjects forty-nine blind males and fifty-four blind females ranging in age from ten to thirty-five with a median C.A. of 16.1 and ranging in I.Q. from 66 to 138 with a median I.Q. of 94. As a control group he used sixty seeing college girls. The median number of correct localizations of the sound of a clicker was 46 for the blind boys, 41 for the blind girls, and 48 for the seeing girls. An analysis of the errors, however, showed that the blind made fewer large errors. Their localizations did not show such wide displacements as did those of the seeing. There was no relation between ability to localize and I.Q. or amount of vision among the blind subjects. This study shows no evidence for the theory of sensory compensation, but it does show that the blind by practice attain to a high degree of proficiency in sound localization. A further article by Hayes (38) describes the work done in this field of sensory compensation, sums up the results, and concludes that there is no evidence to support the theory of sensory compensation. Indeed he raises the question as to whether loss of sight may not in general lead to the impairment of the other senses. To this question there is as yet no answer.

Space Perception. The space perception of the blind has been studied by several German workers who have compared the products of clay-modeling of blind and seeing children. Burde (9) tabulates the kinds of things blind children make when allowed to choose themselves. They make mostly things to eat. They make many mistakes in regard to the proportions of objects. The heads of human beings are frequently too large, probably because there is so much detail to put in. Matz (52, 53) compares the products of the deaf, the blind, and the seeing. Löwenfeld (50) gives numerous examples of the clay-modeling and drawing of the blind and weak-sighted. He differentiates two creative types: the visual type, where visual experience predominates and where the artist wants to bring the world closer to himself; the haptic type, where the artist projects his own inner world into the product. These types are found among the seeing and the blind, but the blind and partially sighted belong mainly to the haptic type. The art of primitive peoples shows many examples of the haptic type.

An attempt to compare the size and space concepts of blind and seeing children has been reported by Hall (23). She constructed a test to measure general orientation, size of objects, estimates of distance, etc. This was given to 166 seeing and 53 blind children in grades V to VIII. In general she finds no statistically reliable differences between these two groups (only one critical ratio is above 3).

The ability of blind children to recognize by touch simple embossed pictures has been studied by Merry (60), who used fifty subjects ranging in age from 6 to 13–9 and in I.Q. from 53 to 137, with a median I.Q. of 97.5. The pictures were embossed with a simple outline of dots. Fifteen, i. e., 30 per cent, of the children did not recognize any of the pictures. The ten pictures in order of difficulty from easy to hard were as follows: (1) wheel; (2) house; (3) shovel; (4) table; (5) chair; (6) fork; (7) apple; (8) hat; (9) cup; (10) horn. Merry found no relationship between intelligence and this ability to recognize pictures.

Memory. Deprived of sight, the blind individual is forced to rely upon his memory for many more things than do seeing individuals. Some blind people, therefore, exhibit great ability in memorizing and in retaining what has been committed to memory. We must inquire, however, whether the blind as a group possess greater inherent ability in this respect or whether they merely learn to develop certain aspects of memory of particular use to them.

There are few objective studies of the memory of the blind. One of the earlier studies by Vertes (74) in Hungary used a method frequently employed in the psychological laboratory. A series of words in pairs is presented to the subject. The examiner then presents the first word of a pair and the subject has to supply the second word of that pair. Vertes used twenty blind children, ages seven to fourteen. The blind scored 89.7 per cent correct as contrasted with 82.9 per cent for the seeing. The poorest blind subject scored 71.8 per cent; the poorest seeing subject, 25.6 per cent. In speed of reproduction the blind averaged 1.6 seconds and the seeing 2 seconds. From these results Vertes concluded that the blind were superior to the seeing. We must, however, keep in mind the very limited scope of this study.

In this country, Bond and Dearborn (5) found the blind to be superior in reproduction of a passage of prose read to them and in retention, but not in immediate memory for numbers. They concluded that the blind are only superior to the seeing in the kinds of memory which they have specifically practiced. Hayes (35) has summarized his results of several memory tests with the blind. His analysis of many cases of blind subjects given the Binet digits and reversed digits tests led him to conclude that the blind were superior to the seeing in short series of digits in direct order, whereas the seeing were superior in long series. Again the blind were superior to the seeing in long series of digits in reverse order, but inferior in short series in reverse order. In Pyle's test of immediate memory for words the blind were inferior to the seeing, but in the Pressey memory test for words the blind were superior.

In general, therefore, there is no great difference between the blind and the seeing. At any rate, the blind are not so conspicuously superior in memory as to support any theory of compensation. On the other hand, there is no evidence of any marked inferiority of the blind to the seeing in regard to memory. The blind seem to possess normal memory ability and they must learn to make use of it for their own particular purposes. If they practice any particular type of memory, they will undoubtedly improve markedly in this particular type. Brilliant feats of memory by blind individuals or by seeing individuals are due to specific practice.

Musical Ability. Music has always been stressed in the education of the blind. Indeed in the early days of this work, music was taught to all or almost all pupils, with the hope that they might make their living by performing or by piano tuning. The educators of the blind, however, soon found that many pupils were not able to profit by this type of instruction. To be sure, many did make excellent instrumentalists and capable pianotuners, but too many were merely average or below in musical talent. The question, therefore, arises as to the amount of musical talent among the blind in general.

The present writers know of no adequate study in this field. Merry (61) has shown that the Seashore Musical Talent Test can with slight modifications be given to the blind. He presents the results for a group of forty-four rather superior individuals. Of this group, 50 per cent ranked above the 75th percentile in all the six Seashore tests. They were, therefore, decidedly superior in musical talent, but from this small group, we can draw no conclusions with reference to the blind in general.

Voice Interpretation. Because of their handicap, the blind must depend upon auditory impressions to recognize their friends and acquaintances, and many of them develop great proficiency in this respect. Whether they become more skillful than the seeing in the general interpretation of the voices of strangers is, of course, another matter. Cantril and Allport (14) have reported one preliminary experiment in this field. They used forty-two blind students and thirty-three seeing students. The task was to judge various voices as to vocation, age, ascendance-submission, introversion-extraversion, interests, and the like. The blind were somewhat better than the seeing in judging vocation, but inferior to the seeing in other respects. In general "67 per cent of their (the blinds') judgments are less accurate than those of the control group." This evidence, the authors point out, relates only to physical and self-expressive characteristics, and the blind may be better at judging other traits, such as friendliness, tact, trustworthiness and the like. More extensive experimentation is required to settle such questions.

Summary. This survey of the psychology of special abilities shows scattered work in many areas. We find no shred of evidence to support the old theory of compensation. Because a person is blind, he does not therefore possess any special ability in other areas. He is not, because of his blindness, more sensitive to auditory or tactual or any other kind of sensations. But, because of his blindness, he must depend upon other than visual sensations to interpret the world around him. He therefore by practice may become much more skillful than the seeing in the use he makes of auditory, tactual, kinaesthetic, and other sensations. Hence he develops the so-called "obstacle" sense. Hence he may develop a prodigious memory for certain types of material. Hence he can recognize many people by the voice alone, and interpret their moods and attitudes. But the blind person must learn how to do this. His handicap, alas, brings him no short cut to proficiency.

MISCELLANEOUS

There are a few miscellaneous studies that have some bearing on the psychology of the blind.

Social Maturity. Social maturity, measured by the Vineland Social Maturity Scale, has been studied with two small groups of blind children. Bradway (6) used seventy-three pupils of a residential school, all blinded at birth or before the age of four years. She found their mean S.Q. or Social Quotient to be 62, indicating an average handicap of 38 per cent as compared with seeing individuals. It was also lower than the mean S.Q. for the deaf, which was 80. She also reports that the S.Q.'s of the blind "showed some tendency to decrease with age, which suggested that blindness results in cumulative social retardation." The other report on the scale is by McKay (57), who experimented with a few preschool blind cases. The scale was administered several times to each case at varying time intervals, and the description of the results would seem to demonstrate its usefulness in measuring the progress of very young blind children.

Phantasies. The phantasy life of the blind has been described by Cutsforth (16). He collected data through personal interviews with forty-eight boys and girls in state schools for the blind. The age range was from seven to twenty-five. He gives examples of different types of phantasy, such as "action," "regressive," "erotic," and the like. He finds a wide range of individual differences among his cases. He believes that qualitative and quantitative differences between the phantasies of the congenitally and accidentally blind exist. The congenital subjects would show fewer violent phantasies. Unfortunately, there is no control group of seeing subjects, so that it is difficult to know how the blindness itself has influenced the phantasy life of the blind subjects as described by Cutsforth.

Reading Interests. Books for the blind are either in braille or on records. Both processes are expensive. The blind individual cannot have his own library. He depends upon the library service which supplies him with braille books or records. What books should be adapted for the blind reader? In an attempt to approach to an answer to this question, Riddell (67) reports the results of a survey of the reading interests of the blind. A questionnaire was sent to 2,419 people on the mailing list of the braille edition of the Readers' Digest. Returns were received from 1,250, or about 52 per cent. The results show that these educated blind people are reading mostly popular recent fiction and desire such fiction in braille and talking-book records. Their next choice is simple nonfiction. The main subjects of interest in reading are classified as "personalities, history, and government." The study concludes by suggesting that the books at present being put into braille for the blind do not seem to conform very much to these expressed interests of the blind. This report is suggestive merely and seems to indicate the need for more rigorous studies of this nature in order to guide the choice of books prepared for the blind.

Occupations. After the blind child leaves school, he tries to find a place in the world outside. Sargent's (68) study shows us what some of the blind are doing after their education in school has been completed. She attempted to follow up 500 children who left the Pennsylvania Institution during the years 1907 to 1922. She obtained personal answers from 185 and information from other sources from 152, a total of 337. Of the remainder 58 had died and 105 could not be traced. The economic status of the 337 is given as follows:

	Percentage
Entirely self-supporting	11.3
Helping in support of others	18.7
Saving money	23.7
Total, self-supporting or better	53.7
Dependent	18.1
Partially self-supporting	17.8
Studying	6.8
Incomplete records	3.6
Total, not self-supporting	46.3

The occupations followed by these individuals include forty different kinds for the men, and twenty-two for the women. For the men the two mentioned most frequently are tuning and caning; for the women, housework and caning.

SUMMARY

The handicap of blindness is generally obvious to the sighted person. This is not so with regard to the handicap of deafness. The latter handicap only becomes apparent when the hearing person begins to communicate with the deaf person. Furthermore, the blind individual is generally very awkward and sometimes quite helpless in moving around and in many bodily activities. And so the blind person strikes the naïve observer as much more handicapped than the deaf. He is more likely to attract attention than is the deaf person. We pity the blind more than we do the deaf. The deaf person does not carry about with him an obvious handicap for all to behold. The naïve observer sees nothing wrong with a deaf man, and often considers him merely stupid or "dumb." Hence, in the history of our subject we note that interest was aroused much earlier in the case of the blind than in the case of the deaf, and philosophers and scientists gave more attention to the problems of blindness than to those of deafness.

In the psychology of blindness, therefore, we note an early interest in problems related to space perception. The blind were frequently studied in order to throw light upon the psychology of normal spatial perception. Again the seemingly miraculous manner in which some blind people avoided obstacles gave rise to the hypothesis of a "sixth" sense and this called for some explanation on the part of normal psychology. In addition we have the old theory of compensation which arose to explain the seemingly miraculous abilities of some blind people. If one sense fails, nature compensates by making the other senses more sensitive.

Interest in these aspects of the psychology of blindness began early, was common both to general psychologists and educators of the blind, and has remained with us down to the present time. A later and somewhat different approach to the psychology of the blind began in the early decades of the present century with the introduction of psychological tests and the growing interest in differential psychology. This approach has led to the study of intelligence, educational achievement, and measurement of personality. It has been intimately connected with the education of the blind. At present we are in the midst of much work representing this newer approach and we can expect many important findings in the future.

Let us, therefore, summarize the results up to date from these two approaches. With reference to the problems of the older approach, we can say definitely that the hypothesis of sensory compensation is now completely discredited. There is no shred of evidence for assuming that because of blindness the individual therefore becomes more sensitive to sounds, tastes, smells, or touch sensations, or is endowed with a better memory. What we find is that in certain practiced tasks the blind are better than the sighted simply because they have practiced them. In unpracticed tasks the blind are no better than the sighted. Indeed there is the suggestion that they may be inherently poorer and we may swing over to a theory of correlation, which would hold that abilities correlate positively and that where one is weak or missing the others are likely to be depressed. But as yet no one has produced any evidence to support this theory.

With reference to facial vision or the sense of obstacles, there is as yet no agreement. The history of research in this problem is a long one, and in spite of carefully controlled experimental procedures we cannot yet be said to understand it fully. We know that audition has much to do with it, and perhaps it is the main factor. But we do not understand the process fully and until we do so, we remain unable to facilitate this useful ability in our education of the blind.

Turning now to the newer approach dealing with tests and educational experiments, we find that much work has been done on the intelligence of the blind. Here the work of Hayes is outstanding. His revision of the Stanford Binet for the blind is the recognized standard scale. From the results of thousands of children tested by this scale, we conclude that the blind on the average are only slightly below the sighted in general intelligence. There would seem, however, to be a larger percentage of dull and feeble-minded cases among the blind. Thus the educators of the blind are not only confronted with the problem of blindness, but also with the problem of low mentality. What to do with the feeble-minded blind is a practical problem that is difficult to solve. It has been suggested that the percentage of such cases may be increasing owing to a decrease in specific localized eye diseases not complicated with general constitutional defects, but the evidence for this trend is very slight. There seems to be no correlation between intelligence and the age at which vision has been lost. No definite conclusion seems to have been arrived at with reference to the average intelligence of the totally blind as compared with those possessing some vision.

In educational achievement the blind are almost always retarded as compared with the sighted of the same chronological age. When blind children in a given grade are compared with the grade norms for standard tests, they frequently are up to the norms. This means that schools for the blind maintain standards similar to schools for the seeing. But the blind children are on the average two or three years older. Reading is one cause of this retardation. Reading braille is difficult and slow. It is at best a tedious process. Experimental work on the reading of braille has begun. Perhaps it may lead to better methods of teaching reading and better techniques of reading.

Very little has been done in the study of the personality of the blind by means of modern techniques. Whether the blind as a group are more introverted or maladjusted than the seeing, it is at present difficult to say. Some evidence points in that direction. Again we are told that blind children in general are very suggestible, lack initiative, are unduly sensitive, and so on. All of these suggestions need to be checked up by better and more comprehensive studies. Perhaps the blind do not differ from the seeing with regard to the amount and frequency of such traits; perhaps they do; and if so, it would be well to know, so that we might try to modify such traits by adequate educational procedures.

From this summary we can see that a good beginning has been made in the psychology of the blind. More knowledge and more accurate knowledge as to the capacities, abilities, and personality traits of the blind will help us to understand them better and to educate them better.

BIBLIOGRAPHY

1. Abel, G. L., "The Educational Achievement of Fifth and Sixth Grade Blind Children," *Teachers Forum* (*Blind*), X (1938), 109–11.
2. Berens, C., "Causes of Blindness," in *What of the Blind?* ed. by H. Lende (Am. Found. for the Blind, N.Y., 1938).
3. Best, H., *Blindness and the Blind in the United States* (Macmillan, N.Y., 1934).
4. Binet, A., "Les proportions du crâne chez les aveugles," *L'année psychol.*, VIII (1902), 369–84.
5. Bond, N. J., and W. J. Dearborn, "The Auditory Memory

and Tactual Sensitivity of the Blind," *J. Educ. Psychol.*, VIII (1917), 21–26.

6. Bradway, K. P., "Social Competence of Exceptional Children. III: The Deaf, the Blind and the Crippled," *J. Except. Child.*, IV (1937), 64–69.
7. Brown, P. A., "Responses of Blind and Seeing Adolescents to an Introversion-Extroversion Questionnaire," *J. Psychol.*, VI (1938), 137–47.
8. Brown, P. A., "Responses of Blind and Seeing Adolescents to a Neurotic Inventory," *J. Psychol.*, VII (1939), 211–21.
9. Burde, M., "Die Plastik der Blinden," *Zeitschr. f. angew. Psychol.*, IV (1910), 106–28.
10. Bürklen, K., *Blindenpsychologie* (Barth, Leipzig, 1924).
11. Bürklen, K., *Touch Reading of the Blind*, trans. by F. K. Merry (Am. Found. for the Blind, N.Y., 1932).
12. Cairns, J. H., "A Survey of Pupils at Perkins Institution with Respect to Vision, Intelligence and Hearing," *Teachers Forum (Blind)*, XI (1938), 14–16.
13. Caldwell, F. F., *A Comparison of Blind and Seeing Children in Certain Educational Abilities* (Am. Found. for the Blind, N.Y., 1932).
14. Cantril, H., and G. W. Allport, *The Psychology of Radio* (Harper, N.Y., 1935).
15. Cutsforth, T. D., "The Unreality of Words to the Blind," *Teachers Forum (Blind)*, IV (1931–32), 86–89.
16. Cutsforth, T. D., *The Blind in School and Society* (Appleton, N.Y., 1933).
17. Dolanski, W., "Les aveugles possèdent-ils le sens des obstacles," *L'année psychol.*, XXXI (1930), 1–51.
18. Farrell, G., "How the Blind See. What Is This 'Sixth Sense'?" *The Forum*, XCVI (1936), 81–86.
19. Fortner, E. N., "A Group Intelligence Test in Braille," *Teachers Forum (Blind)*, XI (1939), 53–56.
20. French, R. S., *From Homer to Helen Keller* (Am. Found. for the Blind, N.Y., 1932).

21. Haines, T. H., "Mental Measurements of the Blind," *Psychol. Monogs.*, XXI (1916), No. 89.
22. Haines, T. H., "Report of New Cases and More Reliable Age Norms of Intelligence by the Point Scale for the Blind," *J. Educ. Psychol.*, X (1919), 165–7.
23. Hall, E., "A Study of the Size and Space Concepts of Blind School Children Compared with Those of Seeing School Children," *Teachers Forum (Blind)*, XII (1940), 42–47.
24. Hall, G. S., "Laura Bridgeman," *Mind, Old Series*, IV (1879), 149–172.
25. Hayes, S. P., "Standard Tests in Elementary Subjects in Schools for the Blind," *Proceedings*, Am. Assoc. of Instructors of the Blind (1918), 42–54.
26. Hayes, S. P., *Self-Surveys in Schools for the Blind*, Pubs. of Pa. Inst. for Instruct. of the Blind, No. 2 (Dec., 1921).
27. Hayes, S. P., *Preliminary Study of the Influence upon School Success of the Age at Which Vision Is Lost*, Pubs. of the Perkins Inst. and Mass. School for the Blind, No. 1 (Jan., 1923).
28. Hayes, S. P., *Ten Years of Psychological Research in Schools for the Blind*, Pubs. of the Pa. Inst. for Instruct. of the Blind, No. 4 (Overbrook, Phil., Jan., 1927).
29. Hayes, S. P., "The New Revision of the Binet Intelligence Tests for the Blind," *Teachers Forum (Blind)*, II (1929), 2–4.
30. Hayes, S. P., *Terman's Condensed Guide for the Stanford Revision for the Blind* (Perkins Inst. for the Blind, Watertown, Mass., 1930).
31. Hayes, S. P., "New Experimental Data on the Old Problem of Sensory Compensation," *Teachers Forum (Blind)*, VI (1933–34), 22–26.
32. Hayes, S. P., "Factors Influencing the School Success of the Blind," *Teachers Forum (Blind)*, VI (1933–34), 91–98.
33. Hayes, S. P., "Where Did That Sound Come From?" *Teachers Forum (Blind)*, VII (1934–35), 47–51.

34. Hayes, S. P., *Facial Vision or the Sense of Obstacles*, Publs. of Perkins Inst. for the Blind, No. 12 (June, 1935).
35. Hayes, S. P., "The Memory of Blind Children," *Teachers Forum (Blind)*, VIII (1935–36), 55–59, 71–76.
36. Hayes, S. P., "Can the Blind Pass in Geography?" *Teachers Forum (Blind)*, X (1937), 22–32, 38.
37. Hayes, S. P., "Words Are Wise Men's Counters (Hobbes): How Rich Are the Blind?" *Teachers Forum*, X (1938), 94–103, 108.
38. Hayes, S. P., "The Psychology of Blindness," in *What of the Blind?* ed. by H. Lende (Am. Found. for the Blind, N.Y., 1938).
39. Hayes, S. P., "What Do Blind Children Know?" *Teachers Forum (Blind)*, IX (1938), 22–29, 32.
40. Heller, T., *Studien zur Blindenpsychologie* (Engelmann, Leipzig, 1904).
41. Holland, B. F., "Speed and Pressure Factors in Braille Reading," *Teachers Forum (Blind)*, VII (1934–35), 13–17.
42. Holland, B. F., and P. F. Eatman, "The Silent Reading Habits of Blind Children," *Teachers Forum (Blind)*, VI (1933–34), 4–11.
43. James, W., *The Principles of Psychology*, Vol. II (Holt, New York, 1890), 203–11.
44. Jastrow, J., "Psychological Notes on Helen Keller," *Psychol. Rev.*, I (1894), 356–62.
45. Knotts, J. R., and W. R. Miles, "The Maze-learning Ability of Blind Compared with Sighted Children," *J. Genet. Psychol.*, XXXVI (1929), 21–50.
46. Koch, H. L., and J. Ufkess, "A Comparative Study of Stylus Maze Learning by Blind and Seeing Subjects," *J. Exper. Psychol.*, IX (1926), 118–31.
47. Lamarque, G., "La sensation des obstacles chez les aveugles," *J. de Psychol.*, XXVI (1929), 494–522.
48. Lende, H., ed., *What of the Blind?* (Am. Found. for the Blind, N.Y., 1938).

49. Lende, H., *Books about the Blind* (Am. Found. for the Blind, N.Y., 1940).
50. Löwenfeld, V., *The Nature of Creative Activity* (Harcourt Brace, N.Y., 1939).
51. MacDougall, R., "Facial Vision," *Am. J. Psychol.*, XV (1904), 383–90.
52. Matz, W., "Eine Untersuchung über das Modellieren Sehender Kinder," *Zeitschr. f. angew. Psychol.*, VI (1912), 1–20.
53. Matz, W., "Zeichen und Modellierversuch an Volksschülern, Hilfsschülern, Taubstummen und Blinden," *Zeitschr. f. angew. Psychol.*, X (1915), 62–135.
54. Maxfield, K. E., *The Blind Child and His Reading* (Am. Found. for the Blind, N.Y., 1928).
55. Maxfield, K. E., *The Spoken Language of the Blind Preschool Child,* Arch. Psychol., No. 201 (N.Y., 1936).
56. Maxfield, K. E., *A Ten-Year Review of American Investigations Pertaining to Blind Children* (Arthur Sunshine Home, Summit, N.J., 1937).
57. McKay, B. E., "Social Maturity of the Preschool Blind Child," *Training School Bulletin,* XXXIII (1936), 146–55.
58. Merry, F. K., "Types of Errors Made in Fundamental Arithmetic Processes by Pupils in Six Schools for the Blind," *Teachers Forum* (*Blind*), III:3 (1930–31), 8–19.
59. Merry, F. K., "A Survey of the Problem-Solving Ability of Pupils in Six Residential Schools for the Blind," *Teachers Forum* (*Blind*), III:5 (1930–31), 12–15.
60. Merry, R. V., "To What Extent Can Blind Children Recognize Tactually, Simple Embossed Pictures?" *Teachers Forum* (*Blind*), III (1930–31), 2–5.
61. Merry, R. V., "Adapting the Seashore Musical Talent Tests for Use with Blind Pupils," *Teachers Forum* (*Blind*), III (1930–31), 15–19.
62. Merry, R. V., *Problems in the Education of Visually Handicapped Children,* Harvard Studies in Educ., No. 19 (Harvard Univ. Press, Cambridge, Mass., 1933).

63. Merry, R. V., and Merry, F. K., "The Finger Maze as a Supplementary Test of Intelligence for Blind Children," *J. Genet. Psychol.*, XLIV (1934), 227–30.

64. Muhl, A. M., "Results of Psychometric and Personality Studies of Blind Children at the California State School for the Blind," *Am. Assoc. of Instructors of the Blind, 30th Biennial Convention* (Vancouver, Wash., 1930), 568–73.

65. Pechstein, L. A., "Factors Influencing the School Success of the Blind," *Sch. and Soc.*, XIX (1924), 47–52.

66. Petzelt, A., *Vom Problem der Blindheit,* Akademie gemeinnütziger Wissenschaften zu Erfurt, Abt. f. Erziehungswissenschaft, No. 26 (1931).

67. Riddell, M., "A Survey of the Reading Interests of the Blind," *Library Journal,* LXV (1940), 189–92.

68. Sargent, R. F., *What Can the Blind Do?* Pubs. of the Pa. Inst. for Instruct. of the Blind, No. 3 (Overbrook, Phil., June, 1924).

69. Sargent, R., "The Otis Classification Test," *Teachers Forum* (*Blind*), IV (1931), 30–33.

70. Scottish Council for Research in Education, *The Intelligence of Scottish Children* (Univ. of London Press, London, 1933).

71. Seashore, C. E., and T. L. Ling, "The Comparative Sensitiveness of Blind and Seeing Persons," *Psychol. Monogs.*, XXV (1918), No. 108, 148–58.

72. Smith, J. M., "Which Hand Is the Eye of the Blind?" *Genet. Psychol. Monogs.*, V (1929), 209–52.

73. U.S. Census, *The Blind and Deaf-Mutes in the United States, 1930* (Dept. of Commerce, Bur. of the Census, Govt. Printing Office, Wash., 1931).

74. Vertes, J. O., "Das Gedächtnis der Blinden," *Arch. gesamte Psychol.*, XXXIX (1920), 214–31.

75. Villey, P., "La perception des obstacles chez les aveugles de la guerre," *Revue Philos.*, XCV (1923), 98–131.

76. Villey, P., *The World of the Blind,* trans. by A. Hallard (Macmillan, N.Y., 1930).

77. White House Conference on Child Health and Protection, *Special Education, The Handicapped and the Gifted* (Century, N.Y., 1931).
78. Wilbur, L., *Vocations for the Visually Handicapped* (Am. Found. for the Blind, N.Y., 1937).

CHAPTER VIII

The Partially Sighted

GENERAL

The partially sighted or the partially seeing are a group of physically handicapped individuals who stand between the blind and the normal seeing in much the same way that the hard of hearing stand between the deaf and the normal hearing. They are individuals whose visual acuity is poor. The group is generally described as including all those whose visual acuity in the better eye after correction or treatment lies between 20/70 and 20/200, and in addition those who have progressive eye difficulties. With reference to educational needs, the partially sighted child is one who has too little vision for normal school work but has too much sight to be educated through the sense of touch. As in the case of the hard of hearing, so with reference to the partially sighted, there can be no sharp dividing line between the normal and the handicapped. Each case must be considered on its own merits. Each child must be studied carefully as to whether he can make best educational progress in a class for the blind or for the partially sighted or for the normal sighted. Standards for admission to classes for the partially sighted vary somewhat from state to state among those states having such classes.

The visual acuity of the better eye of a sample of 2,590 children at the time of entering sight-saving classes is given as follows (11):

Better than 20/70	= 35.2 per cent
Between 20/70 and 20/200	= 55.8 per cent
Less than 20/200	= 9.0 per cent

It will be noted that in this sample 35.2 per cent had visual acuity better than 20/70. These were children whose vision would be likely to become worse under unfavorable conditions.

The special education of the partially sighted is of very recent origin. The first class seems to have been started in England about 1908 and in the United States about 1913. The number of partially sighted children is generally estimated to lie between one in 500 and one in 1,000 school children. The White House Conference Report (11) seems to favor the estimate of one in 500, and from this arrives at an estimated total of 50,359 children in the United States who should be in sight-saving classes. The London Board of Education Report (2) prefers the more conservative estimate of one per 1,000 school children, and according to this estimate, there would be about 25,000 children in the United States in need of special instruction.

The number of children actually in sight-saving classes in 1930 is given as 4,829 in 350 classes (9). Frampton and Rowell (3) report 7,500 children in 571 classes in 1938. This shows a substantial increase in the number of such children being given special educational facilities, but it is still very far from the most conservative estimate of 25,000 who might profit by them.

One value of special classes for partially sighted children is the special attention paid to their physical condition, especially their eyesight. Myers (9) found some improvement of vision in a sample of 1,751 cases at the time of a second vision examination after the children had been in sight conservation classes:

	Better	*Same*	*Worse*	*Total*
Number	462	1,124	165	1,751
Per cent	26.4	64.2	9.4	100.0

The sex distribution of 4,829 cases is according to Myers (9) 50.7 per cent girls and 49.3 per cent boys.

INTELLIGENCE

Very little has been published with reference to the general intelligence of the partially sighted. The largest sample of I.Q.'s has been gathered by Myers (9). He reported the distribution of 709 cases, presumably tested by an individual psychological examination. An additional 261 I.Q.'s are given in the Appendix to Myers' book. These arrived too late to be included in his original distribution. These 261 cases have, however, been added to the original 709 cases and are reported in the White House Conference Report (11). These two distributions are as follows:

	Original Group		*Cases Added*	
I.Q. Interval	*n*	*per cent*	*n*	*per cent*
Below 70	93	13.1	94	9.7
70–80	146	20.6	169	17.4
80–90	179	25.2	245	25.3
90–110	224	31.6	373	38.4
110–120	45	6.3	63	6.5
120–140	22	3.1	26	2.7
Totals	709	99.9	970	100.0

The additional cases added to the original distribution reduce appreciably the percentage of low I.Q.'s. Nevertheless, both distributions show more than 50 per cent of the cases with I.Q.'s below 90. The median I.Q. would be somewhere in the 80's.

The London Board of Education Report (2) gives the results of Stanford-Binet tests (with certain reading and visual tests omitted) of 141 partially sighted children, ages ten to sixteen, compared with a control group of 100 sighted children of similar social status tested by means of a group intelligence test. The following data are given:

	Mean I.Q.	*S.D.*	*n*
Partially sighted in special schools	92.7	15.1	123
Partially sighted in special classes	93.9	11.5	18
Sighted children	94.4	10.3	100

The conclusion drawn is that there is no difference in intelligence between the partially sighted and the sighted.

Hadley (5) describes the procedure for the admission of children into sight-saving classes in Ohio. All who enter are given a Binet test. Without stating the number of cases involved, she says, "The approximate percentages of last year's testing are:"

	I.Q.	*Per Cent*
Superior	110–120	12.6
Normal	90–110	58.6
Dull	80–90	25.4
Borderline	70–80	3.2

The absence of any cases below 70 I.Q. is presumably due to the fact that no feeble-minded children were admitted to sight-saving classes.

These are the only results of intelligence tests given to partially sighted children that we have been able to find in the literature. Obviously they are very unsatisfactory. The large sampling of Myers is based upon the answers to a questionnaire and the original total of 709 I.Q.'s represents only 25 per cent of the cases for whom data were obtained, and only 17 per cent of the pupils enrolled in sight-saving classes at the time of his survey. It is impossible to tell whether the children whose I.Q.'s were given formed a representative sampling of the partially sighted children in special classes. There generally is a tendency to ask for a psychological examination or a mental test if a child is slow in his school work or if he is a "problem" in any sense. The sample may, therefore, contain a preponderance of duller children. The London report contains very few cases and shows that in schools where the mean I.Q. is about 94, the partially sighted do not differ from the sighted.

All of our data seem to have been based upon intelligence tests devised for normally sighted children. It would seem to us that such tests might penalize slightly the partially sighted child. A study of this factor is needed.

At present, therefore, we know very little about the intelligence of the partially sighted child. A thorough and careful survey is badly needed.

EDUCATIONAL ACHIEVEMENT

There are very few published reports of standard educational-achievement tests given to partially seeing children. Probably this is due to the difficulty of procuring test material in large type.

Peck (10) has reported very interesting results on the reading ability of sight-saving class pupils in Cleveland, Ohio. The three reading tests of the Stanford Achievement Test, Form A, were given to 234 children in grades II to IX in January, 1932 and the tests were then repeated with 227 children in January, 1933. The scores were computed for the regular time limits and then for time and a half. The results for the 1932 tests are as follows:

			Median Grade Score			*Median Reading Quotient*	
n	*Grade*	*Grade Norm*	*regular time*	*time and a half*	*Median I.Q.*	*regular time*	*time and a half*
11	2B	2.4	2.8	3.2	98	100	100
16	2A	2.9	2.8	3.0	93	95	100
18	3B	3.4	3.2	3.4	96	95	102
11	3A	3.9	3.3	3.3	84	84	84
20	4B	4.4	4.3	4.4	99	99	100
16	4A	4.9	4.6	5.0	94	98	100
18	5B	5.4	5.2	5.4	91	95	96
13	5A	5.9	5.9	6.1	91	91	96
17	6B	6.4	5.7	6.1	91	91	92
12	6A	6.9	6.0	6.6	90	88	92
13	7B	7.4	7.3	7.3	95	90	91
18	7A	7.9	7.0	7.0	94	92	93
12	8B	8.4	8.5	9.3	83	85	85
9	8A	8.9	8.5	9.3	100	100	103
21	9B	9.4	8.7	8.8	97	96	97
9	9A	9.8	8.8	9.7	98	96	97

The first line tells us that eleven children in grade 2B were tested. The grade norm in January would be 2.4, and median grade scores of our eleven cases were 2.8 for regular time and 3.2 for extended time. This class, therefore, was slightly better than expectation. Furthermore we learn from the table that the median I.Q. on the Binet as reported by the school psychologist is 98, and the median reading quotient 100 for both time intervals. The data show that the reading achievement of these children is on the whole fairly close to the norms for their respective grades. Extending the regular time allows them to increase their grade scores and also their reading quotients slightly. The median I.Q.'s for each class show that these children are on the whole of normal intelligence. No median I.Q. for the 234 cases is given, but the median of the 16 class I.Q.'s given above is 94.

A similar table is given for the 227 cases tested a year later.

The results seem to indicate a slight gain in reading ability. In general, therefore, so far as this sampling is concerned there is no indication of a serious reading deficiency.

Spelling has been tested by Hadley (5) by means of the McCall Spelling Scale. She gives the average scores for 37 classes, and concludes that on the whole the classes are almost equal to the norms for the test. She finds no relation between amount of vision and spelling brightness.

The London report (2) finds the sample of partially sighted children tested equal to the control group of sighted children in arithmetic tests but inferior in reading tests, and argues that, since the two groups are equal in intelligence, the visual handicap of the partially sighted probably causes this reading defect.

The other evidence as to the educational achievement of the partially sighted is derived from the age-grade status of these children. Myers (9) found the following situation for 2,013 cases:

	On Entering Sight-Saving Classes			*At Time of Survey*		
	underage	*normal*	*overage*	*underage*	*normal*	*overage*
n	168	1,219	626	145	1,140	728
%	8.3	60.6	31.1	7.2	56.6	36.2

The percentage of overage cases is very large. After the children have been in sight-saving classes for various lengths of time this percentage increases slightly, but Myers argues that it would have increased still more had they remained in regular classes. The promotion rate of these 2,013 cases was found to be 87.8 per cent, which was about the same as the promotion rate for all pupils in Philadelphia at the time of the survey. Furthermore, the White House Conference Report (11) gives the promotion rate for 356 cases before entering sight-saving classes as 73.7 per cent, whereas it jumps to 91 per cent after these same children have been in sight-saving classes, and concludes that the special classwork helps more children to go on through the regular school.

These few reports on the educational achievement of partially sighted children are very inadequate. Many more and better controlled studies are urgently needed. At present all that we know about the educational status of the partially sighted child is that on the average he seems to be overage for his grade and that possibly the work of the sight-saving class helps him to progress more normally through the grades.

PERSONALITY

We have been unable to find any studies of the personality of the partially sighted. Merry (8) discusses the possibility of personality difficulties arising as a result of visual defect. Constant eyestrain probably causes undue nervous tension. Inability to keep up in school may cause a feeling of mental inadequacy and all sorts of inferiority feelings. Merry suggests the value of a study of personality difficulties of a large number of partially seeing children before they enter a special class and then a follow-up study of them after they have been in such a class for several years. Hearon (7) discusses in general the emotional factors which may arise due to defective vision and cites a few cases where this seems to have been a causative factor in personality maladjustment.

This is all. It would be futile to go on making assumptions in an area in which we have no knowledge. Let us hope that the near future will see many studies on the personality of the partially seeing.

SUMMARY

This chapter shows our ignorance rather than our knowledge. The special education of the partially seeing child is so recent that practically all of the effort and interest in this work has been concentrated on the organization, administration, and equipment of these classes. About the children themselves from a psychological point of view we know practically nothing. It is probable that in general intelligence they differ very little from children with normal vision. If there were a great difference in intelligence, this would certainly have forced itself upon the attention of their teachers. But just what the average I.Q. and the distribution of the I.Q.'s of such children may be, we do not know. As to the educational achievement of the partially sighted there is little that we know definitely. They seem to be slower in moving through the grades, but whether this is due to a lack of intelligence or to their visual handicap or to a lack of adequate instruction in special classes or to any combination of these or other reasons, we do not know. Furthermore, we do not know in any definite sense how much the work of the special class helps the partially sighted child. Again in the field of personality we have no studies at all. We need to know whether there are any peculiar problems that arise owing to defective vision, and, if there are such, how they may be recognized and ameliorated.

A good beginning has been made in the education of the partially seeing, but the study of the psychology of these children has hardly yet begun.

BIBLIOGRAPHY

1. Coffin, H. J., and O. S. Peck, *Sight-Saving Classes in Cleveland Public Schools* (Cleveland Board of Educ., Feb., 1926).
2. England, Committee on Problems Relating to Partially Sighted Children, *Report of the Committee of Inquiry into Problems Relating to Partially Sighted Children* (His Majesty's Stationery Office, London, 1934).
3. Frampton, M. E., and H. G. Rowell, *Education of the Handi-*

capped, Vol. I, *History* (World Book Co., Yonkers, N.Y., 1938).

4. Frampton, M. E., and H. G. Rowell, *Education of the Handicapped,* Vol. II, *Problems* (World Book Co., Yonkers, N.Y., 1940).
5. Hadley, H. C., *Sight-Saving Classes in the Public Schools. Presenting the Ohio Plan* (Heer, Columbus, 1927).
6. Hathaway, W., and H. H. McIntire, *Sight-Saving Classes: Organization and Administration,* Natl. Soc. Prev. of Blindness, Pub. No. 30, revised (1937).
7. Hearon, E. L., *Emotional Factors in Education of the Visually Handicapped,* Natl. Soc. for Prev. of Blindness, Pub. No. 286 (Reprinted from *Sight-Saving Class Exchange,* Feb., 1939).
8. Merry, R. V., *Problems in the Education of Visually Handicapped Children,* Harvard Studies in Educ., No. 19 (Harvard Univ. Press, Cambridge, Mass., 1933).
9. Myers, E. T., *A Survey of Sight-Saving Classes in the Public Schools of the United States* (Thesis, Univ. of Pa., Phil., 1930).
10. Peck, O. S., *Reading Ability of Sight-Saving Class Pupils in Cleveland, Ohio,* Natl. Soc. Prevention of Blindness, Pub. No. 118 (Reprinted from *The Sight-Saving Review,* III (June, 1933).
11. White House Conference on Child Health and Protection, *Special Education* (Century, N.Y., 1931).

CHAPTER IX

The Crippled

GENERAL

There is no single accepted definition of the term "crippled child," but a number of definitions which vary both in content and in emphasis. Some are vague, allowing considerable scope for interpretation; some describe in terms of physical defect alone, while others include educational and vocational aspects. Cardiacs and those with harelip and cleft palate may or may not be included. The following definition is suggested in the report of the White House Conference (31):

"The crippled child, in the orthopedic sense, is a child that has a defect which causes a deformity or an interference with normal functioning of the bones, muscles, or joints. His condition may be congenital, or it may be due to disease or accident. It may be aggravated by disease, by neglect, or by ignorance."

In Michigan (19) the legal definition of a cripple reads, "One whose activity is, or may become, so far restricted by loss, defects, or deformity of bone or muscle as to reduce his or her capacity for education and self-support."

The New York City survey of crippled children (21) used the following definition:

"A crippled child is an individual under 21 years of age who is so handicapped through congenital or acquired defects in the use of his limbs and body musculature, as to be unable to compete on terms of equality with a normal individual of the same age."

In England and Wales the term "crippled child" includes those "crippled in limb, suffering from the sequalae of infantile paralysis and 'heart cases.'"

Estimates of the incidence of crippling conditions vary not only because of differences in definition, but because of the lack of thorough surveys of large areas. The White House Conference (31) estimated 300,000 crippled children in this country, or 3 per thousand. Michigan (19) reported 3 cases per thousand of school age children in some counties, with other counties reporting as high as 9 per thousand when severe posture cases were included. New Jersey (20) estimated 7.24 per thousand eighteen years and younger, and New York City's most recent study (21) estimated 7.2 per thousand under twenty-one years of age.

While estimates of the incidence of crippling vary, surveys are consistent in finding more boys than girls among the crippled group. Cleveland (6) and New York State (22) reported 55 per cent boys; Chicago (29) 53 per cent and New York City (21) 52.4 per cent. Among adult cripples the percentage of males is even greater, due in part to industrial accidents.

The age at which these children become crippled would seem to have important implications for educational programs. In Chicago (29), 83 per cent of cripples under twenty-one years of age were crippled before the age of six. Of a group of children in Wisconsin (32), 79 per cent were crippled before the age of seven. Of 1,277 crippled children studied in New York City (21) "33 per cent were disabled at birth by cerebral palsy or congenital abnormalities. Forty-nine per cent of those with disease other than poliomyelitis were disabled before their fifth and 91 per cent before their tenth birthdays." This suggests the need for early discovery and diagnosis of cases, and for sound educational planning for young cripples.

Statistics concerning the causes of crippling indicate that poliomyelitis ranks first in number of victims. A report (31) which includes 57 public and private teaching centers in 47 cities in 14 states gives the following distribution of causes of crippling:

Cause of Crippling	*Per Cent*
Infantile paralysis	33.7
Bone tuberculosis	12.6
Spastic paralysis	14
Congenital	10
Cardiac *	8
Accidents	6
Others	16

McLeod (17) studying 2,006 crippled children from rural communities arranges causes in this order:

Cause of Crippling	*Per Cent*
Infantile paralysis	21
Congenital deformities	9
Traumatic deformities	9
Bone and joint tuberculosis	8
Osteomyelitis	7
Spastic paralysis	7

The New York City survey reports (21):

Cause of Crippling	*Per Cent*
Poliomyelitis	29
Prenatal influences	18.2
Birth injury	15.7

* This figure does not truly represent the incidence of heart cases since many of these cities do not enroll cardiacs in their crippled classes.

Cause of Crippling	*Per Cent*
Infection	12.9
Trauma or physical agents	6.0
Epiphysical disturbances	4.5
Metabolic disturbances	1.7
New growths	0.5
Unknown and uncertain causes	11.5

More recent surveys tend to show a higher percentage of cerebral palsy cases than did early surveys. This probably does not indicate an increase in the number of cases, but better methods of locating and diagnosing such cases. In the past, the child suffering from cerebral palsy was far too frequently diagnosed as feeble-minded and sent to an institution for the care of the feeble-minded. Dr. Winthrop Phelps (24) estimates that there are between 40 and 50 cerebral palsy cases per 100,000 of population, 30 per cent of whom are impaired mentally.

INTELLIGENCE

Great strides have been made in the care and treatment of crippled children and many studies reported, but very few psychological studies of the crippled have been published.

In 1925 Fernald and Arlitt (8) published a study of the intelligence of a group of 194 children who were enrolled or had applied for enrollment in the Cincinnati School for Cripples. All of these children were tested once with the Stanford-Binet and 66 were retested. For the first test the intelligence quotients ranged from an estimated 30 to 138, with a mean I.Q. of 82.35. The correlation between the first and second test was .90 ± .015.

In order to discover whether or not there was a relationship between type of crippling and intelligence, the group was divided into seven subgroups on the basis of type of crippling condition. The following table shows the mean I.Q. for each of these groups:

Disease Group	*Mean I.Q.*
Poliomyelitis	83.79
Spastic birth paralysis	69.11
Tuberculosis	86.20
Miscellaneous	83.57
Nutritional	86.53
Infectious	85.47
Traumatic	86.00
Central nervous system involvement	75.93

The cerebral palsy group and the group suffering involvement of the central nervous system show the lowest mean scores. When we examine the individual scores we find that the four intelligence quotients below 60 fell in these two groups. No child in these groups tested higher than 110, and only 14 per cent tested above 90 as compared with 44 per cent of the other groups. It should be pointed out that one should not take too seriously intelligence quotients reported for cerebral palsy cases, particularly those having a serious motor or speech involvement. Dr. Elizabeth Lord (15) writes, "As a preliminary step in certain cases, with due consideration for age and physical efficiency, it (Stanford-Binet) often gives valuable leads but the concept of mental age from the clinical point of view is rarely applicable to the cerebral palsied child and is often grossly misleading."

The data of Fernald and Arlitt were examined to discover what, if any, relationship existed between level of intelligence and age at onset of crippling condition. The mean I.Q. for those crippled at birth was 75.75; the mean I.Q. for those crippled after six years of age was 88.32. The interpretation of these differences is ambiguous since all of the cerebral palsy cases are in the first group and the greater number of poliomyelitis cases in the group crippled after reaching school age. Such evidence as we have indicates that on the average the poliomyelitis cases test somewhat higher than other groups of cripples.

A rough scale of degree of crippling was devised and comparisons were made between intelligence level and degree of crippling. There was a slight tendency for the level of intelligence to decrease as the degree of crippling increased. This may or may not be a significant tendency.

An interesting and important part of the study was a comparison of the intelligence of the crippled group with that of their siblings. The siblings of 49 crippled children were tested and the average I.Q. of the noncrippled children in each family was computed. The mean I.Q. for the crippled children was 83.9 and for the siblings, averaged by families, 89.2. This difference of 5.3 points is less than twice the standard deviation of the difference and cannot be considered a reliable difference.

We may summarize the findings of this study thus:

1. The Stanford-Binet appears to be a reliable test for 66 children who were tested twice with the test. The correlation between the first and second test is .90 ± .0.

2. There is no clear indication of a relationship between level of intelligence and age at onset of crippling.

3. There is some tendency for intelligence level to decrease as the degree of crippling decreases.

4. These crippled children tend to resemble their siblings in intelligence.

In 1931 Lee (14) reported the results of the use of the Stanford-Binet with 148 crippled children in the Children's Orthopedic Hospital in Seattle, Washington. The age range was from three to sixteen and the I.Q. range from 35 to 138 with a mean of 86.8. Lee also studied the relationship between level of intelligence and types of crippling conditions.

Crippling Condition	*Mean I.Q.*
Poliomyelitis	92
Spastic paralysis at birth	69
Tuberculosis—bone and joint	88
Miscellaneous	
Nutritional disorders	83
Infections (not central nervous system)	92
Traumatic disorders	86
Central nervous system involvement	74
Congenital deformities	61

The highest I.Q., 138, was a tuberculosis case and the two next highest, 122 and 130, were in the poliomyelitis group. In general these children came from homes of low social-economic status and Lee believes that they might have been of inferior mental ability even if they had not been physically handicapped.

Witty and Smith (33) report the testing of 1,480 children in schools for crippled children in Chicago, St. Louis, Mo., Cleveland, and Toledo. Three hundred and fifty children were tested with the Kuhlmann-Anderson Test, the rest with the Stanford-Binet. The range of I.Q. was from 50 to 130 with a mean of 84.5. The following table shows the *percentage* distribution of in-

Intelligence Quotients	*Percentage Distribution of Intelligence Quotients* I	II	III	IV	V	VI	VII	VIII	Total
130–139	.5	–	.5	1.8	0.4	0.5	2.0	2	.8
120–129	1.0	2	1.0	0.6	0.4	1.0	0.6	3	1.15
110–119	10.0	7	6.0	7.0	6.0	6.0	5.0	2	6.4
100–109	14.0	18	18.0	14.0	15.0	15.0	15.0	18	15.9
90–99	24.0	29	27.0	22.0	25.0	30.0	30.0	28	26.8
80–89	21.0	23	26.0	27.0	23.0	21.0	31.0	31	24.9
70–79	16.0	14	15.0	22.0	20.0	20.0	15.0	13	17.3
60–69	10.0	6	4.0	2.0	8.0	6.0	2.0	2	5.5
50–59	3.0	–	2.5	1.8	1.0	—–	—–	–	1.15
Mean I.Q.:	84.44	93.62	93.57	84.52	84.38	93.53	84.60	93.80	84.5

telligence quotients in grades I–VIII. It is evident that nearly 50 per cent of the cases at each age level fall below 90 I.Q.

The authors compare their crippled group with two groups of unselected elementary school children. The small number of high I.Q.'s among the crippled is very noticeable.

Percentage Distribution of I.Q.'s

Intelligence Quotients Intervals	*1,480 Crippled Children*	*Witty 1,000 Children Grades I–VIII*	*Madsen 880 Children Grades I–VIII*
140–149	0.0	.03	0.2
130–139	.8	2.0	1.7
120–129	1.15	6.5	8.1
110–119	6.4	14.3	17.4
100–109	15.9	31.6	28.5
90–99	26.8	25.3	23.1
80–89	24.9	10.8	12.4
70–79	17.3	7.2	6.4
60–69	5.5	1.7	1.8
50–59	1.15	.3	0.2
40–49	0.00	.2	0.3

A further comparison with Witty's 1,000 unselected school children and 670 blind children is interesting, showing the per cent of blind, sighted, and crippled children in seven I.Q. categories. It seems to indicate that the blind are superior to the crippled, but this apparent difference cannot be accepted at face value. Although the two groups were tested with the Binet the results are not directly comparable, since the Hayes adaptation of the Binet for the blind is somewhat easier than the Stanford-Binet and might thus be expected to yield somewhat higher results. However the study does show that the in-

Classification	*670 Blind*	*1,000 Sighted*	*1,480 Crippled*
Genius	0.3	0.5	0.0
Very superior	1.0	2.0	.8
Superior	5.0	9.0	7.5
Average	68.0	76.0	42.7
Dull	12.0	8.0	24.9
Borderline	7.0	2.0	17.3
Feeble-minded	5.0	0.3	6.7
Median I.Q.	90.0	100.0	85.0

tellectual status of these crippled children is noticeably below that of unselected children.

Gordon, Roberts, and Griffiths (9) tested 98 poliomyelitis cases in the Bath and Wessen Orthopedic Hospital and Clinic. These children ranged in age from four to sixteen. Intelligence quotients, based on the Binet, ranged from 50 to 149 with a mean I.Q. of 103.9. The mean I.Q. for the boys was 105.5 and for the girls 102.1. This difference is not statistically significant. These means are significantly higher than the mean of the school population of Bath, the city from which most of the children came. The mean I.Q. for the total school group was 98.8.

In a partially completed study by Stanton, form L of the Terman-Merril-Binet was administered to 300 crippled children in New York, Connecticut, and Massachusetts. The group included cripples of all types except cerebral palsies. The range of I.Q. was from 35 to 140, with a mean I.Q. of 88. As in the other studies reported, the mean for the poliomyelitis group, 94, was higher than for any other group.

A measure of the intelligence level of the families of these crippled children was obtained by averaging the I.Q. of the next younger and next older sibling of each crippled child. Data are available for 100 families. The mean I.Q. for the crippled children is 86 and that of the families, as represented by average of the next younger and next older sibling, is 90. This is not a statistically reliable difference.

One hundred crippled children whose crippling condition would permit free use of performance-test material have been given the Pintner-Paterson Short Performance Scale. The age range of this group is from seven to twelve, the I.Q. range from 40–150 with a mean of 90.

SCHOOL ACHIEVEMENT

We have been able to find only one report of the school achievement of crippled children. Barbour (2) reported that of 40 poliomyelitis cases, 9 were retarded one year, 4 were retarded two years, and 2 were retarded three years in school. She does not report any acceleration. Employment records indicate considerable variation in educational experience of cripples. Conversations with teachers from various parts of the country reveal a tendency to have crippled children follow the curriculum of normal children. We have no general picture of the educational status of these children. Nilson (23) reports considerable retardation among "physically disabled children" in the Minnesota schools. It is not possible from his figures to sort out different types of handicapped. Hill (11) reports that crippled children in England and Wales are "from one and a half to two years in arrears of average school achievement."

PERSONALITY

Rosenbaum (26) administered the 1929 edition of the Thurstone Personality Schedule to a group of forty-three girls who were spending their third summer in a charity camp for crippled children. These girls ranged in age from sixteen to twenty-five, with a mean of 18.5.

The mean score on the Thurstone was 69. Six months later 36 of these girls, who had returned to their homes, filled out the Thurstone schedule again. This time the mean score was 68. The mean score for college freshmen, a comparable age group, is 40. Thurstone makes the following interpretation of scores:

0–14	Extremely well adjusted
15–29	Well adjusted
30–59	Average
60–79	Emotionally maladjusted
80–	Should have psychiatric advice

Apparently this small group of crippled girls tend, on the average, to be maladjusted. There was a slight tendency for the older girls to be less well adjusted than the younger girls. We must, of course, have more evidence before we can draw any conclusions concerning the emotional adjustment of cripples.

Barbour (2) studied the adjustment of sixty children crippled by poliomyelitis whom she divided into three groups:

1. Educationally paralyzed—paralyzed to such a degree as definitely to impede his educational progress.

2. Occupationally crippled—although the child can lead a quite normal childhood there would be a great possibility of his paralysis prohibiting him from certain occupations in later life.

3. Socially handicapped—a disfiguring paralysis which, although it did not interfere with his physical life, might be a source of social embarrassment.

She compares their condition in 1930 and in 1934, showing considerable physical improvement:

Type of handicap	*Condition in 1930*		*Condition in 1934*	
	number	*per cent*	*number*	*per cent*
Total	60	100	41	100
Educational	16	26.7	1	2.4
Occupational	11	18.3	9	22.0
Social	33	55.0	10	24.4
No paralysis	0	0	21	51.2

She says that the twenty-one children who have completely recovered from the disease "seem to have no darker memories of it than of an attack of measles." They are a normally happy group, one of whom is described by his teacher as the happiest boy in the class. Only six of the group who are still paralyzed are emotionally maladjusted to their handicap.

Strauss (30) suggests that in certain classroom situations the crippled showed a lack of initiative. She reported complete docility in following assignments and states that these children seldom brought in clippings, pictures, or other material unless specifically requested to do so. While the faculty had earnestly set the stage for student government, the children did not ask for the privilege nor were they willing to accept this responsibility when the opportunity was offered them directly.

Alumni of the school showed willingness to follow the suggestions of the case workers but seldom offered any suggestions of their own.

Strauss suggests that lack of experience, oversolicitude of parents, and possible feeling of inferiority may be responsible for a lack of initiative. Often the school and hospital encourage docility to too great a degree. It would seem worth while to determine whether lack of initiative really is a characteristic of crippled children and, if it is, to devise means of overcoming it

Brockway (4), writing of spastic children, reports them to be shy and to have serious feelings of inferiority.

Rogers and Thomas (25) say of spastic children: ". . . as a class these children are unstable emotionally and in most cases this carries over into adulthood."

Two studies of the adjustment of hospitalized children have some significance for the crippled child. Kanner and Lachman (13) discuss the effect of hospitalization upon behavior disorders of children who were ward or dispensary patients at the Harriet Lane Home for Invalid Children. These children seemed to fall into three classes: those with no appreciable aberration of behavior; originally stable children who developed behavior problems while ill; and unstable children in whom illness increased behavior problems. They list as contributing factors:

1. The nature of the illness,
2. The child's personality,
3. Parents' attitude,
4. Physician's influence.

McGrew (16) reports the common fears of 189 hospitalized. She found fear of strangers in 13 per cent of her cases. Fear of the strangeness of the hospital was encountered most often in the group seven to nine years old. Thirty-six per cent of the children were afraid of things they had heard talked about at home and at school, but did not understand. Only one child seemed to be afraid that he would die. Fears were most numerous among the group seven to twelve.

Kammerer (12) reports a study of fifty cases of scoliosis and thirty cases of osteomyelitis at the James Whitcomb Riley Hospital. The mean age for the scoliosis group was 13.76 and for the osteomyelitis group 12.64.

Total scores on the Rogers Test of Personality Adjustment indicate normal adjustment. These children rated within average limits on all of the subtests, and better than average on the Family Relationship Score. He found a low positive correlation between duration of crippling and maladjustment. Interpreting both test results and the results of interviews with the children and their parents, Kammerer concludes that there is no evidence that maladjustment inevitably results from crippling.

SOCIAL COMPETENCE

Bradway (3) used the Vineland Social-Maturity Scale with seven boys at Babbitt Hospital who showed various degrees of crippling associated with intracranial damage at birth. Four of these boys were athetoids affected in all four extremities and in speech. Three were spastics with the handicap confined to the legs. The Stanford-Binet I.Q.'s of these seven boys (corrected to allow for limitations of expression) were between 96 and 107.

The Social Quotients of the four athetoids were about 30; that of the spastics 70. Miss Bradway felt there were no items of the scale which seemed inapplicable to these crippled subjects. Each failure of an item represented a genuine social incompetence. All seven of these boys showed a special difficulty in the locomotion items. The four boys whose arms as well as legs were affected showed additional difficulty with occupation and self-help items.

Another group of twenty-seven children classified both as crippled and feeble-minded were checked on the Vineland Social-Maturity Scale. The degree of crippling in these cases varied from mild tremors to severe crippling of all four extremities. Twenty-three of these children showed no inferiority due directly to crippling, while the remaining four were obviously handicapped on certain items of the scale because of crippling.

Stanton used the Vineland Social-Maturity Scale with the same children, who were compared in intelligence with their noncrippled siblings. The mean social quotient for the crippled group was 80 and for the noncrippled siblings 90. Those who had leg crippling showed the greatest lack in items concerned with locomotion, and those with arm cripplings were most deficient in self-help items.

VOCATIONAL ADJUSTMENT

Hathway (10) reports a study of 50 crippled young men and women who had been referred to the Chicago Division of Rehabilitation by special schools in the city. Included in the group were 8 young women and 42 young men ranging in age from sixteen to thirty. Of the group, 41 were under twenty-one years of age. Crippling had been caused by disease in 37 cases; by public accident in 7 cases; by employment accident in 3 cases; and by congenital defects in the remaining 3 cases.

There was considerable variation in the amount of education: 5 had completed less than the eighth grade; 18 had completed the eighth; 9 the ninth; 4 the tenth; 4 the eleventh; 8 the twelfth; and 2 the first year of college.

Of this group of 50 crippled persons, 30 had made a definite choice as to their training program. In two cases were the choices disapproved. The following training was provided:

7 entered liberal arts courses at an institution of collegiate rank
3 studied law
7 enrolled in courses in business practice
6 were given training in commercial art
4 were trained in mechanical drawing or drafting
2 were given training in millinery
6 were trained in automobile mechanics
7 were trained as commercial telegraphers

2 were trained in radio telegraphy
4 were given music lessons
1 learned watchmaking
1 was placed as a telephone operator

At the time this report was made 19 were still in training; 18 were working: 1 had discontinued his trade because of illness; 2 were not working; and 10 were not located.

Hathway includes in her report a study of a random group of 100 alumni of the Spaulding and Fallon Schools in Chicago. This group consisted of 50 men and 50 women, 79 of whom were between eighteen and twenty-five years of age. The table which follows shows the school grades completed by the group.

School Grade Completed by 100 Crippled Adults	*Total* 100	*Male* 50	*Female* 50
Less than grade VIII	10	5	5
Grade VIII and less than IX	65	31	34
Grade IX and less than X	3	1	2
Grade X and less than XI	10	5	5
Grade XI and less than XII	2	2	0
Grade XII and over	10	6	4

In addition to this academic training 16 of the men and 11 of the women had received additional vocational training.

The crippling in this group varied considerably. Some of the individuals wore braces, used canes or crutches, had artificial limbs, or were confined to wheelchairs. It is interesting to note the occupations in which these people were working successfully. Among the men we find jobs such as office occupations, business proprietorship, express trucking, auto repairing, linotype operating, printing, woodwork, telegraphy, shoe repairing, selling, painting, the designing of greeting cards, tutoring, operating elevator, messenger work, and factory work. Among the women we find office jobs including those of stenographer, file clerk, cashier, business-machine operator, business proprietor, factory worker, dressmaker, milliner, practical nurse, bookbinder, telephone operator, and teacher of shorthand. In all the occupations men reported thirty-five different jobs, and the women twenty-six.

The study points out certain difficulties in the placement of crippled workers: (1) attitude of employers toward handicapped workers; (2) use of physical examinations in eliminating prospective employees; (3) the possible added cost to the employer under the provisions of the Workmen's Compensation Act, and (4) difficulties of transportation to and from the place of work.

Anderson (1) studied the case histories of 4,404 orthopedic disabled men who had applied to the Employment Center for the Handicapped in New York City. These men ranged in age from 14 to 84, with a median age of 31. Of the group, 66 per cent were under 40 years of age. Information concerning formal education was available in only 2,295 or 52 per cent of the cases. We may summarize this information thus:

Amount of Formal Education	*Per Cent of Group*
Sixth grade or less	18
Eighth grade	40
Entered high school	24
Completed high school course	4
Entered college	4
Completed college course	1

In general it would seem that the majority of these men were handicapped educationally as well as physically. Only 11 per cent of the total group reported having received special vocational training after disablement.

The causes of crippling were, in order of frequency: disease 35 per cent, public accidents 30 per cent, industrial accidents

20 per cent, congenital conditions 6 per cent, miscellaneous causes 3 per cent, and 6 per cent no information available. The data showed that 39 per cent of these men were disabled before the age of 15, 13 per cent between 15 and 24 years of age. The median age for all cases was 20.

Considerable variation was noted in the length of time a man held a job. There was a tendency for men with the most serious disabilities to stay longer on a job than did men with lesser disabilities. The weekly earning of these men ranged from $5.00 to $64.00, slightly below the earnings of nonhandicapped workers.

The reports show 1,762 kinds of jobs held by these disabled men of which 70 per cent were unskilled, 12 per cent semiskilled, 6 per cent skilled, and 12 per cent clerical. There was a tendency for men who had held semiskilled jobs before disablement to return to similar jobs after disablement. Some dropped to lower job levels, but it is encouraging to note that many made the adjustment and maintained their occupational status.

This study shows the need to educate employers to accept and use these handicapped workers successfully. In this connection the experience of the Western Electric Company (7) is interesting.

Over a period of a year 652 handicapped and 652 nonhandicapped workers were matched. The investigators concluded: "We are of the opinion that there is no real reason why people possessing certain vocational defects should not be employed by large concerns."

Between August, 1934, and March, 1935, an industrial survey of the physically handicapped was carried on in nineteen California cities (5). Of the population 3.1 per cent in the 15–55 year age group was reported to be physically handicapped; 45.1 per cent of these were classified as crippled.

Many kinds and degrees of crippling were found among the

employed group. About 14 per cent of these workers were using some sort of artificial appliance. This study too indicates that crippled workers are employed at many sorts of jobs. Their wages were reported as standard for the type of work done.

While not all employers were willing to hire handicapped workers, those who had done so found them to be satisfactory and often faithful and conscientious to a greater degree than the nondisabled. The conclusion is drawn that "trained disabled persons placed on suitable jobs make satisfactory employees."

A report on the physically handicapped in Philadelphia (28) indicates that a large number of these people are successfully employed. The crippled held the largest number of jobs, with the deaf next. The smallest group employed were in the tuberculous group. The crippled had a slightly larger proportion of unskilled employees than did the deaf, but they also had a larger proportion of professional workers than any other handicapped group.

The investigators found 708 employers favorably inclined toward handicapped workers; 417 mildly unfavorable; and 34 definitely antagonistic. Employers who had had considerable experience with handicapped workers said that these people were "extra anxious to make good."

Martens (18) suggests, in order of frequency of placements, the fields of service into which crippled children might go:

1. Office work, including bookkeeping, comptometer operation, filing, stenography and typing.

2. Personal service, including art needlework, beauty culture, child care, domestic service, dressmaking, and millinery.

3. Trades and industry, including armature winding, auto mechanics, baking, cabinet making, etc.

4. Professional and semiprofessional service, including chemistry, drafting, library work, music, social work.

5. Selling, including magazine agency, clerk, storekeeping.

6. Factory work, unspecialized as to type.

7. Miscellaneous jobs, including elevator operator, broadcasting worker, switchboard operator, filling-station employee, agricultural worker, chicken raising, etc.

SUMMARY

Studies of the intelligence of crippled children have been consistent in reporting a wide range of intelligence with the average intelligence quotient in the 80's. There is some evidence that children crippled by poliomyelitis are, on the average, superior mentally to other crippled children. We lack definite information concerning the school achievement of these children. In the field of personality so little work has been done that we cannot draw any conclusions. We need to know whether special problems arise with these children, and if so, how to meet them. Vocational studies indicate that there are many occupations in which the crippled may succeed.

BIBLIOGRAPHY

1. Anderson, R. N., *The Disabled Man and his Vocational Adjustment* (Inst. for the Crippled and Disabled, N.Y., 1932).
2. Barbour, E. H., "Adjustment during Four Years of Patients Handicapped by Poliomyelitis," *N. Eng. J. Med.*, CCXIII (1935), 563–5.
3. Bradway, K. P., "Social Competence of Exceptional Children," *J. Except. Child.*, IV:3 (Dec., 1937), 64–69.
4. Brockway, A., "The Problem of the Spastic Child," *J. Am. Med. Assoc.*, CVI (1936), 1635–9.
5. California, State of, *Census and Industrial Survey of the Physically Handicapped in California*, Dept. of Educ. Bull. No. 9 (1935).
6. Cleveland Welfare Federation, *Education and Occupation*

of Cripples, Juvenile and Adult. A Survey of All the Cripples of Cleveland, Ohio, in 1916 (N.Y. Inst. for Crippled and Disabled, May, 1918).

7. Dietz, J. W., "An Experiment with Vocationally Handicapped Workers," *Personnel Journal,* X:5 (1932).
8. Fernald, M. R., and A. H. Arlitt, "Psychological Findings Regarding Crippled Children," *Sch. and Soc.,* XXI (1925), 449–52.
9. Gordon, R. G., J. A. F. Roberts, and R. Griffiths, "Does Poliomyelitis Affect Intellectual Capacity?" *Brit. Med. J.,* II (1939), 803–5.
10. Hathway, M., *The Young Cripple and his Job* (Univ. of Chicago Press, Chicago, 1928).
11. Hill, A. H., "Education of Crippled Children in London and the British Isles," *The Crippled Child,* XVI (1938), 95–96.
12. Kammerer, R. C., "An Exploratory Psychological Study of Crippled Children," *Psychol. Record,* IV (1940), 47–100.
13. Kanner, L., and S. E. Lachman, "The Contribution of Physical Illness to the Development of Behavior Disorders in Children," *Ment. Hyg.,* XVII (1933), 605–17.
14. Lee, M. V., "The Children's Hospital; A Survey of the Intelligence of Crippled Children," *J. Educ. Research,* XXIII (1931), 164–7.
15. Lord, E. E., *Children Handicapped by Cerebral Palsy: Psychological Factors in Management* (Commonwealth Fund, N.Y., 1937).
16. McGrew, J. W., "Emotional Adjustments of the Hospitalized Child," *The Crippled Child,* XVIII (1940), 7–9.
17. McLeod, B., "The Status of Education of Crippled Children in Rural Areas," *The Crippled Child,* XI (1933), 17–20.
18. Martens, E. H., *Occupational Experiences of Handicapped Adolescents in Day School,* U.S. Office of Educ., Bull. No. 30 (1937).
19. Michigan Crippled Children Commission 1932–1934, *Report* (Lansing, Mich., 1934).

20. New Jersey State Crippled Children's Commission, *Report* (Trenton, N.J., 1932).
21. New York City, Commission for the Study of Crippled Children, *The Crippled Child in New York City* (1940).
22. New York State Commission for the Survey of Crippled Children, *Report* (1924–25).
23. Nilson, K., "An Age-Grade Study of Physically Disabled Pupils in Minnesota Public-Schools," *Elem. Sch. J.*, XXIII (1932), 122–9.
24. Phelps, W., "The Treatment of Cerebral Palsy," *The Crippled Child,* XVI (1938), 16–17.
25. Rogers, G. G., and L. C. Thomas, "Emotional Adjustment of the Spastic Child," *The Crippled Child,* XVI (1938), 16–24, 91–93.
26. Rosenbaum, B. B., "Neurotic Tendencies in Crippled Girls," *J. Abn. and Soc. Psychol.*, XXXI (1937), 423–9.
27. Schwendener, N., *Game Preferences of 10,000 Grade Children,* T. C. Contribs. to Educ. (Bur. of Pubs., Teachers College, Columbia Univ., N.Y., 1932).
28. Solenberger, E. R., "Philadelphia Studies Her Physically Handicapped," *The Crippled Child,* XIII (1935), 109, 110, 128.
29. Stevenson, J. L., *A Community Trust Survey of Crippled Children in Chicago* (Community Trust, Chicago, 1925).
30. Strauss, M., "Initiative and the Crippled Child," *The Crippled Child,* XIII:6 (1936), 164, 165, 182.
31. White House Conference on Child Health and Protection, *The Mentally and Physically Handicapped* (Century, N.Y., 1931).
32. Wisconsin, State of, *Care and Education of Crippled Children,* Dept. of Public Instruct., Bull. No. 1 (Madison, Wisc., 1933).
33. Witty, P. A., and M. B. Smith, "The Mental Status of 1480 Crippled Children," *Educ. Trends,* I (1932), 22–24.

CHAPTER X

Other Physically Handicapped Groups

We have included in this chapter a group of physically handicapped children, some of whom fall within the category of the "delicate child."

THE ALLERGIC

General. Allergy is defined as an altered reactivity of the organism. The allergic individual is sensitive to certain substances which are entirely innocuous to the average individual. One may be allergic to a great many substances: to foods, inhalants such as dust, pollen, feathers, and animal dander, or to silk, wool, or chemicals. A person may be sensitive to one or many substances. Some patients appear to be sensitive to such physical agents as heat and cold. It is not known why people are allergic. Estimates of the incidence of allergy vary from 1 to 15 per cent of the population.

Eczema, asthma, hay fever, hives, and swelling of lips and eyelids are common manifestations. In infants, eczema is the most common type.

Nilson (3) studied the evidence of asthma, hay fever, and allergic dermatosis in 1,786 persons and found that in the first decade these conditions appear twice as often in males as in females in a ratio of three to one. After that the sex distribution is approximately equal.

Intelligence. In 1929 Balyeat (1) reported that the "mental activity of allergic children is far above the average normal." He bolsters this opinion with the statement that in spite of the fact that these children are often absent from school they accomplished their schoolwork with ease.

In 1935 Sullivan (5) reported a study of 145 allergic children at the Children's Hospital in Los Angeles. These children ranged in age from 5 to 15–4 with a median age of 8 years, 11 months. Of the group, 75 per cent were asthmatic. In this experiment Sullivan administered the Stanford-Binet Test to 45 cases; the Goodenough Drawing Test to 104 cases; the National Intelligence Test to all children over eight years of age who could read; and the Detroit Primary to all children under eight. The median I.Q.'s are summarized below.

Test	*Median I.Q.*	*No. of Cases*
Stanford-Binet	103	45
Goodenough	100	104
Detroit Primary	103	44
N.I.T.	110	61
Average of three	104	145

He makes a comparison (table, p. 286) between his allergic group and a large group of children in the Los Angeles public schools. He concludes that "children with asthma are very similar in intellectual level to a normal group . . . there may be some indication that the incidence of allergy is less in the feebleminded group."

School Progress. As to school progress, he noted that 22 per cent of these children were retarded one year or more; 11 per cent were accelerated one or more years; and that the remain-

	Allergic		*Los Angeles City School Children*
I.Q.	*Stanford-Binet*	*average of three tests*	*group test*
140 +	.0	.6	
130–139	4.4	5.5	1.2
120–129	8.8	12.4	3.3
110–119	18.0	15.1	10.2
100–109	26.6	27.5	21.8
90–99	25.5	22.7	27.3
80–89	6.6	13.7	20.6
70–79	0	1.3	10.6
Below	0	.6	3.8
No. of cases	45	145	63,114
Median I.Q.	103	104	105

ing 67 per cent were progressing normally in school. He felt that school retardation might be accounted for in part by considerable absence from school.

Relationship between Allergies and Psychological Ailments. Kling (2) reports a study of relationships between neurasthenic, dyspeptic, and allergic symptoms. A questionnaire containing a list of 160 such symptoms was answered by 808 students attending psychology classes at the University of Texas. He concluded that "many of the physiological symptoms of allergy and dyspepsia have a mental origin in the same personality maladjustments, mental stresses, and emotional strains that may produce neurasthenic symptoms, and that, vice versa, a considerable number of neurasthenic symptoms have a physiological origin in obscure and poorly recognized disorders such as allergy.

Thorndike (6) used an abbreviated form of Kling's questionnaire with 594 students at George Washington University. He found the best traits for differentiating between allergic and nonallergic subjects to be:

Slowness in making up mind, difficulty in making decisions;
Difficulty in thinking, need to grope for ideas;
Feeling of general inferiority;
Excessive self-consciousness;
Dreading round of daily tasks;
Feelings of vague uneasiness.

He concludes that there appears to be some relationship between allergy and neurasthenic traits.

THE CARDIAC

General. Adequate statistics are not available to show the incidence of heart disease among children in the United States, but Smith (17) states that it ranks first as the cause of death among schoolgirls and second among schoolboys. The incidence varies from one part of the country, and is highest in the northeastern part of the United States. Master (13) estimates about two million cases in the total population.

The chief cause of heart disease among children is rheumatic fever, an infectious disease, the cause of which is not known. Poverty, poor housing, and cold damp weather are associated with rheumatic fever. Smith (17) notes that the disease is rarely seen among private patients, but is common in the clinic. In spite of the fact that rheumatic fever is an infectious disease it does not run a self-limited course like pneumonia or typhoid, but is a chronic infection. As the infection subsides, the acute process in the heart muscle recovers a large part of its function. The valves, however, become scarred and deformed. Rauh (14) reports that in localities where rheumatic fever is prevalent 80 per cent of the children with organic heart disease have rheumatic valvulitis.

Rheumatic fever is most commonly contracted by young children. An English report (7) states that two thirds of acute rheumatic infections are contracted between the ages of five and fifteen; Wilson, Linogg, and Crawford (18) place onset at six to nine years of age for half of their cases; 75 per cent of De Porte's (11) cases contracted the disease before they were ten years old; and Boas (8) considers the years from five to nine the most common period of onset. Girls are somewhat more susceptible to heart disease than boys.

We have been able to find only one study of the intelligence of cardiacs. Ross (15) tested with the Binet 22 patients, aged five to fourteen, at the Harriet Lane Home in Baltimore. All of these children had organic heart disease. Intelligence quotients ranged from 50 to 117. Only 18 per cent of these children had intelligence quotients between 91 and 110 as against 32 per cent of 1,000 other children tested in the Harriet Lane Psychiatric Clinic.

Schoolwork. Some little information concerning the school work of cardiacs is contained in a report by Brown (9). A report to the New York City Board of Education in 1927 stated that "The school records of children classified as I or IIA in trade classes compare favorably with those of children who do not have heart disease. Those classified as IIB were absent more and could not carry on the normal work without frequent rest periods and constant supervision." It was recommended that only those children classified as I and IIA should take training. These classifications refer to the classification of patients with organic heart disease agreed upon by the Heart Committee of the New York Tuberculosis and Health Association (10). A part of the classification description follows:

Class I. Patients with organic heart disease able to carry on ordinary physical activity without discomfort. Ordinary physical activity does not cause undue fatigue, palpitation, dyspnea, or

chest pain. Patients in this class do not show physical signs of congestion heart failure, or signs of active heart infection.
Class II. Patients with organic heart disease unable to carry on ordinary physical activity without discomfort.

A. Activity Slightly Limited.

Ordinary physical activity causes undue fatigue, palpitation, dyspnea, or chest pain. Patients in this class rarely show physical signs of congestive heart failure or signs of active infection.

B. Activity Greatly Limited.

Less than ordinary physical activity causes fatigue, palpitation, dyspnea or chest pain. Patients in this class usually show physical signs of congestion heart failure, the anginal syndrome, or signs of active heart infection.
Class III. Patients with organic heart disease and with symptoms and signs of heart failure at rest, unable to carry on any physical activity without discomfort.

It was further recommended that children classified as IIB or III should be excluded from trade training. Since children classified as I or IIA did as well as those not suffering from heart disease it was suggested that segregated trade classes for cardiacs be abolished. These classes were discontinued and the boys were sent to the Murray Hill Trade School and the girls were enrolled at the Manhattan Trade School.

Vocational Adjustment. The Cardiac Vocational Guidance Committee followed 477 boys and girls in junior and senior high schools and trade schools for a period of two years. Of the group 29 per cent took the commercial course; 27 per cent took the general course; and 44 per cent took trade courses. The latter included architectural drafting, mechanical drawing, electrical wiring, jewelry making, printing, optical lens work, commercial art, dressmaking, millinery, and novelty work. The only trades from which boys were excluded were automobile mechanics, sheet-metal work, and plumbing. Teaching was the only profession excluded. Few of these children were excused from prescribed curricula, and only a few dropped behind because of illness. The average absence for this group was 11.4 days out of a 200-day school year. Forty-four per cent were rated as unskilled. The mean weekly wage for the skilled was $19.34 and for the unskilled $16.01.

Emotional Adjustment. No study of emotional adjustment was found. Boas (8) says that in his opinion it "is a shock even to a child to be told that he has heart disease, that he must live a life different from that of his playmates, that he cannot join them freely in their daily activities and games. The child becomes heart-conscious and his whole life is colored by the knowledge of his cardiac disability." He suggests, too, that this may be aggravated by overanxious parents. Foster (12) has remarked that children affected with heart disease show a certain diffidence and lack of initiative in school and are prone to attribute any shortcoming to the heart condition. Such a claim should be investigated. Foster believes that considerable fear is associated with awareness of heart disease.

Sigel (16) writes of thirty-one cardiac patients in the Out-Patient Department of the Michael Reese Hospital in Chicago. Each was interviewed by a psychiatrist and fifteen were said to show mental conflict or emotional disturbance.

In spite of the fact that considerable attention has been given to the education of children suffering from heart disease we know remarkably little about them.

THE DIABETIC

General. Diabetes mellitus is a disorder of the functioning of the pancreas. Insulin, the internal secretion of that gland, is produced and absorbed in insufficient amounts. Sugar and starches are not efficiently utilized and indirectly the metabolism of all foods is deranged in time. Insulin obtained from the pancreas of animals can now be used to allow the diabetic patient to eat an essentially normal balanced diet. Joslin, Dublin, and Marks (20) write that with the use of insulin the diabetic child is no longer "marked for death." He is freed from the restricted life of a chronic invalid with a prospect of becoming a useful citizen. With the mortality rates which prevailed in 1933, 26 of every thousand female infants and 15 of every thousand male infants would succumb to diabetes mellitus. The incidence of the disease seems to be increasing in this country and decreasing in Europe. It is more prevalent in urban than in rural areas; more frequent in high social classes than in low; and least frequent in persons engaged in hard manual labor. Joslin, Root, *et al.* (22) reported in 1937 that one of every 8,000 children under fifteen in the United States was diabetic.

Before the use of insulin most diabetic children were underweight, and many were below normal height. Now they more nearly approach height-weight norms. Of forty-nine diabetic children, twenty-five girls and twenty-four boys, the boys more often than the girls were below height norms. One child was classified as a dwarf. Joslin, Root, and White (3) note that under insulin treatment diabetic children gain in weight but are somewhat under the norms.

Psychological Studies. Small groups of diabetics have been tested. In 1922 Miles and Root (24) reported the results of tests used with a group of 39 diabetic patients at the New England Deaconess Hospital. There were 17 men and 23 women ranging in age from fifteen to fifty-five years. They used a control group made up of physicians, nurses, and friends of the patients.

In the Woodworth and Wells Cancellation of Digits Test the diabetics' score was 48 per cent and that of the control group 61 per cent. The diabetics made 3.5 per cent of errors and the controls 3.1 per cent. Memory span for digits was used, with a span up to nine digits. Range for the diabetics was from 30 per cent to 81 per cent with a mean of 56 per cent. For fourteen control subjects the range was from 40 per cent to 100 per cent with a mean of 66 per cent. The average control subject could recall seven digits, while the average diabetic subject could barely recall six digits.

A test of memory span for four-letter words was used in which a list of twenty-five words was read at the rate of one per minute. When the list had been read the subjects wrote as many words as they could remember.

The range for the diabetics was from 0 to 11 with a mean of 3.9; for 18 controls the range was from 3 to 10 with a mean of 6.2; and for a group of medical students the range was from 3 to 13 with a mean of 7.0.

The fourth type of material used was simple one-place number addition. Numbers were printed in 12-point type, ten numbers in a column. A time limit of five minutes was set. The results are summarized below:

Group	*Columns: Range*	*Correctly Added: Mean*	*Average Number Wrong*
30 diabetics	2–28	14.0	3.0
17 controls	4–24	14.7	2.9
27 students	5–28	16.9	4.6

White (26) reports that of 167 cases 23 per cent had intelligence quotients of 110 and more; 54 per cent between 90 and 110 and 13 per cent below 90.

West, Richey, and Eyre (25) reported 60 cases in which the diabetic child was compared with his next older sibling. They used Intermediate and Advanced Otis Group Test and the Stanford-Binet. The distribution of intelligence quotients for the diabetics and their siblings is shown in the table.

	Diabetics			Siblings		
I.Q.	*male*	*female*	*total*	*male*	*female*	*total*
140–		1	1	2		2
130–139	1	2	3		1	1
120–129	4	1	5	2	1	3
110–119	3	5	8	3	2	5
90–109	11	15	26	9	5	14
80–89	3	7	10	1		1
70–79	1	4	5			
50–69		1	1	1	1	2
Total	23	37	60	18	10	28
Median	102.63	95.34	99.5			106.25
Mean	103.5	98.91	100.65			107

Of the diabetic group, 43 per cent fall within the normal range, with some at the upper end of the scale. The differences between the diabetics and their siblings are not significant. McGavin, Schultz, Peden, and Bowen (23) used Form L of the Binet * and Ferguson Form Boards with 49 diabetic children. The mean intelligence quotient was 103 ± 16.8. The correlation between the Binet and the Ferguson tests was .62 ± .06. Brown (19) says that in spite of poorer school attendance diabetic children compare favorably with their nondiabetic siblings. McGavin *et al.* (23) tested the school achievement of 29 diabetics, using the Stanford Achievement test for part of the group and the Metropolitan Achievement test for the others. They report that in 9 cases the achievement of these children was above the average of the grade in which they were placed, and in 9 cases it was below the average for their grade. They computed achievement quotients and found five over 100 and ten under 100.

Brown's (19) comparison of 46 diabetics and 21 siblings on the Woodworth-Cady Psycho-Neurotic Inventory yielded no

* One child was given the Hayes Revision because of a serious eye defect.

striking differences. The only personality changes which parents reported were increased irritability and excitability. McGavin *et al.* (23) report that the Rogers Test of Personality Adjustment (18 cases) showed some tendency toward more social maladjustment and daydreaming than the standardization group. The Bernreuter Personality Scale used with 19 cases showed no definite pattern. In a psychiatric interview 9 of the 44 diabetics expressed a feeling of shame at having diabetes. Two reported that other children avoided them for fear diabetes was "catching." One showed "shut-in personality." The earlier the disease developed the more readily did the child accept his condition emotionally.

White (26) writes that diabetic children should not be permanently excused from school. She finds that most occupations are open to diabetics. He should, however, avoid jobs in which he is open to infections, such as nursing. She also rules out driving an automobile, boat, or plane. Farming is considered an ideal occupation for boys and teaching dietetics, library and secretarial work, and playground and physical education work are highly recommended for girls.

There is so little information available that one cannot safely draw conclusions. Such evidence as we have points toward normal intelligence and satisfactory school adjustment.

THE ENCEPHALITIC

General. Encephalitis is an acute infectious disease of the brain, the cause of which has not been definitely established. Appel (27) writes, "Whether the condition is associated with influenza and its bacillus, with a neurotropic streptococcus, or a filtrable virus is not definitely known."

The Matheson Committee (41) reports that in "epidemic encephalitis the onset is frequently very gradual and the process of the disease slow, in some instances requiring several months to reach its greatest severity." This same committee reported in 1929 that the disease was then more prevalent in the United Kingdom, Sweden, and Switzerland than in other European countries. They stated too that the disease was most prevalent during the winter months and that while it may attack persons of all ages, young adults are most susceptible.

Bond (29) says, "In proportion to the comparatively small number attacked, there is no infectious or contagious disease in this country (England) which produces so much consequent ill-health and disablement as does encephalitis lethargica." The chief sequelae of encephalitis are neurological and personality changes. The Parkinson syndrome is the chief neurological sequela, which Bond and Appel (30) describe as follows: "This consists of the gradual development of a stiff expressionless face which is called 'masklike.' There is general rigidity of muscle. The trunk is often found bent and the patient walks slowly and stiffly and does not swing his arms. Often there is an excessive production of saliva and the voice becomes monotonous. There may be rhythmic jerkings of the arms, hands, head, or jaws."

Changes in disposition may be slight or quite marked. These changes are most likely to happen if the onset of the disease occurs during the period between six and thirteen years. Jenkins and Ackerson (38) note such behavior as listlessness, quarreling, defiant attitude, emotional instability, crying spells, and restlessness. Bond and Appel (30) write that formerly orderly, cheerful children may become disorderly, disobedient, irritable; lie, cheat, steal, and often commit gross sexual offenses. They become brutal and often savage in their attitudes. There is often a marked restlessness with an aggressiveness that brooks no inhibition. Berrien (28) lists similar undesirable behavior. Gibbs (35) describes 144 patients at Kings Park Hospital. He notes some differences between the behavior of these cases and psychotic children.

Intelligence. Table IX summarizes several studies of the intelligence of encephalitic patients.

Hall (36) states that idiocy is practically limited to children who contract the disease at five years and younger. Hallowell (37) listed 24 cases with a battery of tests which included both verbal and performance material. She found some abnormality in 17 cases. Paterson and Spence found a "state of permanent and hopeless idiocy" in 7 of 25 children who were of normal health and intelligence before onset of the disease. Berrien (28) used a large battery of tests with 24 postencephalitic children and found that they rated "consistently below life age on all tests."

Inspection of the table reveals a wide variation in mental ability with a large proportion of the group at the lower end of the scale. Retests indicate a slight tendency toward a decrease in intelligence quotient. This decrease is slightly greater in those who acquire encephalitis before the age of ten.

Obviously these children are difficult to manage and we have no adequate provision for their care. Bond and Appel (30) experimented with a group of encephalitic children at the Pennsylvania Hospital. They concluded that the group method of handling these children under careful supervision is the best.

THE EPILEPTIC

General. Lennox (60) describes epilepsy as "a symptom in which there are recurring lapses of consciousness with or without convulsive manifestations." These lapses vary greatly both in frequency and in severity. Three types of seizures are commonly described in the literature: grand mal, petit mal, and epileptic equivalents.

TABLE IX

SUMMARY OF STUDIES OF INTELLIGENCE OF POSTENCEPHALITIC CHILDREN

Author	*Date*	*Test*	*Number of Cases*	*Age Range*	*Range of Mental Ability*	*Mean I.Q.*	*Retests: Mean Difference 2nd test minus the first*
Robin (44)	1923	Binet	11	7–13	Imbecile to normal	81 *	
Sherman and Beverly (46)	1923	Terman-Binet	20	3–19	High-grade defective to very superior	88	+5.06
Kwint (39)	1926	Binet	13	8–12	Borderline defective to superior	91 *	
Shrubsall (47)	1927	Binet	21	5–14	High-grade defective to average	82	−11.19
Lange (40)	1928	Bebertag-Binet	39	8–15	High-grade defective to average	83	−7.85
Bromberg (32)	1930	Terman-Binet	15	8–21	High-grade defective to average	73	
Scott (45)	1930	Terman-Binet	35	3–24	High-grade defective to very superior	88	−2.0
Bond and Appel (30)	1931	Terman-Binet	48	6–14	High-grade defective to superior	85	+8.2
Dawson and Conn (34)	1931	Burt-Binet	50	3–13	High-grade defective to superior	85	−13÷46
Jenkins and Ackerson (38)	1934	Terman-Binet	57	5–29	Idiot to very superior	75	−2.3

* Median I.Q.

In grand mal there is loss of consciousness, causing the patient to fall. There is a tonic contraction of all the muscles of the body, so that the patient "stiffens out." This is followed by a clonic phase. The patient does not remember what happened during the period of the attack.

In petit mal attacks the patient loses consciousness for only a short time. He may pause in what he is doing, and then go on as if nothing had happened.

In the third type the patient may act with apparent intelligence or he may seem confused. There is amnesia for the period of the attack.

Lennox (60) estimates that 50 per cent of his noninstitutional cases have grand mal seizures, 34 per cent have a combination of grand mal and petit mal, 9 per cent have petit mal alone, and 7 per cent have periods of amnesia without either grand mal or petit mal. Sullivan and Gahagan (68) report that 80 per cent of their cases had major seizures, while at Craig Colony (62) it was reported that 94 per cent were subject to major attacks.

There seems to be no single cause of epilepsy. According to Wilkins (70), "It is generally recognized that the epilepsies may be due to many different causes and may take many different forms."

The true incidence of epilepsy in the general population is not known. Lennox (60) reports that between 2 and 5 per cent of young male adults reporting for military service in several countries have been diagnosed as epileptic. He believes that this estimate is somewhat low. He states also that there is really no significant sex difference in spite of the fact that males outnumber females in institutions for epileptics.

Although epileptic seizures may begin at almost any age, Gowers (57) wrote that in 55 per cent of his cases seizures had begun before the tenth year. Fay (54) found that of 6,075 cases admitted to Craig Colony 30 per cent were known to have had epileptic seizures before the fifth birthday; 18 per cent between the fifth and tenth birthday; and 19 per cent between the tenth and fifteenth birthday. Shanahan (67) reported that in 28 per cent of 7,000 institutional admissions there was a record of epileptic seizure before the fifth birthday. Paskind (65) found that only 11.6 per cent of 304 private patients had seizures before the fifth birthday. Of the cases studied by Sullivan and Gahagan (68) 67.6 had seizures at five years or earlier. They also found a slight tendency for onset to be earlier in males than in females.

Intelligence. There has long been considerable interest in the intelligence of epileptics. In 1881 Gowers (57) reported that 64 cases of a total of 1,450 showed "considerable mental defect." Turner (69) reported that 44 per cent of 159 epileptic patients of all ages were "bright, active and intelligent," except for some defect of memory. We do not know the criteria for these judgments.

Fox (56) reported testing 99 boys and 51 girls in an English training colony for epileptics. These children, who ranged in age from five to sixteen, were tested with the Burt revision of the Binet-Simon Scale. The mean I.Q. for the boys was 71 and for the girls, 65. He found that "tests which epileptic children find harder (than do normal children) include those where immediate memory is concerned, where written language is especially involved, where there are abstract questions to be solved, calling for concentration and reasoning, and finally where the use of coins as in everyday life is tested." It would seem that failure on the last mentioned item might be accounted for in part by the fact that these children lived in an institution and probably had no opportunity to use money.

Ninde (63) used auditory memory span for digits as a measure of intelligence with approximately 2,000 epileptic patients in three state institutions. These patients ranged in age from five to fifty. He found their memory span to be about half of that of normal individuals of the same age. From his data he concluded that 36 per cent of his group were feeble-minded. We may well question the use of this one type of material as a measure of intelligence.

Cookson (52) reported that 26 of 100 epileptics in the Glasgow Royal Hospital for Sick Children showed "a deficiency of mentality more or less marked; in all the others it was normal. When mental deficiency was present it had been noticed as early as the fits."

Patterson and Fonner (66) used the Stanford-Binet with 128 institutional epileptic children and adolescents and found an intelligence quotient range from 38 to 114. Dawson and Conn, using the Burt revision of the Binet with 49 epileptics, report a range of 49 to 117 with a mean intelligence quotient of 80.65 ± 1.43. This was lower than the average of the other hospital children examined.

Fetterman and Barnes (55) found the average intelligence quotient of a group of 105 dispensary patients to be 74 as measured on the Stanford-Binet. The range for this group was from 34 to 133; 40 per cent were below 70 I.Q. and only 17 per cent were of average intelligence.

Sullivan and Gahagan (68) studied the intelligence of 63 male and 40 female epileptic patients at the Childrens Hospital in Los Angeles. The Stanford-Binet was used with most of the group. However, it was necessary to use the Kuhlmann-Binet and the Gesell Normative Schedules of Development to reach a small group. The intelligence quotients ranged from 11 to 141 with a mean of 88 and a median of 92.4. They make an interesting comparison of the intelligence of their epileptic group and several other groups.

		Los Angeles City Schools	*Childrens Hosp. Allergy Group*	*Childrens Hosp. Epileptic Group*	*Dawson & Conn Epileptic Group*
Number of cases		63,147	45	103	49
Classification	*I.Q.*	*Percentage*	*Percentage*	*Percentage*	*Percentage*
Superior	110+	36.5	31.2	19.3	6.1
Average	90–109	47.9	62.1	36.8	20.3
Dull normal	80–89	10.6	6.6	19.4	24.4
Borderline	70–79	3.8	0.0	5.8	26.5
Feeble-minded	below 70	1.3	0.0	18.4	22.4

Brown (51) studied the relatives of 36 patients at the Ohio State Hospital for epileptics and found that 64 per cent had one or more epileptic relatives; 28 per cent had a psychotic relative; 25 per cent had mentally defective relatives; and 89 per cent had relatives who were epileptic, insane, or mentally deficient.

Mental deterioration of the epileptic patient has often been taken for granted. Retests of patients will throw some light on this matter. Fox (56) retested 130 cases with the Burt-Binet after a period of one year. He found that 37 per cent of his cases had lower scores, 22 per cent had higher scores, and 41 per cent had not changed more than 2 points in either direction. Eleven patients lost more than 10 points while only one patient gained more than 10 points. There was marked deterioration in about 8 per cent of his cases.

Patterson and Fonner (66) tested 98 subjects (51 boys, 47 girls) twice, and 30 subjects (12 boys and 18 girls) three times with the Stanford-Binet. For the 51 boys the 22 range for the first test was from 38 to 114, and for the second test 45 to 113. The maximum gaining was 18 points and the maximum loss 17 points. For the 47 girls the range on the first test was from 47–109, and on the second from 42–109. The maximum loss was 9 and the maximum gain was 20. For the 12 boys and 18 girls who were tested three times we find the following record of change from one test to the next:

	Change from First Test to Second		*Change from Second Test to Third*	
	boys	*girls*	*boys*	*girls*
No change	2	10	3	6
Gain	5	6	4	8
Loss	5	2	5	4

They conclude that epileptic children show considerable variation from time to time in either direction.

Lennox (60) cites neurological reports of 1,328 private and clinic patients which found 65 per cent normal mentally, 24 per cent slightly deteriorated, and 11 per cent definitely deteriorated. Patients with petit mal showed the least deterioration. He reports that deterioration increased with the passing of years, but tends to be stabilized after ten years.

Paskind (65) does not tell us how he determined whether or not his "extramural" patients had deteriorated but he states that "93.4 per cent were found to be in excellent mental health, without the slightest trace of deterioration or other psychosis, and engaged in occupations similar to those of the great mass of the population."

Fetterman and Barnes (55) retested 46 patients in a dispensary group. Of these cases 4 had not changed, 19 showed a "slight increase," and 23 a "moderate loss."

Sullivan and Gahagan (68) retested 44 cases at intervals varying from 1 month to 4 years and 11 months. The range for the first test was from 24 to 141 with a median of 95; the range on the second test was from 26 to 130. Sullivan and Gahagan found no characteristic differences between males and females in variability. Barnes and Fetterman (48) retested 35 epileptic patients from three to eight times. They found fluctuations, but only one patient with regular losses. The relationship between deterioration and such factors as severity of attack, age of onset, and frequency of attack is not definitely established. Dawson and Conn (53) and Fetterman and Barnes state that severity of attack and subsequent mental level are not significantly related, while Grinker states that there is some quantitative relationship between mental deterioration and severity of attack. Grinker (58) and Paskind (65) assert that there is a relationship between age of onset and mental deterioration. Sullivan and Gahagan (68) also found a small, but statistically significant difference between the group having onset of convulsions between birth and ten years, and a group having onset between six and twelve years. The mean I.Q. for the former was 82.87 and for the latter 90.43.

Patterson and Fonner (66) and Dawson and Conn (53) report no significant correlation between frequency of attack and subsequent mental level. Grinker (58), on the other hand, reports that the two are related. Paskind (65) found that nondeteriorated patients tended to have fewer attacks than the deteriorated. Worster-Drought (71) concludes that frequency and deterioration are not related.

Personality. Branham (49) in 1926 mentioned emotional instability, stubbornness, willfulness, and boasting as characteristic epileptoid reactions. He said that the epileptic person rushes into things and is easily discouraged, he craves attention and cries easily; sometimes there is unwonted shyness and feeling of uncertainty. Lennox (60) notes that speech is monotonous, and that both mental and physical reactions are sluggish. The patient is unstable, irritable, and subject to fits of anger. He sometimes becomes overdependent. He believes that the treatment which he receives is partly responsible for this. Bridge (50) describes epileptoid personality as "self-centered, constantly demanding his own way and violently resenting interference. He is subject to outbursts of temper and is often moody and peevish." He adds that he is pugnacious, cruel, emotionally unstable, sensitive about his own difficulties. He finds him sluggish in body and mind, but sometimes capable of good mental performance if allowed sufficient time. Bridge believes that these characteristics are present often enough to warrant the assumption they are in some way "bound up in the very nature of the disease."

Grinker (58) writes that epileptics are "said to be egocentric, selfish, seclusive, and show tremendous outburst of emotions."

Harriman (59) used the Kohs Ethical Discrimination Test with 25 patients in a state colony who were subject to grand mal seizures. He used as a control group 25 individuals from a small college community, none of whom were known to have had epileptic seizures. The subjects were males who ranged in age from fifteen through fifty-six with a median age of twenty-eight. School experience ranged from fifth grade through the second year at college with a median of ninth grade. The Kohs Test includes six subtests: social relations, moral judgment, interpretation of proverbs, definition of moral terms, offense evaluation, and moral problems. Time limits were disregarded in administering the test.

The epileptic were markedly inferior on the first test. On the second test the average number of misjudgments for the epileptic was 5.76 and .24 for the controls. The performance on the interpretation of fables showed "utter failure to comprehend the meaning of simple proverbs."

In the definitions of moral terms the superiority of the normal group was "very great." The epileptic seemed greatly confused by the test which asked them to indicate the outcome which society should attach to certain acts. The epileptic group also made a poor showing on the "solutions to a moral problem."

The epileptic patients were inferior to the controls in each subtest and may be said to be inferior in ethical discrimination as measured by the Kohs test.

Sullivan and Gahagan (68) classified 44 of their 103 cases as having serious and continued personality difficulties. The mean intelligence quotient of this group was slightly lower than that of the total epileptic group. Epilepsy had begun earlier in the problem group. Almost without exception these children had come from bad homes.

Makhaeva (61) writing of the motor functions in epileptic children stated that on the whole movements of epileptic children can be characterized as slow, strong, and rather exact. He reports that motor endurance is pathologically high.

Summary. The epileptic are similar to the general population in range of intelligence, but the mean intelligence quotient for epileptic groups tested is lower than for the general population. Average intelligence quotients for the epileptic range from 65 to 88. Since most of these reports are based on studies of institutional cases the averages may be somewhat depressed. There is a greater proportion of epileptic cases at the lower end of the scale than one would find in the general population.

There is contradictory evidence concerning deterioration of epileptics, with the weight of evidence on the side of deterioration. However we cannot predict surely which patients will deteriorate nor how rapid the deterioration will be.

Disorders of personality and conduct may occur in epileptics but such disorders are by no means inevitable. The undesirable behavior most commonly found, namely, lying, stealing, fighting, sex misbehavior, cruelty, and destructiveness, is also found among well children with poor background and training.

THE MALNOURISHED

There has long been interest in the question of the effect of undernourishment on level of intelligence. We have no way of knowing the proportion of children who are undernourished. In periods of war, famine, and financial crises the incidence rises. Malnutrition, however, is not limited to the financially poor of the world.

In 1914 Baker (72) reported malnutrition in 2.9 per cent of school children in New York City. In those children who were retarded in school the incidence of malnutrition rose to 36.1 per cent. In 1929 Hunt, Johnson, and Lincoln (76) tested the intelligence of a small group of undernourished children. They found that in intellect these children "distribute themselves similarly to children of normal height-weight-age index."

Dowd (73) tested 110 New York City children with the Stanford-Binet; 55 of them were from a nutrition clinic and 55 from a general clinic. The two groups showed about the same distribution of intelligence quotients.

Nichols (79) used memory span for digits and opposites tests with 59 fifth-grade children in Baltimore. These children were 9 per cent or more underweight. They were compared with a normal-weight group of the same age. There was no significant difference between the two on memory span for digits and opposites tests, but the underweight group was inferior in tests of steadiness, fatigue, and strength of grip.

Pearson (81) stated in an editorial that "health and intelligence are correlated, but not very markedly. Smith and Field (83) report on 61 children in grades IV to VI who were 7 per cent or more underweight. They were given five months of intensive nutritional work which included instruction, food, and rest. They were tested with the National Intelligence Test at the beginning and end of this period. The children gained in weight beyond expectation but there was no corresponding mental growth. As a matter of fact the control group gained more points of I.Q. on the average than did the nutrition group.

Hoefer and Hardy (75) studied the mentality, school achievement, and nutrition of 450 Joliet children during a three-year health program. They found a consistent tendency for the student in better health to have higher intelligence and educational quotients than the less well nourished. The differences, however, were not statistically reliable. Paterson (80) writes, "We do not have definite evidence that health and intelligence are related, except in certain nonnutritional diseases involving the nervous system." Healy and Bronner (74) wrote in 1932, "The delinquent boy is not the undernourished boy."

McCollum (77) expressed the opinion the "American children cannot subsist upon a diet no better than that of a coolie without increasing the incidence of tuberculosis, dulling the mental capacity and warping the personality." Matitch and Eccles (78) used a large battery of tests with 554 boys at the New Jersey School for Boys at Jamesburg. They found 27 per cent to be of normal intelligence, 47.5 per cent inferior, and 25.1 per cent subnormal. From the point of view of nutrition these boys ranged from 25 per cent underweight to 33 per cent overweight, with a median of 7 per cent overweight. In general they found no significant differences in intelligence between the well and poorly nourished.

Roberts (82) concludes from a survey of the literature that "There is a fairly wide range of nutrition on both sides of normal, in which no appreciable difference in fundamental mental ability or its outward manifestations would be observed." She adds, "Only in extreme and prolonged undernutrition would the nervous system be sufficiently involved to produce demonstrable changes in fundamental ability as indicated by a decrease in the intelligence quotient."

THE TUBERCULOUS

Incidence. Myers (88) wrote in 1930 that "the incidence of infection (tuberculous) among school children has been found to vary from 10 per cent to 90.2 per cent depending upon the opportunities. Dicky and Roland (84) report that of 3,500 children seen at the Children's Clinic at the Stanford University Medical School for all kinds of ailments, 23.5 per cent reacted positively to tuberculin tests. Drolet (86) found that of 6,080 children admitted to three general hospitals in New York City there was a positive reaction to tuberculin tests in 13 per cent of the boys and in 15 per cent of the girls. Downes and Price (85) report 30 to 33 per cent positive tuberculin reaction in a poor section of New York.

Intelligence. We have been unable to find much information concerning the intelligence of this group. In 1929 Muhl (89) reported that of 25 children suffering from incipient tuberculosis 11 had intelligence quotients between 90 and 100; 10 between 80 and 90; and 4 below 70. We do not know what test was used. Neymann (91) found 300 patients in the Chicago Municipal Tuberculosis Sanatorium to be, on the average, of normal intelligence as measured by the Alpha Test of Yerkes and Yocum. He states that obviously feeble-minded patients are not accepted at this institution.

Seidenfeld (92) used the higher form of the Otis Self-Administering Test of Mental Ability with 42 female and 62 male patients in the National Jewish Hospital at Denver. The average age of the females was approximately twenty-nine years, and of the males approximately thirty-one. Somewhat less than half of the patients were Jewish. The amount of schooling varied considerably; about 13 per cent had not attended secondary school; 54 per cent had had one or more years of college; and 37 per cent had had some college work. The median score on the Otis was 46; for the males 47.7; and for the females 42. These patients tended to test slightly above the Otis norms. Seidenfeld found a correlation of .07 between scores on the Otis and length of hospitalization. He found little or no relationship between Otis scores and degree of tuberculosis.

Personality. Muhl (89) reports such personality trends as inertia, oscillating moods, irritability, suggestibility, daydreaming, in 30 females ranging in age from four to sixty. She states that the so-called optimism of the tuberculous patient is largely a myth.

Neymann (91) used the Neymann-Kohlstedt Diagnostic Test for Introversion-Extroversion with 300 tuberculous patients. He reports 46 per cent introverts, 39 per cent extroverts, and 15 per cent neutroverts. This is not very different from the distribution which he reports for the general population: 40 per cent introverts, 40 per cent extroverts, and 20 per cent neutroverts.

Eyre (87) states that tuberculosis is a condition which involves financial worry, shifts of home relationships, and segregation. He reports that fear is practically universal in tuberculous patients.

Strecker, Braceland, and Gordon (94) write of interviews with 75 tuberculous patients in small sanatoriums and wards of city hospitals. Only 11 showed personality changes. Remarks of the patients indicate their feeling of change.

"I have become more sociable. I was formerly quite shy."

"I am not as friendly and trusting as I was."

"I feel so alone that I prefer my own company."

"My friends have deserted me. I am much quieter than I used to be and a hundred times more bitter."

Each patient was asked how he felt when he first learned

that he had contracted tuberculosis. The replies varied from "a feeling of physical and moral catastrophe" to relief that one might give up and be taken care of.

The moods of these patients were summarized as:

Fatalistic, making the best of it	35 cases
Depressed	29 cases
Marked swings of mood	4 cases
Happy (euphoria)	7 cases

The depressed group represented many gradations of depression including suicidal tendencies. Economic worries were often responsible for feelings of depression. There was a small group who admitted daydreaming of various sorts. Certainly the tendency of this group is not toward a feeling of happiness and well-being but rather toward a feeling of fatalism and depression.

Employment Opportunities. Not only is there financial worry during the period of illness but there is some prejudice among employers against employing a person who has had tuberculosis. The Philadelphia survey (92) of handicapped workers showed that the crippled held the largest number of jobs and the tuberculous the least. The National Tuberculosis Association reports a large number of patients under thirty-five years of age who have little education, have no vocational plans, and need vocational training. They emphasize the need to combat prejudice of employers.

Summary. Again we have a group of whom educators have been aware for some time, but about whom we know very little. It seems essential to know what problems may be common to a large group of these children, in order that we may plan their educational program intelligently.

BIBLIOGRAPHY

THE ALLERGIC

1. Balyeat, R. M., "The General Health and Mental Activity of Allergic Children," *Am. J. Diseases of Child.* (June, 1929), 1193–7.
2. Kling, C., "A Statistical Study of Neurasthenic, Dyspeptic and Allergic Symptoms," *J. Genl. Psychol.*, X (1934), 328–43.
3. Nilson, T., "Constitution and Allergic Manifestations: Sex-Age of Allergic Conditions," *J. Allergy*, V (1934), 124.
4. Slesinger, H. A., "The Allergic Child," *Hygeia*, XVII (Aug., 1939), 704–6.
5. Sullivan, E. B., "Allergy in Relation to Intelligence and School Success in Children," *J. Juv. Research*, XIX (1935), 173–9.
6. Thorndike, R., "A Note on the Relationship of Allergy to Neurasthenic Traits," *J. Genl. Psychol.*, XVII (1937), 153–5.

THE CARDIAC

7. *Acute Rheumatism in Children in Relation to Heart Disease*, Reports on Public Health and Medical Subjects, No. 44 (His Majesty's Stationery Office, London, 1927).
8. Boas, E. P., "Heart Disease in Childhood," *J. Except. Child.*, IV (Oct., 1937), 25–32.
9. Brown, M., *The Effect of School and Industry on Young People with Heart Disease* (N.Y. Tuberculosis and Health Association, Vocational Guidance and Service, 1931), 42.
10. *Criteria for the Classification and Diagnosis of Heart Disease* (Paul B. Hoeber, N.Y., 1928).
11. De Porte, J. V., "Heart Disease Among Children of School Age," *N.Y. State J. of Med.*, XXXI (May 15, 1934), 448–50.
12. Foster, N. B., "Psychic Factors in the Course of Cardiac

Disease," *J. Am. Med. Assoc.*, LXXXIX (Sept. 24, 1927), 1017–118.

13. Master, A. M., "Optimism in Heart Disease," *Hygeia*, XVI (July, 1938), 594–6.
14. Rauh, L. W., "The Incidence of Organic Heart Disease in School Children," *Am. Heart J.*, XVIII (1939), 705–13.
15. Ross, M., "Mental Retardation Associated with Congenital Heart Disease," *J. Pediat.*, XIV (1937), 21–24.
16. Sigel, E., "The Mental Hygiene Problems of Cardiac Patients," *Smith College Studies in Social Work*, II (June, 1932), 336–57.
17. Smith, C. H., and L. P. Sutton, *Heart Disease in Infancy and Childhood* (Appleton, N.Y., 1930).
18. Wilson, M. G., C. L. Linogg, and G. C. Crawford, "Heart Disease in Children," *Am. Heart J.*, IV (1928), 164–95.

THE DIABETIC

19. Brown, G. D., "The Development of Diabetic Children, with Special Reference to Mental and Personality Comparisons," *Child Develop.*, IX (1938), 175–84.
20. Joslin, E. P., L. Dublin, and H. Marks, "Studies in Diabetes Mellitus Characteristics and Trends of Diabetic Morality throughout the World," *Am. J. Med. Sci.*, CLXXXVI (1933), 753.
21. Joslin, E. P., H. F. Root, and P. White, "The Growth, Development and Prognosis of Diabetic Children," *J. Am. Med. Assoc.*, LXXXV (1925), 420–2.
22. Joslin, E. P., H. F. Root, P. White, and A. Marble, *The Treatment of Diabetes Mellitus*, 6th ed. (Lea and Febiger, Phil., 1937).
23. McGavin, A. P., E. Schultz, G. W. Peden, and B. D. Bowen, "The Physical Growth of Intelligence and the Personality Adjustment of a Group of Diabetic Children," *N. Eng. J. of Med.*, CCXXIII:4 (1940), 119–27.
24. Miles, W. R., and H. F. Root, "Psychologic Tests Applied to

Diabetic Patients," *Arch. Internatl. Med.*, XXX (1922), 767.

25. West, H., A. Richey, and M. B. Eyre, "Study of Intelligence Levels of Juvenile Diabetics," *Psychol. Bull.*, XXXI (1934), 598.
26. White, P., *Diabetes in Childhood and Adolescence* (Lea and Febiger, Phil., 1932).

THE ENCEPHALITIC

27. Appel, K. E., "Encephalitis in Children," *J. Pediat.*, VII (1935), 478–87.
28. Berrien, F. K., "Psychological Differences in Psychopathic and Post-Encephalitic Children," *J. Appl. Psychol.*, XVIII (1934), 536–49.
29. Bond, E. D., *After Histories of Persons Attacked by Encephalitis Lethargica*, Reports on Public Health and Medical Subjects, No. 49 (His Majesty's Stationery Office, London, 1928).
30. Bond, D., and K. E. Appel, *The Treatment of Behavior Disorders following Encephalitis* (Commonwealth Fund, N.Y., 1931).
31. Bond, E. D., and G. E. Partridge, "Post-Encephalitic Behavior Disorders in Boys and their Management in a Hospital," *Am. J. Psychiat.*, VI:1 (1926), 25–103.
32. Bromberg, W., "Mental States in Chronic Encephalitis," *Psychiat. Quart.*, IV (1930), 537.
33. Brown, A. W., R. I. Jankins, and L. E. Cisler, "Influence of Lethargic Encephalitis on Intelligence of Children," *Am. J. Diseases of Child.*, CV (1938), 304–21.
34. Dawson, S., and T. C. M. Conn, *Intelligence and Disease*, Medical Research Council, Special Report Series, No. 162 (His Majesty's Stationery Office, London, 1931).
35. Gibbs, C. E., "Behavior Disorders in Chronic Epidemic Encephalitis," *Am. J. Psychiat.*, IX (Jan., 1930), 619–36.
36. Hall, A. J., "The Mental Sequelae of Epidemic Encephalitis in Children," *Brit. Med. J.*, I (1925), 110–11.

37. Hallowell, D. K., "24 Cases of Acute Epidemic Encephalitis," *Psychol. Clinic,* XVI (1925), 167–85.
38. Jenkins, R. L., and L. Ackerson, "The Behavior of Encephalitic Children," *Am. J. Orthopsychiat.,* IV (Oct., 1934), 499.
39. Kwint, L., "Beiträge zur Klinik und Pathogenese der Folgeerscheinungen von epidemischer Encephalitis bei Kindern," *Zeitschr. f. Kinderk.,* XL (1926), 678.
40. Lange, W., "Die Entwicklung der Intelligenz bei Kindern nach Encephalitis epidemica," *Psychiat.-neurol. Wochenschr.,* XXX (1928), 579.
41. Matheson Committee, *Epidemic Encephalitis—Ecology—Epidemiology—Treatment* (Columbia Univ. Press, N.Y., 1929).
42. Parsons, A. C., "Report of an Inquiry into the After Histories of Persons Attacked by Encephalitis Lethargica," Reports on Public Health and Medical Subjects, No. 49 (His Majesty's Stationery Office, London, 1928).
43. Paterson, D., and J. C. Spence, "The After-Effects of Epidemic Encephalitis in Children," *Lancet,* II (1931), 491.
44. Robin, G., *Considérations sur les troubles mentaux liés aux formes prolongées de l'encéphalite épidémique chez l'enfant,* Thèse de Paris, No. 380 (1923).
45. Scott, L. M., *The Role of the Psychiatric Social Worker in the Treatment of Post-Encephalitis,* Smith Coll. Studies in Social Work (1930).
46. Sherman, M., and B. T. Beverly, "The Factor of Deterioration in Children Showing Behavior Difficulties after Epidemic Encephalitis," *Arch. Neurol. and Psychiat.,* X (1923), 329.
47. Shrubsall, F. C., "The Sequelae of Encephalitis Lethargica," *Brit. J. Med. Psychol.,* VII (1927), 210.

THE EPILEPTIC

48. Barnes, M. R., and J. L. Fetterman, "Mentality of Dispensary Epileptic Patients," *Arch. Neurol. and Psychiat.,* XL (1938), 903–10.

49. Branham, V. C., "Epileptoid Reactions in Children," *Am. J. Psychiat.*, LXXXII (Jan., 1926), 423–29.
50. Bridge, E. M., "Mental State of the Epileptic Patient," *Arch. Neurol. and Psychiat.*, XXXII (Oct., 1934), 723–36.
51. Brown, R. R., "A Study of the Mental and Physical Traits of the Relatives of Epileptics," *J. Appl. Psychol.*, XIV (Dec., 1930), 624–36.
52. Cookson, S. H., "An Analysis of One Hundred Cases of Fits in Children," *Arch. Diseases of Child.*, II (1927), 178–85.
53. Dawson, S., and J. C. M. Conn, "The Intelligence of Epileptic Children," *Arch. Diseases of Child.*, IV (1929), 142–51.
54. Fay, T., "Convulsive Seizures, Their Production and Control," *Am. J. Psychiat.*, X (1931), 551–66.
55. Fetterman, J., and M. R. Barnes, "Serial Studies of the Intelligence of Patients with Epilepsy," *Arch. Neurol. and Psychiat.*, XXXII (1934), 797–801.
56. Fox, J. T., "The Response of Epileptic Children to Mental and Educational Tests," *Brit. J. Med. Psychol.*, IV (1924), 235–48.
57. Gowers, W. R., *Epilepsy* (Churchill, London, 1881).
58. Grinker, R. R., *Neurology* (C. C. Thomas, Baltimore, 1934).
59. Harriman, P. L., "The Ethical Discrimination of the Epileptic," *J. Abn. and Soc. Psychol.*, XXX (March, 1935), 411–18.
60. Lennox, W. G., "Epilepsy," Ch. XXXI in *Nelson New Loose-Leaf Medicine* (Nelson, N.Y., 1932), 621–46.
61. Makhaeva, E. A., "On the Condition of the Motor Functions in Epileptic Children," *Nov. Psikhonevrol Det. Vozr.* V (1935), 107–75.
62. New York State, *Forty-fifth Annual Report of the Department of Mental Hygiene, July 1, 1932 to June 30, 1933* (Lyon, Albany, 1934).
63. Ninde, F. W., *The Application of the Auditory Memory Span Test to Two Thousand Institutional Epileptics: A Study in Relative Associability* (Temple Press, Westchester, Pa., 1927).

64. Notkin, J., "Is There an Epileptic Personality Make-up?" *Arch. Neurol. and Psych.*, XX (Oct., 1928), 799–803.
65. Paskind, H. A., "Extramural Patients with Epilepsy with Special Reference to the Frequent Absence of Deterioration," *Arch. Neurol. and Psychiat.*, XXVIII (Aug., 1932), 370–85.
66. Patterson, H. A., and D. Fonner, "Some Observations on the Intelligence Quotients in Epileptics," *Psychiat. Quart.*, II (1928), 542–8.
67. Shanahan, W. T., "Convulsions in Infancy, and their Relationship, if any, to Subsequent Epilepsy," *Psychiat. Quart.*, II (1928), 27–41.
68. Sullivan, E. B., and L. Gahagan, "On Intelligence of Epileptic Children," *Genet. Psychol. Monogs.*, XVII (1935), 309–76.
69. Turner, W. A., *Epilepsy: A Study of the Hiopathic Disease* (Macmillan, London and N.Y., 1907).
70. Wilkins, L., "Epilepsy in Childhood," *J. Pediat.*, X (1937), 317–57.
71. Worster-Drought, C., "Hystero-Epilepsy," *Brit. J. Med. Psychol.*, XIV (1934), 50–82.

THE MALNOURISHED

72. Baker, J., "The Physical Condition of Retarded School Children," *Med. Rec.*, LXXXV (1914), 64.
73. Dowd, H. L., "Relation of Mental Retardation to Nutrition," *Hosp. Soc. Serv.*, VI (1922), 92.
74. Healy, W., and A. Bronner, *Delinquents and Criminals* (Macmillan, N.Y., 1932).
75. Hoefer, C., and M. Hardy, "The Influence of Improvement in Physical Condition on Intelligence and Educational Achievement," *Nat. Soc. for Study of Educ.*, XXVII (1928), 371–87.
76. Hunt, J. L., B. J. Johnson, and E. M. Lincoln, *Health Education and the Nutrition Class* (Dutton, N.Y., 1921).

77. McCollum, E. V., "Fundamentals of Nutrition," *Internatl. Clinic,* II, 42nd Series (1932), 1–17.
78. Matitch, M., and A. K. Eccles, "The Relation between Nutrition, Mental Level and Delinquent Boys," *J. Nerv. and Ment. Disorders,* LXXVIII (1933), 123.
79. Nichols, E., "Performance in Certain Mental Tests of Children Classified as Underweight and Normal," *J. Comp. Psychol.,* III (1923), 147.
80. Paterson, D. G., *Physique and Intellect* (Century, N.Y., 1930).
81. Pearson, K., "The Health and the Intelligence and Physique of School Children," *Brit. Med. J.,* II (1923), 334.
82. Roberts, L. J., *Nutrition Work with Children* (Univ. of Chicago Press, Chicago, 1935).
83. Smith, A. J., and A. M. Field, "A Study of the Effect of Nutrition on Mental Growth," *J. Home Econ.,* XV (1926), 686–90.

THE TUBERCULOUS

84. Dickey, L. B., and R. P. Roland, "The Incidence of Tuberculosis Infection in Children Based on 3,500 Intracutaneous Tuberculin Tests," *Am. Rev. Tuberculosis* XXIII (1931), 13–21.
85. Downes, J., and C. R. Price, "T.B. Control in the Mulberry District of N.Y.C.," *Milbank Memorial Fund Quart.,* XV:4 (1937), 319–47.
86. Drolet, G. J., "The Incidence of Tuberculosis among Children in N.Y.C.," *Am. Rev. Tuberculosis,* XXX (1934), 1–32.
87. Eyre, M. B., "The Role of Emotions in Tuberculosis," *Am. Rev. Tuberculosis,* XXVII (1933), 315–29.
88. Myers, J. A., *Tuberculosis among Children* (C. C. Thomas, Baltimore, 1930).
89. Muhl, A. M., "Fundamental Personality Trends in Tuberculous Women," *Psychoanalytic Rev.,* X (1935), 380–430.
90. National Tuberculosis Association, Rehabilitation Depart-

ment, "The Social and Vocational Rehabilitation of the Tuberculous," *Occupations*, XV (1937), 581–633.

91. Neymann, C. H., "The Relation of Extroversion and Introversion to Intelligence and Tuberculosis," *Am. J. Psychiat.*, IX (1930), 687–96.
92. Seidenfeld, M. A., "Some Psychometric Observations on the Tuberculous Patients in a National Institution," *J. Gen. Psychol.*, XXI (1939), 447–55.
93. Solenberger, E. R., "Philadelphia Studies Her Physically Handicapped," *The Crippled Child*, XIII (1935), 109, 110, 128.
94. Strecker, E. A., F. J. Braceland, and B. Gordon, "Mental Attitudes of Tuberculous Patients," *Ment. Hyg.*, XXII (1938), 529–43.

CHAPTER XI

The Defective in Speech

PRELIMINARY CONSIDERATIONS

THE NATURE OF SPEECH

Before we can enter into a discussion on speech defects it might be well for us to decide what we mean by the term *speech.* Speech may be considered that form of language which man produces without resorting to agencies outside of his own organism. In speech only those oral and visible symbols are used which the individual can produce without the use of tools. The elements of speech are action (gesture), voice, and articulated sounds (words). The third element differentiates man's use of speech from lower animals. Only man is capable of producing finely differentiated sounds which we have come to recognize as words and which have become organized into spoken language. This achievement enables man to use speech for social control and communication, the highest and most civilized of the functions of speech.

THE NATURE OF SPEECH DISORDERS

What Is a Defect of Speech? To define a defect of speech is as subtle and as difficult a problem as defining the term abnormal. We probably all have some vague notion of what an abnormal person is, at least in our own usage of the term, and perhaps we have even set up some vague criteria by which we judge a given individual as being normal or abnormal. Let us do as much for speech and set up minimum standards for "normal" speech. Normal speech must be audible and intelligible to the hearer. The voice must not only be adequate in intensity but not unpleasant to hear. The speaker should be able to produce speech easily and readily according to the exigencies of the speaking situation. "Normal" speech varies with the speaker: it should be appropriate to the mental and chronological age, the physical development, etc., of the individual. By setting up the converse of the criteria for normal speech we can arrive at criteria for defective speech. Speech may be considered defective when it is not easily audible and intelligible to the listener. Speech is defective if it is vocally or visibly unpleasant or labored in production. Finally, speech is defective if it is inappropriate to the individual in regard to his mental and chronological age, sex, and physical development.

Two terms, defects and disorder, which are frequently used interchangeably, might better be defined and differentiated. A defect of speech is what one observes when speech is atypical. It does not include or even presuppose the existence of an organic cause. For example, a person's voice may have peculiarities of pitch because he carries over into one language the pitch patterns of another. This would constitute a defect called foreign intonation. If, however, the pitch of an individual's voice is monotonous because he is deaf or hard of hearing, we have a speech disorder. A disorder, then, includes the cause and audible end result; a defect is only the result. A speech defect may exist without a disorder, but all disorders entail speech defects.

THE DEFECTIVE IN SPEECH

INCIDENCE AND DISTRIBUTION OF SPEECH DEFECTS

The White House Conference Report (23, p. 353) indicated that about 1,000,000 school children between the ages of five to eighteen were so defective in their ability to speak as to be in need of remedial treatment and training. The number of defective speaking children between five and eighteen who were not attending school was not included in the estimate. In New York City alone, about 50,000 children constituting approximately 5 per cent of the school population, were found to be defective in speech. This percentage is smaller than *the average* (6.9) percentage of speech defectives in the school population of forty-eight of the larger cities of the United States. Little more need be said to indicate how widespread and serious a problem defective speech is among the children of this country.

The types of speech defects, according to the White House Report, tended to be distributed as follows for every 10,000 cases:

Oral inactivity	4,851
Articulatory disorders on a structural basis	1,059
Stuttering	1,029
Sound substitution	1,014.3
Voice disorders on a functional basis	1,014.3
Dialectal	470.4
Voice disorders on a structural basis	441
Articulatory disorders (paralytic)	58.8
Aphasic disorders	29.4
"Hard-of-hearing" speech	14.7
Voice disorders (paralytic)	14.7

The incidence of speech defects was found to be greatest in the first year of school, with the exception of stuttering, which showed its greatest incidence in the fifth school year. In general, speech defects occur more frequently among boys than among girls.

RELATIONSHIP OF SPEECH TO OTHER DISORDERS

Intelligence and Speech Defects. Although speech defects may be found on any level of intelligence, there is a greater incidence of defective speech among the mentally defective than among the mentally normal. Carrell (3) reports the results of a study of a school population of 1,174 children in which the type and frequency of speech defect and the intelligence of all defective children were determined. The speech defective children in the school population were found to have lower intelligence quotients than the general school population. Kennedy (6) made a study of the speech of mental defectives ranging from the level of the moron to the idiot. She found that of the 249 morons, ranging in I.Q. from 50 to 69, 42.57 per cent had speech defects; 31 of 32 imbeciles ranging in I.Q. from 21 to 47 had speech defects; and all of the 32 idiots ranging in I.Q. from 20 to below test level had defective speech. In a study of the defective in speech in a whole school system, of 89,057 elementary and high school pupils, Wallin (20, pp. 454–5) found that 2.8 per cent of children in the regular grades had speech defects compared with 26.3 per cent in the special schools for the mentally deficient. Further, Wallin found that, of 2,774 cases referred to a psychoeducational clinic because of suspected mental deficiency, 19.6 per cent were found to have defective speech.

On the higher educational level, Travis and Davis (17) found that among 546 university freshman, normal speakers were superior in intelligence to speakers with functional disorders of speech. In a study of freshmen at Mt. Holyoke College, however, Stinchfield (14) discovered that there were as many girls of good intelligence in the groups needing corrective speech instruction as in the superior speech groups.

The conclusions in regard to the inferiority of intelligence of the speech defectives do not pertain to stutterers. The consensus of evidence supports the view that stutterers as a group are normal or better in intelligence. McDowell (36, p. 9) administered the Stanford Revision of the Binet-Simon Intelligence Test to fifty New York City stutterers attending the public elementary schools. She found that the stuttering children had a mean I.Q. of 101.9 and a standard deviation of 19.87. This compared with an average I.Q. of 102 for the control group and a standard deviation of 20.26. West, Travis, and Camp (23, p. 320) report a median I.Q. of 96.5 in a group of 4,059 stutterers. On the college level, findings indicate that stutterers are somewhat superior in intelligence to the nonstutterers. Steer (38) found the average I.Q. of eighty-seven college stutterers to be 116.5. In another study Johnson (34) found the I.Q.'s of college stutterers to range between 105–136. In general, we may conclude that though speech defectives as a group are inferior in intelligence to normal speakers, the distribution of intelligence among stutterers is at least as good as that of normal speakers.

Despite the high incidence of speech defects among the feeble-minded, amentia per se is probably not a direct cause of defective speech. West, Kennedy, and Carr (22, p. 138) state: "It is because the aments are not *merely* aments that the lay person believes that articulatory defects may be ascribed to feeble-mindedness." Directly, feeble-mindedness will be causally related to deficiencies of language usage rather than to defects of speech. The ament's vocabulary is small, but only because he has few ideas. The low-grade idiot may not speak at all because he has *no ideas.* The paucity of his ideas may, however, cause him to develop feelings of inferiority and inadequacy which may manifest themselves in disorders of speech.

Such disorders are indirectly caused by the amentia and are psychogenic rather than organic in origin.

Organic disorders of speech among the feeble-minded are concomitantly rather than directly the results of amentia. A spastic individual may be feeble-minded because of a brain lesion responsible for both spasticity and feeble-mindedness. Similarly, a brain injury may at once be the cause of blindness or deafness and mental deficiency. Cretinism and mongolism are special organic conditions which are associated with defective speech. In such cases speech defects are to be considered associated with feeble-mindedness rather than directly caused by it.

Educational Achievement and Speech Defects. The consensus of findings of research workers seem to indicate that the defective in speech do not make as rapid progress in school as do children with normal speech. In Carrell's study (3) the speech defectives were found to be inferior in school achievement to the general school population. Root (13), in a survey of speech defectives in South Dakota public elementary schools, found speech defectives to be six months retarded compared with average pupils without defects in speech. At Mt. Holyoke College, Stinchfield (14, pp. 38–9) found that the girls needing corrective speech training failed in their school work despite their high intelligence.

Stutterers fall into a somewhat special group in regard to educational accomplishment. In the McDowell study (36, p. 48) in which scores on standard achievement-tests were used as a basis for comparison, the findings indicated that there were no significant differences between the stutterers and non-stutterers. Studies on higher educational levels, however, indicate that the reading ability of stutterers is below that of normal speakers. Murray (37) found college stutterers to be deficient both in rate of silent reading and comprehension of silent-reading material.

Chronological Age and Speech. The age of an individual and his level of speech development are closely related because of the presence of other determinants which accompany the process of growing up. Normal children, those who are neither defective nor accelerated intellectually and physically and who receive an adequate amount of linguistic stimulation, generally begin to use conventional language during the second half of the second year. But the use of language is characterized by an array of errors and faults which, for an older child or adult, would constitute definite speech defects. These speech inadequacies—defects in the adult sense only—continue for some time. At the age of two, for example, a child is very likely to lisp. His sibilants may be produced with a lingual protrusion, or perhaps *t* and *d* sounds may be substituted for them. Occasionally both sibilants and substitutes are entirely omitted. Guttural sounds, which are produced with the back of the tongue and the soft palate, are likely to be faulty in their production, with dental substitutions occurring quite frequently (*dood* for *good* is an example of such substitutions). In the speech of a two-year-old the presence of one sound may unduly influence and distort the production of neighboring sounds. So a small child may say *kucking* instead of *sucking* and *bumb* instead of *thumb.* Another characteristic speech error of small children is the transposition of sounds within a word. The word *ask,* for example, is frequently pronounced as *aks* by many children, and occasionally so pronounced by adults.

The types of errors just considered should give us no cause for real concern if they appear while a child is learning to speak. They should, however, disappear rapidly as the child approaches school age. By the time a normal child is ready for school infant inaccuracies should have entirely disappeared. His speech should then be clear and easy to understand. Persistence of infantilisms at school age becomes a matter of real concern for the parent, the teacher, and the child.

Physical Defects and Speech. We find an increased percentage of speech disturbance among the physically defective. Frequently the cause of the physical defect is directly the cause of the speech defect. Such physical abnormalities as tongue-tie, harelip, cleft palate, malocclusion, or other mouth deformities are likely to cause disturbances in the production of speech. Pharyngeal and laryngeal deformities are likely to result in voice defects. Blindness, deafness, and spasticity (see pp. 364–79) are responsible for associated voice and articulatory defects. Endocrine disturbances, especially those involving the pituitary and thyroid glands, are likely to result in disorders of voice and articulation. Neurological disturbances are frequently the cause of defective speech. Brain lesions, tumors, brain inflammations, etc., may directly affect those parts of the nervous mechanism which control the organs of phonation and articulation (vocal folds, tongue, lips, palate, etc.). Neuropathologies without specific lesions of the central nervous system may also be indirectly responsible for speech disturbances. Pathological conditions such as chorea and epilepsy present a picture of excessive nervous irritability and are indirectly responsible for disturbed speech. The speech of some of these physically defective types of individuals will be treated in some detail later in our discussion.

Sensorimotor Efficiency and Speech Defects. In regard to motor and sensorimotor efficiency, the defective in speech fall below the norms of children without speech defects. Carrell (3, pp. 179–203) found that the speech defectives were inferior to normal controls in both physical and psychophysical items in anthropometric measurements. In a foreign study of the motor efficiency of grade-school children, involving such tasks as running, jumping, balancing, and climbing, Arps (1) found that the motor efficiency of speech defectives, and more especially of stutterers, was much lower than that of pupils with normal speech. It is likely that the high incidence of speech defects among the physically defective accounts in part for the lowered motor and sensorimotor efficiency of the defective in speech.

Personality and Speech Defects. In any consideration of the personality traits of the speech defective, we must constantly bear in mind the close relationship between physical defects and personality (see pp. 11–17). A physical deficiency of severe degree will necessitate new methods of adjustment on the part of the physically handicapped individual. An individual's personality, we recall, may be defined as the sum total of his reactions as he adjusts to his environment. Because speech is fundamental in almost all of a person's adjustments, changes in speech accompany changes in personality. The speech of a physically handicapped individual may be considered an integral part of his personality. The blind, we shall later learn, develop speech defects for reasons peculiar to their methods of adjusting to their environment. The irritability of the hyperthyroid individual and his rapid speech rate are both intimately associated with the glandular dysfunction.

With respect to the personality traits of speech defectives who do not present organic involvements, there is a paucity of experimental evidence, except in regard to stutterers. For the most part, college students have been the subjects of study. During the fall terms of 1930 and 1931 the Thurstone Personality Schedule, 1929 edition, was given to forty-six Freshman students who were doing speech-corrective work at Mt. Holyoke College (48, pp. 207–15). The Thurstone Schedule consists of 223 questions which may be answered by either *Yes,*

No, or ?. A *Yes* answer is considered unfavorable for each of the questions. Stinchfield reports that 60 per cent of the questions which Thurstone considered most significant appeared in the positive list of high-frequency answers. She concludes that "This in itself is a strong argument for the need of mental hygiene as well as corrective speech work with these students."

In an earlier study (48, pp. 215–21), Stinchfield arranged a Trait Inventory consisting of a list of forty-six desirable and undesirable traits. The list was given to three groups of Freshman students during the fall of 1926. One group was composed of 33 students who had been classified for speech-correction work, a second group was made up of 33 students who had superior speech, and the third group consisted of 204 students of average speech attainment. The trait list included such items as even disposition, tact, courtesy, control of behavior (emotionality), undue sensitivity, etc. Stinchfield found that "the corrective group had checked off a considerable number of questionable or negative traits, as compared with the superior speech group and the average group." The girls in the corrective group rated themselves lowest compared with the other two groups in regard to such questions as "Do you make contacts easily; are you close-mouthed, easily satisfied, calm, communicative, unselfish, original?" The scores for the traits of even disposition, courtesy, quietness, good memory, good control, and normal sensitivity indicated that the members of the speech-correction group considered themselves below the level of the superior and average groups. The girls in the speech-correction group considered themselves somewhat more aggressive than the members of the other two groups. Though Stinchfield is skeptical about the technique she employed in her study, in which students were permitted to score themselves in regard to a list of traits, she found that later records and studies tended to uphold the students' original ratings of themselves.

Templin (15) studied the aggressiveness of a group of seventy-one students enrolled in the Speech Clinic at Purdue University, who were compared with forty-nine students with normal speech. Both groups included men and women students of freshmen, sophomore, junior, and senior standing. The revised Moore-Gilliland test for aggressiveness was used as a measuring instrument. The results, summarized in the table below, indicate that the normal group was more aggressive than the speech-defective group. Among the group with speech defects, the stutterers tended to be more aggressive than the voice defectives, and the voice defectives more so than the students with articulatory defects. It should be noted, however, that the differences between and among all the groups are too small to be considered statistically significant.

Comparison of Average Aggressiveness Scores of Normal and Defective Speakers

Group	*Number*	*Average*	*S.D.*
Normal speakers	49	70.88	18.58
Defective speakers	71	64.68	21.15
Articulatory defectives	37	63.49	22.35
Phonic defectives	15	65.00	20.15
Rhythmic defectives	19	66.74	19.20

There have been a number of significant experimental studies to determine the personality traits of stutterers. Among these, McDowell's (36, Ch. V) study is outstanding for the pre-pubescent stutterer. McDowell administered a combination of the Woodworth-Matthews Questionnaire and the Woodworth-Cady Questionnaire, the Kent-Rosanoff Free-Association Test, and a teacher's rating made on the basis of a trait inventory used by Terman in a study with gifted children, to forty-six stutterers and forty-six equated control subjects. McDowell's general conclusion was that there were no significant differences in personality between the stutterers and the normal speakers. In the traits of self-confidence and sensitiveness, however, there were differences which favored the control group. Johnson (34) studied the personality problems of eighty male and female stutterers ranging in age from seven to forty-two years. On the basis of results obtained with the Maturity section of the Woodworth-House Mental-Hygiene Inventory, Johnson found differences unfavorable to the stutterers in regard to health, nervousness and irritability, shyness, vocational anxiety, secretiveness and depression, and in the feeling of satisfactory adjustment to life. The unfavorable differences were greater for the mature stutterers than for the prepubescent stutterers.

Bender (24, Ch. VIII) conducted a carefully controlled study in which the Bernreuter Personality Inventory was given to a group of 249 stutterers and 303 nonstutterers, all male freshmen students at the College of the City of New York. The stutterers ranged from 14 years to 23 years, 7 months, with an average age of 17 years, 2 months. The control group ranged from 14 years, 5 months to 24 years, 5 months, with an average age of 17 years. Bender's results indicated that "the stuttering group was significantly higher neurotically, more introverted, less dominant, less self-confident, and less sociable" than the nonstuttering group.

In summarizing the findings of experimental studies to determine the personality traits of stutterers, it may be concluded that mature stutterers present a picture of greater maladjustment than prepubescent stutterers. In regard to speech defectives other than stutterers, present findings indicate that they make less adequate adjustments than do normal speakers. There is, however, a significant need for further experimentation and research, especially with speech defectives in the lower school grades.

THE MAJOR TYPES OF SPEECH DISORDERS

Organic vs. Functional Disorders. All speech disturbances may be classified under one of two broad major headings: (1) those which are fundamentally physical or organic in origin and (2) those which are psychogenic or functional in origin. Accurate classification under either of these headings is not always possible. In a strict sense, no speech difficulty is either completely organic or entirely functional in its etiology. A defect, such as lisping, may arise originally because of an organically bad arrangement of teeth, but the tooth arrangement may make the individual self-conscious and so affect his habitual way of reacting to his environment. This reaction may be reflected in his speech. It is conceivable that a child or an adult may enjoy the attention his faulty speech brings him and so persist and refuse to correct an error of organic origin.

It is convenient, and often necessary for the speech therapist to determine under which of the two major classifications a given speech disturbance may be included. In general, we may say that if a disturbance in speech is never exhibited unless associated with a physical defect such as an organic spasm of nervous origin, as in the spastic, or a defective speech organ, as in the individual with a cleft palate, we may consider the disturbance to be basically *physiogenic* or *organic.* If, however, we observe that the speech disturbance is associated with difficulties which are basically emotional, if the speech defective's case history reveals a psychoneurotic personality, if the difficulty shows marked fluctuations in severity which are concurrent with emotional rather than physical disturbances, the speech disturbance may be considered to be fundamentally *psychogenic* or *functional.* Whenever the admixture of causes and associations with a speech deficiency do not permit of ready classification, we may consider the disturbance as psychophysiogenic. In all cases, regardless of classification, the speech therapist is likely to employ both psychotherapy and organic retraining. Classification is useful in that it may indicate which of the two therapies needs greater emphasis.

In the discussion of the major types of speech disorders which follows we shall confine ourselves for the most part to speech disturbances which are known or thought to have organic bases. We see no good reason for speech-defective persons whose defects are not causally related to organic anomalies to be included under the general category of the physically handicapped.

Types of Speech Disorders. We will consider four major classifications of speech disorders: (1) Stuttering (stammering), which includes defects in rhythm of speech, intermittent blocking of speech sounds, hesitation, and repetition of sounds once initiated. (2) Articulatory defects (dysarthrias and dyslalias) which may result in making an individual's speech indistinct or confusing because of a failure or an inability to produce the commonly accepted speech sounds. Articulatory defects include lisping, cluttering, and sound substitution. (3) Disorders of voice (dysphonias), which include any failure to produce smooth, even, vocal tones sufficiently audible to meet conversational needs. Huskiness, shrillness, weakness, and nasality are examples of voice defects. (4) Language impairment (dysphasias), in which the symbolic meaning of language is disturbed.

STUTTERING *

Overt Symptoms of Stuttering. Stuttering in its broadest sense is arhythmic vocal expression. Usual symptoms of stutter-

* The definitions of the terms used to indicate the various speech disorders are not to be considered final. Speech pathologists frequently disagree and use different terms for the same speech disorder. We shall make it a practice in this chapter to use what we consider to be the most widely accepted term for each disorder.

ing include involuntary, spasmodic repetitions of sounds, or an inability to produce certain sounds. The stutterer seems to be blocked when he speaks. Sometimes a stutterer will experience difficulty with a few speech sounds such as *b, p, d,* and *t,* or certain combinations of sounds. Occasionally there will be blocking on any and all speech sounds, though most stutterers will generally be able to produce one or two favorite sounds or sound combinations without evidence of difficulty. Frequently the stutterer's blocking will be accompanied by muscular spasms, especially of those muscles involved in the production of speech sounds. Occasionally, the spasm will include muscles not in any way involved in the producing of speech sounds but which have, through habit, become associated with the act of speech. These may include ticlike movements of the individual limbs, the head, or the body as a whole.

In addition to those speech symptoms, stutterers present an interesting physiological picture. The stutterer exhibits peculiarities of breathing, at least when he speaks. In normal speech the ratio of inspiration to expiration is about one to five; the stutterer's ratio has been found to be about one to two. Speech, normally, is produced on expired breath, but many stutterers have been found to exhale almost completely and then attempt to speak while inhaling. In general, breathing is arhythmic; the stutterer often interrupts inhalation to exhale, or an incompleted exhalation to inhale. A considerable amount of breath is often wasted before the speech act is initiated, so that vocalization, perforce, stops short.

Biochemistry of Stutterers. There have been interesting and perhaps significant findings in studies made on heart rate and blood distribution of stutterers. The pulse rate of stutterers has been found to increase from the normal 72 to as much as 129 per minute. Inorganic phosphates and sugar have been found in excess of normal in the blood of stutterers; potassium and protein are below normal in quantity. Calcium has been found to be excessive in total amount, but normal in regard to the quantity which is capable of diffusion through the body membranes (35). The significance of the components in the blood chemistry of the stutterer lies not in the amount of each blood component but rather in the proportions of the components to one another. For example, in the normal blood picture, the proportion of inorganic phosphates decreases as the calcium content of the blood is increased. An examination of the blood of the stutterer, however, reveals that the amount of inorganic phosphates increases as the calcium content increases. According to West, Kennedy, and Carr, "These findings seem to show that the linkings among certain elements of the blood are significantly different from those of the nonstutterer's blood. These patients (if they can be so labeled) seem to exhibit a different metabolic mechanism from that of the normal speaker." (22, p. 59.)

Muscular Movements of Stutterers. A number of experiments have been performed to investigate voluntary muscular movements among stutterers. West (40) found that stutterers were slower than nonstutterers in their rate of repetitive, muscular movements. The experimental task involved control of the muscles of the jaw and eyebrow. Hunsley (33) required a group of twenty mature stutterers to follow a pattern of clicks according to a presented auditory pattern. The muscles of the jaw, lips, and tongue were involved. The stutterers were found to be inferior to a control group of normal speakers in their ability to follow the presented pattern. In another experiment, the voluntary movements of the diaphragm, tongue, lips, and jaw of a group of stutterers and a control group of normal speakers were studied by Blackburn (25). The findings indicated that the stutterers differed from normal speakers in the regularity and rate of their muscular movements. The results of the several experiments are consistent in their findings. Stutterers are generally found to be inferior to nonstutterers in their ability to control voluntary movements of such muscles as the eyebrow, tongue, lips, jaw, and diaphragm even when these muscles are not being used for speech.

Motor Ability of Stutterers. In Arps' study (see p. 327) it was found that stutterers were inferior to children without speech defects in such motor tasks as running, jumping, balancing, and climbing. American studies, in which standardized motor tests were used, generally indicate that differences exist between stutterers and nonstutterers in regard to motor ability. In a study by Westphal (42) twenty-six male stutterers ranging from eight to seventeen years in age were matched with a control group of male nonstutterers. The motor ability of the groups was examined by a series of test situations which included: (1) The Smedley Dynamometer to measure hand grip; (2) a Bead-Tossing Test; (3) The Goddard Norsworthy Revision of the Seguin Form Board; (4) Simultaneous Writing of Digits with both hands by blindfolded subjects; (5) The Stoelting Nine-Hole Steadiness Plate used with the subject's alternating hands. Westphal found that only in the use of the Stoelting Plate did the stutterers show themselves to be superior to the nonstutterers. In the other tasks the nonstutterers as a group were superior to the stutterers.

Cross (30) tested the motor capacity of twenty-one college stutterers by means of the Stanford Motor-Skills Tests. The stutterers were matched with a control group of thirty-one right-handed and eleven left-handed normal speakers. Cross found significant differences between the two groups in regard to their motor ability. The stutterers were found inferior to the normal speakers in bimanual activity and in the rate of movement of the right hand and the left hand. The differences between the right and left hands of stutterers were found to be less than that for normal speakers.

The results of tests of the motor ability of stutterers indicate that they compare unfavorably with normal speakers. This is what we should expect in the light of the experimental findings in tests of muscular movements of stutterers.

Psychological Characteristics of Stutterers. The psychological picture of the stutterer is an interesting one. In our discussion of personality traits of the defective in speech (see pp. 329–30) we found that there were several unfavorable traits which appeared to be more characteristic of the mature stutterer than of the prepubescent stutterer. Among these traits were anxiety, undue sensitivity and embarrassment, fears, and depression. The findings do not make it clear, however, whether the undesirable traits are the causes of stuttering or evolve as consequents. We know that normal speakers may stutter on occasions when they are temporarily embarrassed or afraid; we can recognize also that habitual stuttering with its many uncomfortable visible as well as audible elements, may give an individual due cause for fear and anxiety about himself in social, educational, and vocational situations. This, of course, is much more likely to be the case with adults than with stuttering children who have not yet become aware of the effect of their speech upon other persons in their environment. It is undoubtedly true that part of the adjustment difficulty experienced by the adult stutterer is directly related to the stutterer's own reaction to his defective speech.

Incidence and Distribution of Stuttering. Figures for the incidence of stuttering in the population vary somewhat with the investigators. McDowell (36, p. 6) found that in a school population of 7,138 children, .87 per cent presented symptoms of stuttering which were sufficiently marked to be noted by their teachers or the speech correctionist. Smiley Blanton (26) in an earlier study found stutterers to comprise .72 per cent of the school population in Madison, Wisconsin. A rather high percentage (2.64) was found by Camp (29) in her study of the school population of Grand Rapids, Michigan. Rogers (12) estimated that the number of stuttering children in the United States is five times as many as the combined numbers of blind and deaf children.

Stuttering, it is generally agreed, is more prevalent among boys than among girls. McDowell (36, p. 7) found the ratio of boys to girls to be 2.9 to 1. Blanton (26, p. 584) found the ratio to be about 3 to 1 in his study. West, Kennedy, and Carr (22, p. xix) make the observation that stuttering is a speech problem faced particularly by males.

The greatest age incidence of stuttering is at about eleven years (22, p. xx), though many children begin stuttering at the ages of five or six, and some children do not show definite symptoms of stuttering until after adolescence. In general, we find fewer stutterers in the grammar-school grades than in the primary grades, and fewer in the high schools than in the grammar schools. Though not confined to childhood, stuttering usually has its onset before the close of adolescence.

From the point of view of intelligence, we have noted (p. 323) that stutterers as a group are at least normal. They are superior in intelligence when compared with other speech defectives.

Types of Stuttering. Froeschels describes two rather well-defined types or stages of stuttering. In the first stage stuttering is characterized chiefly by sound repetition. This is a type of stuttering that almost all children demonstrate at some time during their early speech development and which adults exhibit when embarrassed or lost for words. The sound repetition is *not* accompanied by muscular cramps or by any special awareness or self-consciousness as to the manner of speech itself. This is termed *initial stuttering* and may well be considered a normal phase of speech development. In the second stage of stuttering the appearance of cramps is the outstanding symptom. Muscular rigidity, at first restricted to the organ of articulation and later frequently extended to other sets of muscles, accompanies attempts at speech. In this stage the individual becomes acutely aware of his speech, partly because of the effect his speaking has on his listeners. This second phase is termed *developed stuttering.*

Theories as to Causation of Stuttering. In keeping with our earlier indicated intention, we shall consider only those theories which suppose stuttering to be associated with special organic conditions to which the defect is related.

Cerebral Dominance Theory. Professor Lee Edward Travis (16, p. 42) believes that stuttering is a result of a conflict between the two brain hemispheres. According to Travis the central nervous system functions under a dominant gradient which is located in the left brain hemisphere for right-handed people and in the right hemisphere for left-handed people. Cerebral dominance is necessary for properly co-ordinated muscular activity. If there is interference with natural cerebral dominance as a result of brain injury or disease, or an original lack of such dominance because both brain hemispheres are equally potent in their ability to send out nervous currents to control muscular activity, a conflict in leadership will result. Each brain hemisphere will send out its own nerve impulses according to its own rhythmic pattern. The muscles on the right side of the body will receive impulses and be innervated according to a pattern different from the muscles on the left side of the body. For normal, rhythmic speech, however, it is necessary for the brain to send out identical patterns of nervous currents to paired muscles on both sides of the body. This is possible only when there is a dominant gradient, with one hemisphere taking the lead, and the other following this lead. Thus, a lack of cerebral dominance results in muscular spasm which in speech is recognized as stuttering.

A change in handedness, or the development of incorrect handedness as a result of environmental pressure, is associated with stuttering because there is an interference with natural brain dominance. An individual who has a natively right cerebral dominance should naturally be left-handed. If, as a result of injury or training, he is forced to become right-handed, the interference with brain dominance will frequently manifest itself in stuttering.

Stuttering as a Manifestation of Dysphemia. Dr. Robert West holds that stuttering is a manifestation of an inner psychophysical condition known as dysphemia. "Dysphemia is the condition; stuttering is the manifestation of that condition. Stuttering we can describe exactly; dysphemia is as yet shrouded in mystery. Stuttering is a phenomenon; dysphemia is an inner condition" (22, p. 53).

West believes that the dysphemic individual represents a *different* rather than a pathological personality. The dysphemic is different from most individuals in regard to certain physiological factors including blood composition and metabolism. In addition, West holds that the condition underlying dysphemia is biologically inherited.

The physiological condition of dysphemia does not significantly affect the basic biological functions (respiration and digestion) of the muscles of the speech mechanism. Dysphemia, however, does frequently interfere with and disturb the functioning of the muscles in speech—a learned activity. Emotional situations, especially those in which fear is a factor, contribute to the picture of dysphemia. Under stress of emotion the speech symptom of dysphemia is aggravated, and stuttering is manifest. Because so much of speech is emotional, the opportunity for speech disturbance is frequent and great.

The physiological and psychological symptoms we have described may be considered causally related to primary stuttering. West believes that there is a secondary phase of stuttering which evolved out of the individual's reaction to his own speech. "The occurrence of the spasm of stuttering causes the patient greater social anxiety than he would otherwise experience; this anxiety, in turn, makes the speech less efficient; and as soon as he becomes oppressed by the potency of this vicious cycle, a definite psychoneurosis develops. This is spoken of as the secondary phase of stuttering. With many adults it is doubtless the larger aspect of the problem; but with children it may be almost wholly lacking" (22, pp. 62–3).

Stuttering as a Manifestation of Perseveration. Eisenson (31, pp. 168–72), like West, considers stuttering to be a manifestation of a special type of personality for whom stuttered speech is normal under certain conditions. Perseveration may be defined as a tendency to react to stimuli or situations when the physical cause for such reaction has been removed. It is a tendency for original reactions to continue autonomously, resisting change, so that other reactions to new and changing stimuli cannot readily take place. In a series of experiments involving sensory and motor tasks Eisenson found that stutterers as a group are more influenced by stimuli which were *once present* but which were *no longer physically present* at the moment of reaction than were normal speakers.

Stuttering itself is considered a manifestation of perseveration. The production of a speech sound is the result of the excitation of a set of neurons. When the state of excitation continues autonomously, resisting change, the result is either a repetition of the original sound produced or, if that is inhibited by the speaker, a blocking of further production of articulated sound.

The tendency to perseverate is exhibited by most people, stutterers and nonstutterers alike, when they are fatigued or under emotional strain. Frequently the tendency is revealed in nonspeech activities such as walking or skating or writing. The seagoer takes some time to find his "land legs"; we continue to feel that we are on skates after the skates have been removed; most of us repeat letters or words in writing and later wonder why. The stutterer, however, perseverates more consistently and to a greater degree than the nonstutterer. Stuttering, for the perseverator, is therefore as normal a manner of speaking as is nonstuttering for others.

ARTICULATORY DEFECTS

In order for speech to be produced the stream of breath must be modified by the action of the organs of articulation. This is accomplished by the movements of the jaw, lips, tongue, and soft palate. For the proper production of speech sounds the organs of articulation and the nervous mechanism controlling these organs must be organically sound. Any failure of the articulatory organs to make the appropriate modifications may be considered a defect of articulation. Failures may occur because (1) the organs of articulation may be defective in structure or in their relationship to one another; (2) the neurological mechanism controlling the articulatory movements may be impaired so that normal muscular innervation or inhibition is not possible; or (3) incorrect habits of articulation may have been established even though the speech mechanism is not impaired.

Organic Causes: Oral Deviations.

1. Cleft Palate and Harelip. The articulatory disturbances resulting from cleft palate and harelip are probably greater than

those caused by any other organic malformation. (For a discussion of the voice of the cleft-palate patient see p. 351.) The degree of disturbance is largely determined by the severity of the physical injury. If the soft palate alone is involved, the most seriously defective sounds are the *k, g,* and *ng*. If the hard palate is also involved, sounds which are produced as a result of contact between tongue and hard palate, such as *sh,* and *r,* will also be defective. If the injury includes the upper gum ridge and upper lip the involvement will include such sounds as *p, b, m, t, d, s, z,* etc. If the cleft is sufficiently extensive, the articulatory involvements may be so great and the sounds produced so abnormal in their acoustic aspects as to make the normal comprehension of articulated speech impossible.

2. Malocclusion. A normal jaw adjustment for articulation requires that the upper jaw be slightly anterior to the lower jaw when the jaws are closed. When the opening between the jaws is too great because the lower jaw protrudes past the upper jaw (prognathic), or does not come sufficiently forward to the upper jaw, or the teeth formation is such that the jaws cannot approximate properly, the result is a malocclusion. The effect of malocclusion upon speech depends upon the size of the resultant opening. The sounds most usually defective are the *s* and *z*. If the opening between the jaws is wide enough, the lip-teeth sounds *f* and *v* may also be defective.

3. Tongue-tie. The tongue is attached to the floor of the mouth by a fold of connective tissue called the frenum. If the frenum is too short, or is attached too far front in the mouth, free tongue action which is necessary for proper articulation will be impeded. Sounds which require tip of the tongue action such as *t, d, l, s,* and *z* are likely to be defective in the event of tongue-tie.

4. Tumors of the Tongue. The result of abnormal growths of the tongue is to reduce ease and precision of movement. The

general effect is to cause speech to be thick and indistinct. Sounds directly involving lingual activity will be those chiefly defective. Articulation in general may suffer because the speaker will experience awkwardness and difficulty in producing speech sounds.

Neurological Deficiencies.

1. Dysarthrias. The production of articulated speech sounds calls for a neurological mechanism capable of being stimulated and of making adequate and appropriate responses to the stimuli received. The organs of articulation are directly controlled by nerves emanating from the basal ganglia and the cerebellum. Deficiencies in these centers result in defects of articulation classified as dysarthrias which, like dysphasias (see p. 352), are not in themselves disease entities but rather a symptom complex resulting from disturbances of the neurological mechanism. The disturbance may be caused by trauma, tumor, infectious diseases such as encephalitis, blood-vessel diseases, or degenerative diseases involving the brain centers controlling articulatory movements.

2. Cerebellar Lesions result in staccato, scanning, explosive speech. There is considerable slurring of both consonant and vowel sounds. Generally, the patient with a cerebellar lesion finds no difficulty in uttering isolated speech sounds, but experiences considerable difficulty in producing sounds in a continuous stream of speech. Excessive facial grimacing frequently accompanies the production of articulated speech.

3. Lesions of the Medulla Oblongata. The motor neurons leading from the medulla control many vital functions which involve the muscles used in speech. Movements of the tongue, the lips, and the larynx are controlled in the medulla. Lesions of neurons innervating lip and tongue activity will result in indistinct and labored speech. If the lesion is extensive and of great degree, speech may become entirely unintelligible.

VOICE DEFECTS

Voice Production. Voice, as sound in general, must have the following as essentials for its production: (1) a body capable of vibration (vibrator); (2) a source of energy to be applied to the vibrator; (3) a medium of transmission to a receptor, and (4) resonators to reinforce the original sound produced. The last is an aid, though not an essential. Voice is produced when the stream of breath expelled from the lungs (the source of energy) is directed under pressure through the windpipe to the larynx. In the larynx the stream of breath is forced through the narrow opening between the vocal folds or voice lips (vibrator). When the breath is forced through the narrow opening between the vocal folds they are forced into vibration and sound (voice) is produced. The voice is reinforced essentially by the cavities of larynx, pharynx, mouth, and nose (see diagram below). A disorder of voice may result from any disturbance in the expulsion of the stream of breath, interference with the vibrator, or failure of the sound to be properly resonated.

Characteristics of the Normal Speaking Voice. The speaking voice should be loud enough to meet the needs of normal speech situations, have a pitch appropriate to the age and sex of the individual, be clear in tone, and characterized by sufficient variety of intensity and inflection to make listening easy. Any significant deviations from these attributes may be considered a defect of voice.

Types of Voice Defects (Dysphonias).

1. Inadequate Loudness. A voice may be considered lacking in loudness if it is not easily audible in ordinary conversational situations. The terms *weak* or *thin* are generally used to describe such voices.

2. Inappropriate Pitch. Voices which are either too high or too low in pitch for the sex and age of the individual may be

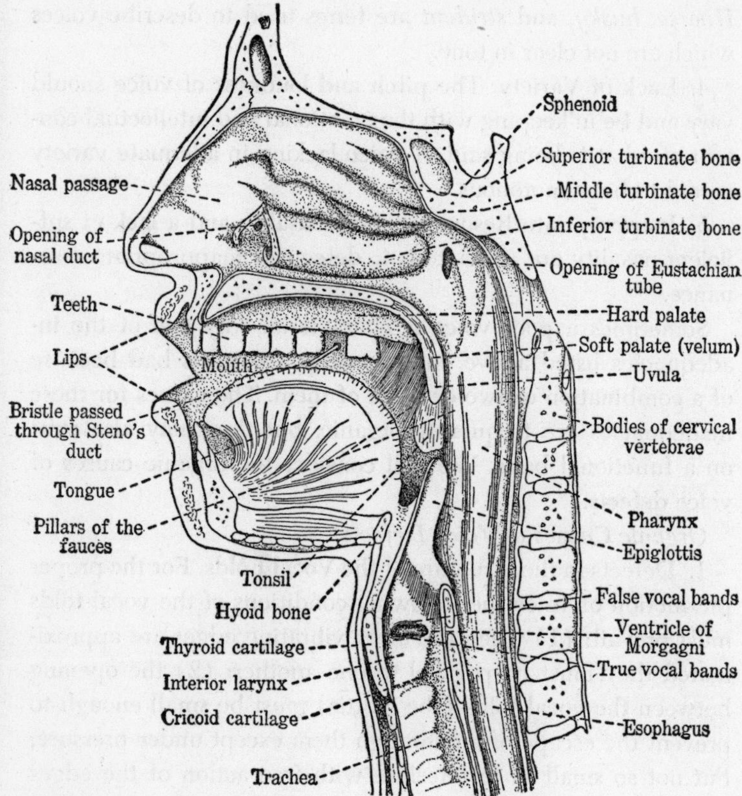

FIG. 10. THE SPEECH MECHANISM

(From West, Kennedy, and Carr, *The Rehabilitation of Speech.* Reproduced by permission of Harper & Brothers.)

considered inappropriate in pitch. The abnormally high-pitched voice is the more common defect and is described by such terms as *shrill* and *treble.*

3. Unclear Tone. A voice that is lacking in clearness of tone contains discordant elements which are displeasing to hear.

Hoarse, husky, and *strident* are terms used to describe voices which are not clear in tone.

4. Lack of Variety. The pitch and loudness of voice should vary and be in keeping with the emotional and intellectual content of what is being said. A voice lacking in adequate variety is said to be monotonous.

5. Inappropriate Resonance. Overnasality and a lack of sufficient nasality are characteristic defects of inappropriate resonance.

Sometimes a poor voice is characterized by one of the inadequacies listed above, more usually a voice is bad because of a combination of two or more of them. The causes for these inadequacies are frequently organic, but they may also exist on a functional basis. We will consider the organic causes of voice defects.

Organic Causes of Voice Defects.

1. Defects in the Structure of the Vocal Folds. For the proper production of voice the following conditions of the vocal folds must prevail: (1) when the inner vibrating edges are approximated they must be parallel to one another; (2) the opening between the vocal folds (the glottis) must be small enough to prevent the escape of air through them except under pressure; but not so small as to interfere with free action of the edges when they are set into vibration by the column of air coming from the lungs.

Any irregularity in the structure of the vibrating edges of the vocal folds which prevents parallel or close approximation will result in a defect of voice. Possible irregularities include depressions of the vocal edges which result in a small gap through which air escapes when the vocal folds are approximated, or growths on the vibrating edges of the vocal folds which prevent regularity of vibration. The causes of the deficiencies may be congenital, developmental, or pathological.

Among the pathological causes are paralysis, syphilis, tuberculosis, tumorous growths, and mechanical injury. The last cause is generally restricted to small children who are all too likely to inhale what they cannot swallow and so will have foreign objects stuck in the larynx. The irritation of the vocal folds by the object, or the violent coughing which is a consequent, may cause injury which will result in defective voice production.

2. Inadequate Breath Supply. In order to have the vocal folds vibrate with sufficient vigor to produce voice the supply of breath must be enough to set the vocal folds into vibration. Any disorder that weakens the bellowslike action of the thoracic cavity will prevent or impede the building up of adequate pressure in the chest to cause vigorous vibratory action of the vocal folds. Such disorders include diseases of the lungs, such as tuberculosis, which directly cause part of the lungs to be useless; disorders which reduce the muscular activity of the diaphragm, such as paralysis of the diaphragm; and chest involvements, such as enlarged heart, which prevent adequate lung expansion. The voices of patients with such disturbances are weak and thin and are likely to be inadequate for even ordinary conversational needs.

3. Defective Control of the Phonating Mechanism. Frequently the organs of the phonating mechanism may be structurally intact but be unable to function properly because of related muscular and neurological disturbances. A few of the more prevalent of these disturbances will be considered.

a. Spastic vocal paralysis, caused by an upper motor-neuron disturbance, frequently results in the vocal folds approximating so closely that the stream of air cannot readily set the vocal folds into vibration. Voicelessness (aphonia) is the consequent. On the other hand, lower motor-neuron lesions are likely to prevent the vocal folds from approximating closely enough to offer sufficient resistance to the stream of air to set the vocal folds into vibration. Voiceless, hoarse, whispered speech is the result.*

b. Choreatic speech (see also p. 370) is characteristically jerky and irregular, as a result of the abnormal respiratory movements of the patient. Short quick gasps and sudden increases in voice intensity are symptoms of choreatic speech when the muscular spasms affect the respiratory muscles. When the spasms involve the soft palate, intermittent nasalization and denasalization occur during speech. Spasms which involve the vocal folds, common in Sydenham's chorea, result in sudden changes in the pitch and intensity of voice.

c. Cerebellar lesions result in a voice production characterized by a lack of muscular co-ordination. For normal voice production, the process of respiration must be subordinated to the breath needs of speech. Such subordination is possible only when an individual can co-ordinate his muscular activities according to functional needs. An individual with a cerebellar lesion is incapable of co-ordinating muscular activity. As a result, the respiratory process is dominant rather than subordinate to the act of speaking. Smooth, freely flowing utterance is not attained. The voice is nasal, staccato, and jerky. The intensity changes of the voice are characteristic and interesting. When speech is initiated the intensity is normal, but it becomes deficient as the patient continues to speak and his supply of breath is diminished.

d. Paralysis agitans, resulting from lesions in the corpus striatum (see p. 51), may involve a rigidity of the vocal folds. The voice is consequently high pitched, shrill, and monotonous.

e. Endocrine disturbances may affect voice by influencing muscular activity. Hypertonicity and excessive activity may result from a hyperactive thyroid gland and be reflected in an

* For a more detailed discussion of spastic speech see pp. 369–70.

overtense, overloud voice. On the other hand, a hypothyroid condition resulting in sluggish muscular activity is likely to become manifest in a dull, lifeless, monotonous voice. Such a voice is characteristic of the cretin.

4. Defects of the Resonating Cavities. The cavities of the larynx, pharynx, mouth, and nose are concerned with the modulation of the tones of the voice. The modulation of pitch and voice quality result from variations in the size and shape of the resonating cavities and in the texture of the wall of these cavities. The laryngeal and nasal cavities are relatively inflexible and cannot be appreciably varied in either size or shape. The pharynx is capable of great variation by means of the action of the tongue and soft palate; in addition, textural modification of the pharyngeal cavity may take place as a result of the changes in the tension of the muscles which form the walls of the pharynx. The mouth is capable of the greatest amount of variation of all the resonating cavities as a result of the action of the lips, tongue, soft palate, and lower jaw.

Defects of the resonating cavities may result either from physical anomalies or from improper functioning of physically normal cavities. Among the most common physical anomalies are abnormal growths in the cavities. Growths such as hypertrophied adenoids or tonsils, polyps, and spurs interfere with the normal response of the resonating cavities by changing their size and shape and preventing normal modifications. The effect of an abnormally large amount of adenoidal tissue is to close off, partially or completely, the cavities of the pharynx and nose. As a result, sound cannot readily enter and be reinforced by these cavities. The voice produced by a person suffering from growths in the nasal or pharyngeal cavities is lacking in nasal resonance. Tones are "dead" and "flat." In addition, the consonants *m*, *n*, and *ng* [ŋ], which are dependent upon nasal resonance for their production, cannot be produced properly.

Deviated septum and high palatal arch are frequent causes of improper nasal resonance.

A deviation of the septum (the bony and cartilaginous partition separating the two nares of the nasal passage) results in improper nasalization and muffling of voice similar in effect to the presence of abnormal growths. The voice defects of a deviated septum are frequently aggravated by chronic colds and catarrh with which the structural anomaly is often associated.

Another common cause of deficient nasal resonance arises from affections of the membranes lining the nose and throat. Inflammations of the membranes result in swelling and in an exudation of mucus. The voice may show signs of both excess nasality and a lack of nasality, depending upon the accompanying speech sounds. The irritation caused by the exudation of mucus may prevent the soft palate from functioning properly, resulting in partial nasality on nonnasal sounds; on the other hand, the swollen and inflamed condition of the walls of the nose and pharynx do not permit these cavities to reinforce nasal sounds normally and fully. The irritation frequently results in a huskiness in addition to improper nasal resonance.

The laryngeal cavity may be obstructed by nasal discharges dropping into the larynx or by tumorous growths which are comparatively rare in children. Chronic catarrh may cause an inflammation of the walls of the larynx, occasionally to such a degree that there is an interference of free vibration of the vocal folds. Hoarseness, tenseness, and intermittent vocalization are the most common voice symptoms resulting from laryngeal obstructions.

Oral deviations such as cleft palate, insufficient palate, or an abnormally large uvula are other common organic causes of voice defects. Cleft palate may vary in extent from a mere pinhole perforation in either the hard or soft palate to a complete fissure extending from the upper lip through the base of the nose to the uvula. The outstanding voice symptom of cleft palate is excessive nasality resulting from an inability to block off the nasal passage by velar activity. A short, soft palate, even though uncleft, is also likely to result in excessive nasality. An abnormally large uvula may cause the velum to be pulled down and so also result in nasality. In addition, a large uvula may irritate the membranes of the pharynx and cause chronic coughing and huskiness.

DYSPHASIA

The term dysphasia is applied to those states or conditions in which the patient experiences difficulty in the comprehension and use of spoken or written language. Dysphasia is in itself not a disease, but rather a symptom complex related to a physiological disorder involving the brain mechanism. The disturbance in language function is only *one* of the symptoms of dysphasia; others include changes in intellectual and emotional behavior and changes in the general personality make-up of the individual. All of these elements in the symptom-complex must be considered if we are to get a true picture of the dysphasic and understand the nature of his disability.

Etiology. Early students of dysphasia inclined to the belief that the disturbance was a result of a lesion in a localized area of the brain. Broca, in 1864, demonstrated that the speech of right-handed persons was affected by injuries to the left hemisphere of the brain, whereas lesions in the right hemisphere did not affect the speech of right-handed persons. Following Broca, Bastian, Kussmaul, and Wernicke attempted to demonstrate that localized and *specific* brain areas were responsible for different aspects of speech, and injuries to the given brain areas resulted in the various types of dysphasic disturbances. More recent workers, including Hughlings Jackson and Henry Head, are opposed to the localization theory, though they agree that the brain area on the side opposite to the dominant hand controls the speech functions. Head (64) believes that the capacity to use language in any form is the result of physiological activities of certain parts of the *brain cortex.* When these parts are disturbed, no matter the cause, the result is a disorder of some degree in the language capacity *as a whole,* rather than in any isolated manifestations.

The possible causes of cerebral cortex disturbance with which dysphasic symptoms are associated are many and varied. They include tumors, trauma, hemorrhages, embolisms, and thromboses of blood vessels supplying the cerebral cortex. Infectious diseases such as meningitis and encephalitis are frequently associated etiologically with dysphasias. Degenerative diseases of the brain such as multiple sclerosis are associated with dysphasia in older persons. Epilepsies and allergies affecting the nervous system are also causally associated with dysphasias. Of the causes just enumerated, the vascular disturbances, embolisms, hemorrhages, and thromboses, are probably the most common etiological associates.

Personality of the Dysphasic. When considering the speech of a dysphasic patient we must bear in mind that the speech is more than the result of a neurological disturbance. The speech of the dysphasic is rather a revelation of a new personality which evolved partly because of events experienced prior to the cause of the dysphasic condition, and partly as a result of the cause itself. Dysphasic patients demonstrate disturbances of thinking which are especially apparent in the sphere of the abstract. Abstraction, generalization, and organization show the greatest deficiency. The dysphasic's thinking, and hence his use of language, proceeds on a concrete level. Dr. Goldstein (65) holds that dysphasic patients have lost "categorical" behavior and are reduced to a more concrete level of behavior. The loss of the meaning of words and the inability to name objects, especially characteristic of the amnesic patient, is accompanied in dysphasics by a great change in their world. The new language used indicates that the dysphasics are building up a world in a particular, concrete way rather than in the more general, abstract way. The tendency of the dysphasics to resort to gesture and pantomime when they wish to express themselves may be considered another indication of their reversion to an elementary and concrete mode of behavior.

The dysphasic patient almost invariably demonstrates a disturbance in his emotional behavior. He is likely to be unstable and to "fly off the handle" readily and frequently. Under excitement the dysphasic's speech may not be impeded; the speech content, however, is not articulate and remains on a nonintellectual level, sometimes consisting almost entirely of a stream of strikingly intoned swear words. In his thinking, speaking, and in his general overt behavior the dysphasic indicates to the trained observer that he has evolved a personality different in part from his old self, and related to the cause which brought about his speech deficiency.

The Linguistic Aspect of Dysphasia. From the linguistic point of view, dysphasia represents a disorder of symbolic formulation and expression, and indicates an inability of the patient to execute readily and easily acts connected with the production and comprehension of spoken and written speech. Both perception and perceptual responses are disturbed, so that dysphasic persons usually suffer from a general impairment in all functions involving the use of language, including reading, writing, speaking, and the comprehension of speech.

The degree of language impairment is usually difficult and frequently impossible to determine. Unless the clinician can obtain reliable information as to the patient's language ability previous to the onset of his difficulty, it is not possible to determine the extent to which the language function has been impaired. An individual with a rich vocabulary, who has been able to use many different words to express the same notion, may not readily demonstrate impaired speech because he is still able to express himself. On the other hand, a person with a limited vocabulary readily demonstrates speech disability because even a slight impairment interferes significantly with oral expression. In the case of dysphasias beginning in infancy, measurement of language disturbance (retardation) is almost impossible because there is no basis for comparison. At most, a mental examination may roughly indicate the degree of *expected* linguistic development. But because good mental tests are largely language tests, and because dysphasic patients also suffer a degree of impairment in motor activities, only the crudest sort of estimate can be made.

The form assumed by a dysphasic disturbance depends not only upon the site, extent, and severity of the brain injury, but also upon the experiences, habits, education, and intelligence of the patient, which are best reflected in the content and manner of his speech. Because the speech characteristics of no two persons are alike, dysphasic manifestations are different for each individual so that there are really as many kinds of dysphasias as there are dysphasic patients. In a strict sense, therefore, classification into discrete types is not possible. Usually, however, one of the language functions shows greater impairment than the others, and, on the basis of the functions most impaired, Weisenberg and McBride (67) have classified dysphasias into four major types. These we shall consider.

Predominantly Expressive Type. In this type of dysphasia the most serious disturbance lies in the patient's inability to express ideas in speech and in writing. In addition, articulation is likely to be defective and word formation and sentence structure to be similarly impaired. Verbal and structural confusion is present which results in erroneous use of words and in the employment of ungrammatical forms. The difficulty of evoking words seems to be equally great for names, objects, and conditions. The following specimen of conversation (67, p. 164) is that of a patient with a predominantly expressive disorder.

> *Patient—Male, white, age 49; Professor of Romance Languages with Ph.D. degree.*
>
> (Do you sometimes think of words more easily in some other language besides English?) Yes . . . yes . . . constantly . . . the . . . I feel . . . the "family" . . . er, "members of the family" . . . I get in Spanish . . . and French rather . . . rather . . . er rather than in English . . . an' English is not coming . . . (Does the German come easily?) No! . . . (Or Italian?) No . . . Except in "ausgegangen" . . . and so forth . . . I *study* my German *for* eight and nine and ten and eleven . . . and so forth . . . an' humorously . . . "ausgegangen" . . . an' my German . . . I . . . er *learn* it at school for six years . . . an' Junior and Senior in college . . . I took it up again.*

The above specimen contains some examples of the verbal errors characteristic of the expressive type of dysphasia. We should note the repeated use of "yes" when "no" was appropriate, and the use of the preposition "for" when "at" was needed to express the proper meaning of the sentence. Grammatical errors are to be observed in the use of the verb *learn* for "taught" and the use of the verb in the present tense when the sentence called for the past tense.

Predominantly Receptive Type. The patient suffering from the receptive type of dysphasia may be able to express himself fairly well, but will have difficulty in understanding spoken

* From T. Weisenberg and K. E. McBride, *Aphasia.* Reprinted by permission of the Commonwealth Fund.

speech or written symbols. The degree of difficulty in regard to the comprehension of the spoken and written symbols varies with the patients. Some have relatively little difficulty in reacting to the written symbols, while in other cases the patient's difficulty may be as extensive in reacting to the written word as it is to the spoken word.

Though the receptive type of dysphasic patient is likely to have some degree of impairment in regard to expression, he is not apt to speak hesitantly or to slur his utterances in the manner of the expressive dysphasic. The most striking defects of expression of the receptive dysphasic are grammatical and verbal confusions. Word-order confusions are also apt to characterize the spoken speech of the receptive dysphasic. The specimen of conversation which follows (67, p. 225) contains some of the characteristic expressive errors of receptive dysphasics.

> *Patient—Male, white, age 57; lawyer; high-school education.*
>
> I just sat here last night by *himself* . . . wrote these things that I told myself . . . now they're things that I just *made* lying here in the night while I had no one *to live* . . . didn't want anyone . . . she really wasn't fit for it . . . she ought to have been in bed several *months* . . . several days . . . (Gestured to indicate behavior of nurse who had a bad cold in her head.) . . . like this all night . . . and I couldn't *stay awake* . . . I couldn't sleep, *with all that thing to have her.**

Verbal confusions in the specimen are to be observed in the use of the word "months" for "days," and "stay awake" for "sleep." Both of these errors were spontaneously corrected by the patient. The grammatical confusion of the last quoted phrase

* *Ibid.*

"with all that thing to have her" is so great as to obscure completely the meaning of the utterance.

Expressive-Receptive Type. All language processes, both expressive and receptive, are extremely limited in this type of dysphasia. In individual instances, the expressive-receptive speech characteristics may really represent the most severe stage of the dysphasic's disorder, which will change either to predominantly expressive or predominantly receptive as the patient shows improvement. There are cases, however, where both expressive and receptive processes continue to be so severely disturbed as to make it difficult to decide whether the expressive aspect is superior or inferior to the receptive aspect of the disturbance. Such cases may be classified as expressive-receptive patients.

The linguistic impairments of the expressive-receptive patient are those which characterize the severe cases belonging to the predominantly expressive and predominantly receptive types. Except under emotional stress, verbal expression may be limited to a few words which the patient will overwork, and which may be poorly articulated. Under emotional stress, the patient may swear with a remarkable degree of fluency, or may even utter a meaningful sentence such as "Don't bother me!" as a response to an annoying situation. Another type of response which may be evoked is the automatic word series such as counting or reciting the letters of the alphabet. The specimen of speech which follows (67, p. 550) represents the longest and best verbal expression produced by the patient during a two-week period of study.

> *Patient—Male, white, age 41; skilled mechanic, high-school education at least.*
>
> Patient had been writing numbers to dictation and after writing "1,000,000" correctly, he spontaneously wrote "93,000,000," pointed to the sun and said: "Old,

old . . . not here . . . earth here one . . . sun . . . old here, lessein . . . here . . . earth hot." *

The specimen, even though a comparatively good one for the patient, still reveals how inadequate his speech was for the situation. We may note that one or two "key" words such as "here" and "earth" tend to be used many times, supplemented by a few other words.

Amnesic Type. The patient's greatest difficulty consists in a marked inability to evoke words as names for objects, conditions, qualities, relationships, etc. The amnesic dysphasic has relatively little difficulty in calling forth familiar and colloquial expressions and automatic responses. Emotionally colored speech can usually be called forth quite readily. In general, the type of words which seem most impaired are those which are precise in their significance for a given speech situation; the type of linguistic responses which remain fairly undisturbed are those which are lacking in precise intellectual significance. The speech which is produced is fairly free of word confusion or grammatical distortion. Articulation is good, especially when compared with the expressive dysphasics.

The amnesic patient is superior to the receptive type in his ability to recognize the correct word both when he hears it spoken by another person or uttered by himself. In general, the comprehension of spoken and written speech is relatively good. Despite this, the amnesic patient often finds himself unable to repeat words he hears and understands, or to write the symbols for words he can read.

An analysis of the sample of conversation (67, p. 312) will reveal the amnesic patient's difficulty in spontaneously producing the correct word for an object and his retained ability of recognizing the precise word when he hears it spoken by another person.

* *Ibid.*

Patient—Male, white; age 35; salesman; two years at high school.

(Patient is asked to name a large pocketbook) . . . I fell, down on this all right . . . well, I guess we're outa luck . . . (Is it a *map*?) No . . . (A *trunk*?) No . . . (A *purse*?) . . . Yeah, well, you can use it that way but that isn't . . . that isn't what . . . what's the proper name? . . . (*Money*?) No . . . (*Bag*?) . . . Well, you can call it that . . . (*Pocketbook*?) Yeah! *

BIBLIOGRAPHY

THE DEFECTIVE IN SPEECH

1. Arps, W., "Motor Efficiency of Elementary Grade Pupils in Speech Corrective Schools, in the Common School, and in Schools for Handicapped Children," *Lehrzeitung*, XIII (Hamburg, 1934), 597–9.
2. Bender, J. F., and V. Kleinfeld, *Principles and Practices of Speech Correction* (Pitman, N.Y., 1938).
3. Carrell, J. A., "A Comparative Study of Speech Defective Children," *Arch. Speech*, I (1936), 179–203.
4. Eisenson, J., *The Psychology of Speech* (Crofts, N.Y., 1938).
5. Greene, J. G., *The Cause and Cure of Speech Disorders* (Macmillan, N.Y., 1927).
6. Kennedy, L., *Studies in the Speech of the Feebleminded*, Thesis (Univ. of Wisconsin, Madison, Wisc., 1930).
7. Manser, R., *Speech Correction on the Contract Plan* (Prentice-Hall, N.Y., 1935).
8. McCullough, G., and A. Birmingham, *Correcting Speech Defects and Foreign Accent* (Scribner, N.Y., 1925).
9. Peppard, H., *The Correction of Speech Defects* (Macmillan, N.Y., 1931), Ch. 6.
10. Raubicheck, L., E. Davis, and L. Carll, *Voice and Speech Problems* (Prentice-Hall, N.Y., 1939).

* *Ibid.*

11. Robbins, S., and R. Robbins, *Correction of Speech Defects of Early Childhood* (Expression Co., Boston, 1937).
12. Rogers, J. F., *The Speech Defective School Child,* Office of Education, Bull. No. 7 (Wash., 1931).
13. Root, A. R., "A Survey of Speech Defectives in the Public Elementary Schools of South Dakota," *Elem. Sch. J.,* XXVI (March, 1926), 531–41.
14. Stinchfield, S., *Speech Pathology* (Expression Co., Boston, 1938).
15. Templin, M. A., "A Study of Aggressiveness in Normal and Defective Speaking College Students," *J. Speech Disorders,* IV:1 (March, 1938), 43–49.
16. Travis, L. E., *Speech Pathology* (Appleton, N.Y., 1931).
17. Travis, L. E., and M. G. Davis, "The Relation between Faulty Speech and Lack of Certain Musical Talents," *Psychol. Monogs.,* XXXVI:168 (1926) 71–81.
18. Twitmyer, E. B., and Y. S. Nathanson, *Correction of Defective Speech* (Blakiston, Phil., 1932).
19. Van Riper, C., *Speech Correction* (Prentice-Hall, N.Y., 1939), Ch. XI.
20. Wallin, J. E. W., *Clinical and Abnormal Psychology* (Houghton Mifflin, Boston, 1927).
21. Ward, I. C., *Defects of Speech* (Dutton, N.Y., 1927).
22. West, R., L. Kennedy, and A. Carr, *The Rehabilitation of Speech* (Harper, N.Y., 1937).
23. White House Conference on Child Health and Protection, *Report of the Committee on Special Classes, Special Education* (Century, N.Y., 1931).

STUTTERING

24. Bender, J. F., *The Personality Structure of Stuttering* (Pitman, N.Y., 1939).
25. Blackburn, W. B., "A Study of Voluntary Movements of Diaphragm, Tongue, Lips, and Jaw in Stutterers and Normal Speakers," *Psychol. Monogs.,* XLI (1931), 1–13.

26. Blanton, S., "A Survey of Speech Defects," *J. Educ. Psychol.*, VII (1916), 581–92.
27. Bluemel, C. S., *Stammering and Allied Disorders* (Macmillan, N.Y., 1935).
28. Boone, E. J., and M. A. Richardson, *The Nature and Treatment of Stammering* (Dutton, N.Y., 1932).
29. Camp, P. B., "Survey of Speech Defects," *J. Speech Educ.*, XI (1923), 280–3.
30. Cross, H. M., "Motor Capacities of Stutterers," *Arch. Speech* (1936), 112–32.
31. Eisenson, J., *The Psychology of Speech* (Crofts, N.Y., 1938), 168–72.
32. Froeschels, E., *Psychological Elements in Speech* (Expression Co., Boston, 1932), 132–7.
33. Hunsley, Y. L., "Disintegration in the Speech Musculature of Stutterers during the Production of a Non-Vocal Temporal Pattern," *Psychol. Monogs.*, XLIX (1937), 32–49.
34. Johnson, W., "Influence of Stuttering on the Attitudes and Adaptations of the Stutterer," *J. Soc. Psychol.*, V (1934), 415–20.
35. Kopp, G. A., "Metabolic Studies of Stutterers," *Speech Monogs.*, I:1 (Sept., 1934), 117–32.
36. McDowell, E. D., *Educational and Emotional Adjustments of Stuttering Children*, T.C. Contribs. to Educ., No. 314 (Bur. of Pubs., Teachers College, Columbia Univ., New York, 1928).
37. Murray, E., "Disintegration of Breathing and Eye Movements in Stutterers during Silent Reading and Reasoning," *Psychol. Monogs.*, XLIII (1931), 218–75.
38. Steer, M. D., "The General Intelligence of College Stutterers," *Sch. and Soc.*, XLIV (1936), 862–4.
39. Travis, L. E., *Speech Pathology* (Appleton-Century, N.Y., 1931), Ch. V.
40. West, R., "A Neurological Test for Stutterers," *J. Neurol. and Psychopathol.*, XXXVIII (London, 1929), 10–14.

41. West, R., L. Kennedy, and A. Carr, *The Rehabilitation of Speech* (Harper, N.Y., 1937), Ch. IV.
42. Westphal, G., "An Experimental Study of Certain Motor Abilities of Stutterers," *Univ. of Iowa Studies in Child Devel.*, IV (1933), 214–21.

ARTICULATORY DEFECTS

43. Bender, J. F., and V. M. Kleinfeld, *Principles and Practices of Speech Correction* (Pitman, N.Y., 1938).
44. Manser, R., *Speech Correction on the Contract Plan* (Prentice-Hall, N.Y., 1935), Ch. IX.
45. Peppard, H., *The Correction of Speech Defects* (Macmillan, N.Y., 1931), Ch. VI.
46. Raubicheck, L., E. Davis, and L. Carll, *Voice and Speech Problems* (Prentice-Hall, N.Y., 1939).
47. Robbins, S., and R. Robbins, *Correction of Speech Defects of Early Childhood* (Expression Co., Boston, 1937).
48. Stinchfield, S., *Speech Disorders* (Harcourt Brace, N.Y., 1933), 58–115.
49. Van Riper, C., *Speech Correction* (Prentice-Hall, N.Y., 1939), Ch. XI.
50. West, R., L. Kennedy, and A. Carr, *The Rehabilitation of Speech* (Harper, N.Y., 1937), Ch. V.

VOICE DEFECTS

51. Barrows, S. T., and A. N. Pierce, *The Voice: How to Use It* (Expression Co., Boston, 1933), 145–55.
52. Jackson, C., "Your Voice," *Hygeia* (Feb., 1939), 110–12.
53. Jackson, C. and O. L., *The Larynx and its Diseases* (Saunders, Phil., 1937).
54. Negus, V., "The Significance of Hoarseness," *N.Y. State J. of Med.* (Jan., 1939), 9–12.
55. Orr, F. W., *Voice for Speech* (McGraw-Hill, N.Y., 1938).
56. Orton, H., "Cancer of the Larynx," *Arch. Otolaryngology*, XXVIII (1938), 153–92.

57. Orton, H., "Diseases of the Larynx: Material Abstracted during 1938," *The Laryngoscope* (Feb., 1939), 69–101.
58. Raubicheck, L., E. Davis, and L. Carll, *Voice and Speech Problems* (Prentice-Hall, N.Y., 1939).
59. Russell, G. O., *Speech and Voice* (Macmillan, N.Y., 1931).
60. Van Riper, C., *Speech Correction* (Prentice-Hall, N.Y., 1939), Ch. XII.
61. West, R., L. Kennedy, and A. Carr, *The Rehabilitation of Speech* (Harper, N.Y., 1937), Ch. VII.

DYSPHASIA

62. Ewing, A. W. G., *Aphasia in Children* (Oxford Univ. Press, London, 1930).
63. Froeschels, E., *Psychological Elements in Speech* (Expression Co., Boston, 1932).
64. Head, H., *Aphasia and Kindred Disorders of Speech* (Cambridge Univ. Press, Cambridge, 1926).
65. Goldstein, K., "The Problem of the Meaning of Words Based upon Observations of Aphasic Patients," *J. Psychol.*, II (1937), 301–16.
66. Osnato, M., *Aphasia and Associated Speech Problems* (P. H. Hoeber, N.Y., 1920).
67. Weisenberg, T., and K. E. McBride, *Aphasia* (Commonwealth Fund, N.Y., 1935).

CHAPTER XII

Speech Involvements of Special Types of the Physically Handicapped

THE BLIND

Speech Development of the Blind. Learning to speak, for the small child, is largely a matter of imitation. The child with normal vision who is learning to speak learns speech sounds and word contexts as they are accompanied by visible activity of the face, arms, and hands, and the action of the body as a whole. The visible aspect of speech is absent for the blind. In developing speech the congenitally blind must learn to imitate movements of the speech mechanism that they have never seen; they must depend completely on the acoustic aspects of speech production.

The normal seeing child receives speech stimulation from many people who vary among themselves in respect to voice quality, manner, and articulatory ability and accuracy. The environment of the congenitally blind child is much more limited. Fewer people see the blind child, and fewer still speak to him. The speech development of the blind child is likely to be neglected so that he begins to talk at a later time than does the seeing child. The developed speech of the blind is likely to be imitative of the speech characteristics of the few people who have afforded him speech stimulation. If these characteristics are desirable, the blind child is fortunate; if they are faulty, the blind child will probably develop faulty speech. Cutsforth (1, p. 114) makes the observation that in institutional schools for the blind there is frequently an institution-wide imitation of the mannerisms and language of a favorite teacher or popular older pupil. The seeing child can ape what he hears or sees; and so may imitate the speech or dress or walk of a favorite older person; the blind child is limited in his mimicry to what he hears, and so may learn to imitate mannered speech.

Vocalized speech, to the blind child, is an even more important avenue of communication than for the seeing child. Once verbal utterance has been attained, the blind child is more likely to speak than the visually normal child. Speech, to the blind child, is his only effective way of stimulating his environment and eliciting responses from it. As a social being, a blind person ceases to exist when he is not actively engaged in verbal communication. It is not enough for a blind person to be near other persons, he must be engaged in conversation with them, to stimulate and be verbally stimulated by them, in order to assure himself that he is socially alive.

Despite the importance of vocal communication for the blind, there is a greater prevalence of voice and articulatory errors among the blind than among the normally sighted. In a survey conducted by Stinchfield (5, p. 70) which included 400 children of the Pennsylvania School for the Blind at Overbrook and at Perkins Institution for the Blind at Watertown, Massachusetts, 49 per cent of the children were found to have some form of speech defect. Surveys indicate that defective speech is more prevalent among blind children than among seeing children of the same age and same school grade from the kindergarten to high school (3).

Psychological Causes of Speech Defects among the Blind. One of the most significant causes for the existence of speech defects among the blind, aside from causes inherent in the very development of their speech, lies in the personality of the blind. As we have indicated elsewhere (see p. 13), the blind tend to be egocentric, and hence are likely to overlook or be unaware of their own shortcomings though highly sensitive to the deficiencies—including speech defects—of others in their environment. Occasionally, a blind person may be aware of his defects but indulge in practicing them for the sake of whatever emotional satisfaction they afford him. Parents, friends, and even the teachers of a blind person may hesitate to correct his speech for fear of hurting his feelings or meeting with an attitude of antagonism.

Another basic psychological reason for the defective speech of the blind lies in the inability of the blind person to analyze the sounds he hears. A seeing person not only hears a sound but can also observe how it is produced. For many of the English sounds, especially those produced by lip-teeth activity, this observation is very helpful. Thus, a seeing person has a twofold basis for speech analysis. A blind person can hear a sound but he cannot see how the sound is produced. Because of this, his basis for analysis is incomplete and his imitation of the sound may be faulty.

Organic Causes of Speech Defects among the Blind. Somatic deficiencies that are frequent accompaniments of congenital blindness or blindness acquired because of illness are underlying organic causes for the defective speech of the blind. Nasal, oral, pharyngeal, and laryngeal malformations, as well as poor neuromuscular control, which result in sluggish and uncertain reactions, may be caused by such diseases as spinal meningitis, infantile paralysis, and rachitis. The sphenoidal sinus may become infected because of its closeness to an infected optic tract, and so disturb the speech mechanism. Lack of muscular stimulation because of limited opportunity for exercise results in muscular immaturity, poor muscle tone and general flaccidity. These muscular deficiencies make difficult the task of correct voice production and accurate, precise articulation.

Articulatory Defects. Infantilisms such as lisping, sound transposition, and sound omission are frequently heard in the speech of the blind. Slovenly, muffled speech resulting from insufficient oral activity is common among the blind students. Elliot (2) reports that many blind persons ". . . attempt articulation with their lips barely apart."

Voice Defects. An outstanding voice characteristic of the untrained blind person is referred to by Cutsforth (1, p. 117) as the "broadcast voice." It is overloud, probably because of the inability of the blind to localize the auditor and to direct and project the voice with reference to him. The "broadcast voice" insures the blind person that he is being heard and so affords him a feeling of greater security which he might not otherwise have. In addition to its loudness, a blind person's voice is apt to be flat and monotonous, lacking appropriate modulation. The flatness and monotony are probably the results of the muscular hypotension and general flaccidity which are characteristic of the blind.

Special Problems in the Correction of the Speech of the Blind. The speech teacher of the blind has to cope with problems which lie partly in himself as an individual, partly with the personality of the blind person, and in part with the physical and social situation in which both teacher and blind student find themselves. To begin with, the teacher must develop a personality that is emotionally controlled. The teacher must sympathize with the blind but must be careful not to substitute pity for sympathetic understanding. Blind children need more speech correction than do the normally sighted; they come to school with poor speech habits which indulgent parents and siblings have not attempted to correct. The teacher must appreciate the need for early and intensive corrective work, even though he realizes that the blind child might find speech therapy irksome.

The blind person, we have already indicated, is not likely to be sensitive to his own errors or objectively critical about his speech. He has "gotten by" with his speech for several years with little or no criticism so that he is apt to meet criticism of his speech with more than a normal amount of antagonism. Living in a limited and special environment centered about themselves, the blind do not find their own speech objectionable. Moreover, they do not have sufficient social insight to perceive that their speech is faulty from the point of view of the larger social group. Sankey sums up some of the reactions of the blind to speech training by such expressions as: "Who wants to talk like a sissy," or, "Oh, in that class they teach you to put on airs." (4, p. 81.) The blind must be furnished with strong motivating drives to overcome the effects of their egocentricity and their feelings of antagonism in order to make the attainment of correct speech a worth-while acquisition. Dramatic and radio work have been found to be successful devices in motivating speech work for the blind.

In the correction of the speech of the normally sighted, the use of mirrors, pictures, and the observation of the speech teacher are important. These corrective materials cannot be used by the blind for whom speech correction must proceed largely on tactual, kinesthetic, and auditory bases. Tongue depressors, applicator sticks, and fingers help in the development of the tactual sense. Repetitive articulatory drills help to develop the kinesthetic image. The "talking book" is coming into wide use as an auditory aid. Even when the blind person is cognizant of his faults and is desirous of correcting his speech, he is beset with hindrances. Because of the poor tonus of the muscles used in articulation, drills and exercises are tiresome. Only when the general health and muscle tone of the blind person is at a high level will speech training result in maximum benefit for the blind.

THE SPASTIC

The speech involvements resulting from spasticity will be determined by the amount and degree of brain injury. When the injury involves large cerebral areas the spastic may display the language retardation of the ament as well as the voice and articulatory defects commonly associated with spasticity itself. A contributing and complicating factor in the speech of the spastic originates on a psychogenic basis. The intellectually normal or even superior spastic individual may develop speech peculiarities because of a feeling of self-consciousness arising from his appearance. We shall consider here only those defects in speech that are directly caused by the paralysis.

Voice. The voice of the spastic individual, if laryngeal muscles are involved, will be symptomatic of his general inability to make fine muscular movements and so control variation in pitch and intensity. Voice pitch is dependent upon a fine balance between two sets of laryngeal muscles. One set raises the framework of the larynx and tenses the muscle bands. In spasticity with laryngeal involvement both sets of muscles are apt to be hypertonic. Thus changes in voice pitch cannot easily take place. The level of pitch can be changed only with difficulty. Muscle changes are gross in nature so that the resultant pitch is likely to be either too high or too low. Slight and subtle pitch changes which characterize normal inflectional patterns are practically impossible of voluntary attainment. Under emotional stress inflection changes may occur, but then they are uncontrolled, exaggerated, and likely to be characterized by marked tremor.

The voice of the spastic is likely to be too loud and unvarying in intensity. Changes in loudness which characterize normal voice and which normal speakers employ for emphasis are missing. The voice of the spastic will frequently be husky in quality. Occasionally the spastic can speak only in a husky whisper and is unable to produce vocalized speech. In general the voice is labored, jerky, and unrhythmic.

Articulation. Because intricate muscular movements are not possible for the spastic, speech sounds involving precise and delicate adjustments of the articulators cause the spastic the greatest amount of difficulty. Consonant sounds such as *s* and *t* require special arrangements of the muscles involved in articulation for their correct production. Such sounds are likely to be faulty. If there is a general rigidity of the facial muscles, sounds involving lip movements, such as the consonants *b, p, f, v, m,* are likely to be defective. In general, the articulation of the spastic is lacking in precision and marked by sound substitutions and omissions.

THE CHOREATIC

The specific defect in speech of the choreatic patient is determined essentially by the particular muscle groups which are involved in and disturbed by the choreatic spasms. If the respiratory muscles are affected, speech is likely to be produced in a jerky, gaspy manner, with sudden and explosive increases in the volume of the voice. If the spasms involve the larynx, incorrect voicing and unvoicing of speech sounds are likely to take place. In cases where there is an involvement of the soft palate (palatal nystagmus), sounds produced with palatal contact are likely to be defective. Incorrect nasalization of non-nasal consonants, and interruption and denasalization of nasal consonants constitute characteristic defects. Where the spasms involve facial muscles, vowel sounds and lip consonants are likely to be distorted.

THE DEAF *

SPEECH AND HEARING

Speech development, as we have indicated earlier, is normally an imitative process. Hearing is the most important sensory avenue through which sounds are learned and upon which sound imitation, including articulation and voice inflection, is based. Although vision is unquestionably a very important sensory avenue for speech learning, it is possible through the visual sense alone to produce only such consonants as *p, f, th* [θ], etc., which involve overt articulatory movements. For the most part, however, vowel sounds and many consonants, such as *l, n, t, d, g, k, s,* etc., are produced in a manner which is not entirely discernible to the eye. For example, the lip positions for *d, l,* and *n* are essentially the same. The acoustic differences are the result of adjustments of articulatory organs—the tongue and the parts of the hard and soft palate—which the eye cannot easily observe. A person depending upon vision for sound discernment is likely to confuse such words as *dough, low,* and *no,* because the visible aspects of these words are similar.

It is recognized, of course, that when the hearing loss occurs after normal speech has been developed there is likely to be no immediate or appreciable difficulty in the production of articulated speech sounds. Voice production, however, may

* Our discussion will be concerned essentially with the speech of the hard-of-hearing and the deafened.

readily be affected. The individual who cannot hear and react to his own voice or to the voices of others is likely to develop a monotony of pitch even though his voice was sufficiently varied before his hearing became affected. Eventually, in severe cases of deafness, articulation may also become affected because the failure to perceive complete speech patterns may result in the individual's producing only those sounds which he is able to hear. The Ewings (15, p. 41) report that more than 50 per cent of the severely deaf patients tested in their clinic had developed defects of speech of which, in a majority of instances, they were not aware. As a rule, however, patients who suffer from only a slight degree of deafness develop no appreciable defects of speech.

SPEECH DEFECTS ASSOCIATED WITH DEAFNESS

The speech involvements associated with deafness vary according to the type, severity, and onset of the hearing deficiency. In general, as we would expect, deaf children are decidedly retarded in speech development. The defects of speech include vocal defects such as monotony, slowness of rate,* defects of nasality, extremes in pitch and intensity. Defects of articulation are numerous, especially in regard to the production of the following sounds (14, p. 233): *s*, *sh* [ʃ], *ch* [tʃ], *ng* (ŋ), *t*, *l*, *r*, *d*, *z*, *zh* [ʒ], *j* [dʒ], and *y* [j]. Defects of intonation and the persistence of infantilisms in speech were also found to be common characteristics of the speech of the deaf.

SPEECH INVOLVEMENTS ARISING OUT OF THE DIFFERENT TYPES OF DEAFNESS

Conduction Deafness. In general, the individual suffering

* Voelker (23) reported deaf persons to speak at an average rate of 67 words per minute compared with 164 words per minute for normal-hearing persons.

from conduction deafness exhibits speech defects resulting from reduced acuity of hearing. Speech sounds which are not visible in their production are not "heard," and because they are not "heard," they are not properly learned and tend to be produced inaccurately. Visible sounds which are more easily learned, viz.: *p, f, w,* etc., may frequently be substituted for the consonants partly resembling them, viz.: *k, th, r,* etc. For example, a conduction deaf person may say "dot" for "got," or "wag" for "rag."

The *voice* of the conduction-deaf person is characteristically of weak intensity. Sounds which are transmitted to the ear through the temporal bones are seemingly increased in intensity whereas sounds which are transmitted through the air are diminished in intensity. A conduction-deaf person has difficulty in estimating the loudness of his voice. Usually he reacts to his own voice (transmitted to himself through the bones) as if it were louder than it actually is. On the other hand, the voices of other persons, which are transmitted to him through the air, appear to be less loud than they actually are. Any increases in intensity of his own voice cause unpleasant reverberations in his head. Consequently, to avoid this sensation, the conduction-deaf person develops the habit of speaking in a voice which is subdued and too weak in intensity for others to hear him with ease. The lack of pitch variety is an added factor making it difficult to listen to the conduction-deaf person. Monotony of both pitch and volume are the chief characteristics of the voices of persons suffering from reduced acuity arising out of conduction deafness.

Perception Deafness. The articulatory defects of the perception-deaf individual are similar to those of the conduction-deaf person. The voice, however, is different for reasons arising out of the type of the deafness. Whereas the conduction deaf person hears his own voice as louder than those of his hearers, the severely perception-deaf person cannot hear his own voice unless he speaks very loudly. This is so because the auditory nerve has lost its normal sensitivity. Only an increased intensity of sound will result in the nerve being stimulated to a degree sufficient to bring about a mental reaction to sound. Consequently, the person suffering from severe perception deafness speaks very loudly. Unless he hears himself speak he cannot be sure that others can hear him.

Deafness to Special-Frequency Ranges. The speech involvements in special-frequency ranges will be determined by the extent and range of frequency to which the individual is deaf. We will consider the characteristic speech difficulties involved in low-, middle-, and high-frequency deafness.

1. *Low-Frequency Deafness.* A person who is insensitive to pitches in the low-frequency range is unable to hear the fundamental tones of the voice which range between 100 to 400 vibrations per second. The fundamental tones of the voice arise as a result of the vibration of the vocal folds and accompany the pitches of articulated voiced consonants, such as *d, g, v, l, m,* etc., and vowels. From the point of view of comprehension, the effect of low-frequency deafness lies in the emotional rather than the intellectual sphere, because the fundamental voice tones convey the feelings and emotional implications of the speaker. The intellectual content of speech is not greatly affected because articulated sounds, which convey the intellectual meanings, are in the higher pitch frequencies.

All speech is perceived as whispered when the vocal tones are not heard. The different vowels can be recognized by a person deaf to low frequencies much as persons with normal hearing recognize whispered vowels. Confusion exists in the perception of cognate consonants, those which are alike as to place and manner of production but which differ in regard to the absence or presence of voice. The consonants *t* and *d, k* and *g, p* and *b, s* and *z* are examples of pairs of cognate sounds. Consequently a person who is unable to hear the fundamental voice tones will not be able to distinguish between such words as *pin* and *bin, palm* and *balm, tin* and *din.* Comprehension of speech, despite the possibility of cognate confusion, is not likely to be significantly impaired if the topic of discourse is *known.* Thus, the individual will have little difficulty in engaging in a self-initiated conversation or in one on a familiar topic, but he is likely to have considerable difficulty in participating in a conversation he has not initiated if the topic is unfamiliar to him.

The articulation of the person with low-frequency deafness will reveal his confusion in regard to the hearing of cognate sounds. Consonants such as *t* and *d, k* and *g, p* and *b, s* and *z* are likely to be interchanged in speech. The voice of the person is likely to be dull, strident, and uninflected, lacking almost completely in capacity for subtle implications which normally result from changes in the pitches of the voice.

2. Middle-Frequency Deafness. The resonating cavities of the human speech mechanism—the cavities of the larynx, pharynx, mouth, and nose—reinforce sounds in the middle-frequency pitch range. Within this range are included the various vowel sounds and the vowellike consonants *h, m, n, ng* [ŋ], *r, w, l,* and *y* [j]. Deafness to the middle-frequency pitches would make a person unable to perceive by ear differences between sounds included within this range. Some compensation for a hearing loss in the middle-frequency range may take place through "lip reading" because of the characteristically different positions of the lips and shape of the mouth in producing the vowels and vowellike consonants.

3. High-Frequency Deafness. With the exception of the vowels and vowellike consonants, most speech sounds are in the upper pitch frequencies, ranging from 2,400 to 8,000 vibrations per second. An individual deaf to frequencies within this range

is unable to distinguish between sounds falling within the range of frequencies to which he is deaf. For example, the differences between *s* and *sh* [ʃ] or *f* and *v* may not be perceived by the ear. If the deafness includes the entire high-frequency range speech is heard as a jumble of noises, such as the normal person may hear when a radio is not "tuned in" properly.

A person with "pure" high-frequency deafness can perceive the emotional implications of speech carried by the low frequencies of the voice but can only partly comprehend the ideational content conveyed by articulated speech. High-frequency deaf patients, however, very often manifest some involvement in the low-frequency ranges as well, so that comprehension of both the emotional and ideational content of speech is impaired.

In producing speech, the high-frequency deaf person has especial difficulty with those sounds which are not readily visible in their production. Sounds such as *s, z, f, v, t, d, k,* and *g* are inaccurately produced or may be entirely omitted. The more easily observable sounds such as *p* and *b* are generally produced accurately because the articulatory movements are easy to imitate.

Deafness to Low Intensities. Intensity or phonetic power is the least reliable of the characteristics by which speech sounds may be recognized. Speech sounds vary in intensity of production from individual to individual and in the same person from time to time, according to the manner and content of speech. Such factors as emphasis and syllable stress are important in determining the audibility of sounds in the syllable. A vowel sound in an accented syllable may have three or four times the phonetic power of the same vowel in an unaccented syllable. There is, however, a consistent difference in intensity between the vowel sounds and the consonants. Fletcher (17, p. 74) has determined that all vowel sounds are phonetically stronger than any of the consonants except *l*.

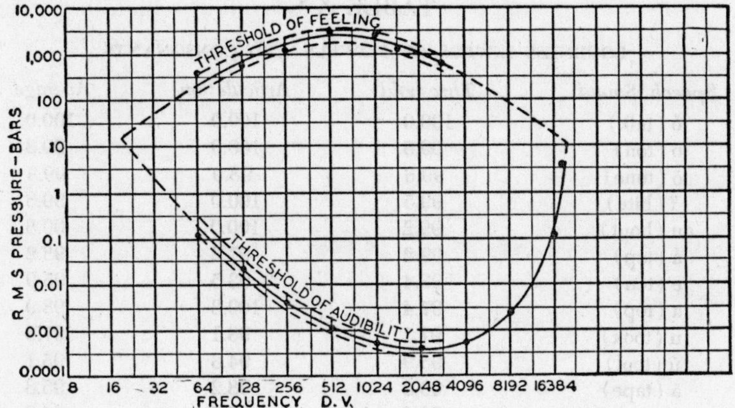

FIG. 11. THE THRESHOLD OF AUDIBILITY
FOR SOUNDS IN RELATIONSHIP TO THEIR PITCH

(From Harvey Fletcher, *Speech and Hearing,* by courtesy of D. Van Nostrand Co., Inc.)

A complicating factor in regard to the intensity of sounds is that sounds of different frequencies are audible at *varying intensities* (see Fig. 11). Attempts to increase the audibility of sounds of low phonetic value by loud speaking frequently results in overintensifying other sounds in the context of speech which are initially of high phonetic value. Loud speaking, if it is to be of help to persons who are deaf to sounds of low intensities, must be practiced so that the weak sounds can be brought up to the level of phonetically strong sounds, without accompanying increase in the intensity of the naturally strong sounds.

SPEECH TRAINING FOR THE DEAF

The type and course of training prescribed for any individual with a hearing loss will depend primarily upon the type and the

TABLE X *

LOUDNESS LEVELS OF VOWELS AND CONSONANTS

Speech Sound	*Threshold*	*Articulation*	*Average*
ó (talk)	100.0	100.0	100.0
o (ton)	99.6	100.0	99.8
ō (tone)	99.6	98.9	99.3
ī (bite)	99.5	100.0	99.8
ou (bout)	99.2	100.0	99.6
á (tap)	99.2	97.2	98.2
e (ten)	98.4	93.5	95.9
a (top)	97.4	100.3	98.9
u (took)	97.1	98.1	97.6
ū (tool)	95.9	94.3	95.1
ā (tape)	93.3	98.2	95.8
i (tip)	92.6	95.5	94.0
ē (team)	89.4	96.3	92.9
r (err)	96.0	95.5	95.8
l (let)	93.5	92.6	93.1
ng (ring)	88.9	93.8	91.4
sh (shot)	88.9	93.2	91.1
ch (chat)	87.2	89.7	88.5
n (no)	86.8	86.7	86.75
m (me)	85.4	85.1	85.3
th (that)	84.2	....	84.2
t (tap)	84.1	86.4	85.3
h (hat)	83.9	81.7	82.8
k (kit)	83.8	85.3	84.6
j (jot)	83.7	89.7	86.7
f (for)	83.6	77.7	80.7
g (get)	82.9	86.9	84.9
s (sit)	82.4	78.1	80.3
z (zip)	81.6	81.6	81.6
v (vat)	81.4	80.1	80.8
p (pat)	80.6	81.4	81.0
d (dot)	78.9	87.8	83.4
b (bat)	78.8	83.7	81.3
th (thin)	78.7	71.2	75.0

* From Harvey Fletcher, *Speech and Hearing*, by courtesy of D. Van Nostrand Co., Inc.

degree of the deficiency. It is obvious that the *deaf* who have never reacted to oral speech as such will need a course of training different from the *deafened* who have lost their hearing after they had acquired speech. Similarly, the hard-of-hearing who still hear and react to oral speech, though their hearing is impaired, will require training and therapy different in many respects from that intended for the deaf and deafened.

The cause of the hearing loss must be considered in devising a program of speech training for the deaf. The perception-deaf, the conduction-deaf, and the individual suffering from high-frequency deafness require programs arranged for the special needs arising out of the cause of the difficulty. Though it is not within the limits of this text to prescribe detailed speech-training programs for the deaf, the deafened, and the hard-of-hearing, general principles may be indicated. First, the hearing that the individual possesses must be utilized to the fullest extent. Remnants of hearing should be reinforced by appropriate mechanical hearing aids.* Secondly, other senses should be developed and utilized to replace or assist hearing in learning and establishing habits of oral speech production. The kinesthetic (muscle), the tactual (touch), and the visual sense must be employed in the speech education of persons with reduced acuity of hearing. The individual must be taught not only how to hear a speech sound but how to feel and to see it and how to place and move his articulatory organs in the production of speech sounds.

* For a discussion of hearing aids for the deaf see the Ewings (15, pp. 110–27).

BIBLIOGRAPHY

THE BLIND

1. Cutsforth, T. D., *The Blind in School and Society* (Appleton-Century, N.Y., 1933).
2. Elliot, R., "Spoken English at the Oklahoma School for the Blind," *Teachers Forum (Blind)* XI:1 (Sept., 1938).
3. Fladeland, S. V., "Speech Defects of Blind Children," *Teachers Forum (Blind)*, III (1930), 6–8.
4. Sankey, A. M., "Problems in Teaching Speech to the Blind," *Quart. J. Speech*, XXIV:1 (Feb., 1938), 77–83.
5. Stinchfield, S. M., *Speech Pathology* (Expression Co., Boston, 1928).

THE SPASTIC

6. Carroll, R. L., "Speech Training in the Child Crippled by Spastic Paralysis," *J. Speech Disorders,* II (Sept., 1937), 155–7.
7. Fagan, H. R., "Methods of Treatment for Spastic Speech," *J. Speech Disorders,* IV (March, 1939), 25–31.
8. Palmer, M. F., "Spastic Paralysis from the Point of View of the Speech Pathologist," *J. Speech Disorders,* IV (Dec., 1939), 294–6.
9. Pusitz, M. E., "Speech Correction in Cerebral Palsies," *J. Speech Disorders,* IV (Sept., 1939), 205–18.
10. Robbins, S. D., "Speech of the Spastic," *J. Speech Disorders,* IV (March, 1939), 32–33.
11. Rutherford, B. R., "Frequency of Articulation Substitutions in Children Handicapped by Cerebral Palsy," *J. Speech Disorders,* IV (Sept., 1939), 285–7.
12. West, R., L. Kennedy, and A. Carr, *The Rehabilitation of Speech* (Harper, N.Y., 1937), 108–19.
13. Zentay, P. J., "Motor Disorders of the Central Nervous Sys-

tem and Their Significance for Speech," *The Laryngoscope*, XLVII (1937), 421–30.

THE DEAF

14. Bender, J. F., and V. M. Kleinfeld, *The Principles and Practices of Speech Correction* (Pitman, N.Y., 1938).
15. Ewing, A. W. G., *Aphasia in Children* (Oxford Univ. Press, London, 1930).
16. Ewing, I. E., and A. W. G. Ewing, *The Handicap of Deafness* (Longmans, Green, N.Y., 1938).
17. Fletcher, H., *Speech and Hearing* (Van Nostrand, N.Y., 1929).
18. Goldstein, M. A., *Problems of the Deaf* (Laryngoscope Press, St. Louis, Mo., 1933).
19. Goldstein, M. A., "Defective Speech in Relation to Defective Hearing," *Arch. of Otolaryngology* (Jan., 1940), 38–41.
20. Hudgins, C. V., "A Comparative Study of the Speech Coordinations of Deaf and Normal Subjects," *J. Genet. Psychol.*, XLIV (1934), 3–48.
21. Hudgins, C. V., "Voice Production and Breath Control in the Speech of the Deaf," *Am. Annals of the Deaf*, LXXXII (Sept., 1937), 338–63.
22. Newhart, H., "Hearing Deficiencies in Relation to Speech Defects," *The Laryngoscope*, XLVIII (1938), 129–36.
23. Voelker, V. A., "A Preliminary Strobophotoscopic Study of the Speech of the Deaf," *Am. Annals of the Deaf*, LXXX (May, 1935), 243–60.
24. Voorhees, I. W., "Defects in Speech in Relation to Defects in Hearing," *Arch. Otolaryngology* (Jan., 1940), 7–15.
25. West, R., "Speech and Hearing," *Quart. J. Speech* (April, 1935), 178–88.
26. West, R., L. Kennedy, and A. Carr, *The Rehabilitation of Speech* (Harper, N.Y., 1937), Ch. X.

Subject Index

Acromegaly, 65
Adrenal glands, 67
Allergic, 284-7; definition of, 284; intelligence of, 285-6; personality of, 286-7
Articulatory defects, 341-3; organic causes of, 341-3
Autonomic nervous system, 40-41

Babbitt Hospital, 15
Behavior patterns, development of, 61-62
Blind, articulatory defects of, 367; educational achievement of, 219-29; intelligence of, 212-19; learning ability of, 217-18; memory of, 236-8; musical ability of, 238; occupations of, 241-2; organic causes of speech defects of, 366-7; personality development of, 13-14; personality of, 229-31; phantasies of, 240; psychological causes of speech defects of, 366; psychology of, 207-51; reading ability of, 219-21; reading interests of, 240-1; social maturity of, 239-40; space perception of, 235-6; special abilities of, 231-9; special problems in correction of speech of, 367-9; speech development of, 364-5; speech of, 364-9; spoken language of, 226-7; touch reading of, 222-5; vocabulary ability of, 221-2; voice defects of, 367
Blindness, causes of, 208-9
Brain, 38, 49, 56-57; stem, 38
Broca's area, 54

Cardiacs, 287-94; classification of, 288-9; emotional adjustment of, 290; intelligence of, 288; school achievement of, 288-9; vocational adjustment of, 289-90
Central nervous system, 38-40
Cerebellar lesions, and speech, 343; and voice, 348
Cerebellum, 38, 52
Cerebral dominance, 338-9
Cerebrospinal nerves, 38
Cerebrum, 38, 52-53
Choreatic speech, 348, 370-1
Cleft palate, 350; and harelip, 341-2
Compensation, 25-26
Compulsion neurosis, 33-34
Conduction deafness and speech defects, 372-3
Cortex, areas of, 53-56
Cortin, 67
Cranial nerves, 38, 40
Cretin, 349
Cretinism, 66
Crippled, 262-83; definition of, 262-3; intelligence of, 265-71; personality of, 272-5; school achievement of, 271; social com-

Crippled (*continued*) petence of, 275-6; vocational adjustment of, 276-81
Crippling, causes of, 264-5; incidence of, 263
Cycloid, 8-9

Deaf, Binet tests of, 110-12; educational achievement of, 130-50; emotional stability of, 157-62; general adjustment of, 152-7; group intelligence tests of, 117-22; intelligence of, 110-30; language tests of, 138-43; learning tests of, 122-4; lip-reading tests of, 144-8; mechanical ability of, 168-70; memory of, 170; miscellaneous tests of, 124-6; motor ability of, 166-8; performance tests of, 112-17; personality of, 150-65; psychology of, 101-87; reading of, 143-4; special abilities of, 166-71; speech tests of, 144-8; speech training of, 377-9; vocational training of, 171-5
Deafness, causes of, 103-4; incidence of, 102-3; speech defects associated with, 372-7; to low intensities, and speech defects, 376-377; to special-frequency ranges, and speech defects, 374-7
Decussation, 57, 59-60
Deviated septum, 350
Diabetes mellitus, definition of, 290-1
Diabetic, 290-4; intelligence of, 291-3; personality studies of, 293-4
Dysarthrias, 343
Dysphasia, 351-9; linguistic aspect of, 353-4; types of, 354-9
Dysphasic, personality of, 352-3
Dysphemia, 339-40
Dysphonias, 344-6

Encephalitic, 295-6; definition of, 294; intelligence of, 296-7; sequelae of, 295
Endocrine disturbances and voice, 348-9
Endocrine system, 62-69; nature of, 62-63
Epileptic, 296-305; deterioration of, 301-3; intelligence of, 299-301; personality of, 303-5
Epilepsy, age at onset of, 298-9; incidence of, 298; type of seizures, 297-8
Escape reactions, 26-28

Facial vision, 231-3
Fears and phobias, 32-33
Froelich's syndrome, 65
Fundamental human drives, 21-23

Gigantism, 65
Goiter, 66

Hard of hearing, educational achievement of, 192-5; intelligence of, 189-92; personality of, 195-204; psychology of, 188-206
Hearing aids, 379
High-frequency deafness as cause of speech defects, 375-6
Hyperthyroidism, 66
Hypothalamus, 51-52
Hypothyroidism, 66

Identification, 28
Internal mechanisms of behavior, 37-71

Laryngeal obstructions, 350
Low-frequency deafness and speech defects, 374-5

Malnourished, 306-7; intelligence of, 306-7
Malocclusion, 342
Mechanisms of adjustment, 23-34; determinants of a choice of, 34-35; undesirable, 35
Medulla oblongata, 38, 50-51; lesions of, and speech, 343
Memory distortion, 32
Mental hygiene, 19-36; aims of, 19-20; defined, 19; program for the physically handicapped, 20-21
Middle-frequency deafness and speech defects, 375
Myelin, 42
Myxedema, 66

Nerve fibers, 41
Nervous system, 37-62; anatomy of, 41-43; co-ordinating centers of, 49-56; general topography of, 37-41
Neurilemma, 41
Neurological deficiencies and speech, 343
Neuron, 41
Neurons, interconnections of, 43-49; types of, 43-45
Normal speaking voice, characteristics of, 344

Obstacles, sense of, 231-3
Oral deviations, 350-1

Pancreatic Islands, 68
Paralysis agitans, and voice, 348
Parasympathetic system, 40
Parathyroid glands, 67
Partially sighted, the educational achievement of, 256-9; intelligence of, 254-6; psychology of, 252-61
Perception deafness and speech defects, 373-4
Performance scales, 77-80
Perseveration, 9
Personality, and endocrine system, 4-5; and physical deficiencies, 11-17; defined, 1-2; development, 1-18; factors of, 2-10; normality and abnormality of, 10-11; types, 7-11
Physical handicaps and social competence, 15-16
Pineal gland, 68-69
Pituitary dwarfism, 65
Pituitary gland, 63-64
Projection, 29; areas, 53, 55
Prolactin, 64

Rationalization, 30
Reflex arcs, 45-46
Regression, 27-28
Repression, 30-32
Resonating cavities, defects of, 349-51
Rheumatic fever, 287-8

Schizoid, 8-9
Sensory compensation, 233-5
Sex glands, 67-68
Spastic, speech of, 369-70; vocal paralysis of, 347-8; voice of, 370
Speech, and chronological age, 325-6; and hearing, 371-2; and physical defects, 326
Speech defects, and educational achievement, 324-5; and intelligence, 322-4; and personality, 327-30; and sensorimotor efficiency, 326-7; incidence and distribution of, 321-2
Speech disorders, major types of, 331-58; nature of, 319-20; rela-

Speech (*continued*) tionship to other disorders, 322-30
Spinal cord, 38, 40, 46; and its tracts, 46, 56-60; effects of lesions of, 60-61
Striate bodies, 51
Stutterers, biochemistry, 333-4; motor ability, 335-6; muscular movement of, 334-5; psychological characteristics of, 336
Stuttering, as a manifestation of dysphemia, 339-40; as a manifestation of perseveration, 340-1; defined, 332; incidence and distribution of, 336-7; overt symptoms of, 332-3; theories as to causation of, 338-41; types of, 337-8
Subcortical centers, 56
Sublimation, 24-25
Sympathetic system, 40
Synapse, nature of, 48-49

Talking book, 368
Tests, educational, 75; for blind, 90-91; for deaf, 83-84
Tests, intelligence, 73-75; for blind, 88-90; for deaf, 77-83
Tests, list of, 94-97
Tests, personality, 75-76; for blind, 92; for deaf, 84-86
Tests, special ability, 76; for blind, 92; for deaf, 86-87
Thalamus, 51
Thymus gland, 69
Thyroid gland, 65-67
Tongue-tie, 342
Tracts of the cord, 56-60
Trial behavior, 23-24
Tuberculosis, incidence of, 308
Tuberculous, 308-10; employment possibilities of, 310; intelligence of, 308-9; personality of, 309-10
Tumors of the tongue, 342-3

Voice defects, 344-51; organic causes of, 346-51; types of, 344-6
Voice production, 344

Author Index

Abel, 245
Ackerson, 295, 297
Allport, 238, 246
Amoss, 79, 97, 116, 117, 180
Anderson, 278, 279
Appel, 294, 295, 296, 297
Aretz, 189, 206
Arps, 327, 335, 359
Arthur, 79, 97

Baker, 306
Balyeat, 285
Barbour, 272, 273
Barnes, 300, 302, 303
Beilinsson, 145, 180
Bell, 206
Bender, 330, 360
Berens, 208, 245
Berrien, 295, 296
Best, 208, 209, 245
Beverly, 297
Binet, 72, 111, 131, 180, 211, 245
Blackburn, 334, 360
Blanton, 337, 361
Boas, 288, 290
Bock, 192, 205
Bond, E. D., 295, 296, 297
Bond, N. J., 237, 245
Boulware, 84, 99, 141, 182
Bowen, 293, 294
Bowers, 115, 185
Braceland, 309, 310
Bradway, K. P., 163, 164, 180, 239, 246, 275
Bradway, L. M., 15, 17
Braille, 210
Branham, 303
Bridge, 303, 304
Bridgman, 116, 117, 180
Brigham, 90, 97
Brockway, 274
Bromberg, 297
Bronner, 307
Brooks, 19, 36
Brown, A. W., 82, 88, 97, 98, 124, 180
Brown, G. D., 293, 294
Brown, M., 288, 289, 290
Brown, P. A., 92, 97, 98, 230, 231, 246
Brown, R. R., 301
Bruner, 108, 109, 183
Brunschwig, 85, 98, 99, 150, 152, 153, 154, 159, 162, 181, 184, 229
Burde, 235, 246
Bürklen, 222, 223, 224, 234, 246

Cairns, 216, 246
Caldwell, 220, 246
Camp, 337, 361
Campbell, 10, 17
Cantril, 238, 246
Caplin, 193, 205
Carr, 334, 337, 362
Carrell, 326, 359

Coffin, 260
Collins, 78, 79, 98, 113
Conklin, 145, 181
Conn, 297, 300, 303
Conway, 189, 205
Cookson, 300
Crawford, 288
Cross, 335, 361
Cutsforth, 228, 240, 246, 365, 380

Davidson, 88, 98
Dawson, 297, 300, 303
Day, 181
Dearborn, 237, 245
De Porte, 288
Dickey, 308
Diderot, 104, 181, 209
Dietz, 279, 280
Dolanski, 232, 233, 246
Doll, 15
Dowd, 306
Downes, 308
Drever, 78, 79, 98, 113, 181
Drolet, 308
Dublin, 291

Eatman, 248
Eccles, 307
Eisenson, 340, 361
Ewen, 9, 17
Ewing, A. W. G., 138, 181, 372, 381
Ewing, I. R., 138, 181, 372, 381
Eyre, 292, 309

Farrell, 246
Fay, 298
Fernald, 265, 266, 267
Fetterman, 300, 302, 303
Field, 306, 307
Fletcher, 378, 381
Fonner, 300, 301, 302, 303
Fortner, 89, 98, 214, 246
Foster, 290
Fox, 299, 301
Frampton, 98, 253, 260, 261
French, 246
Froeschels, 337, 361
Fusfeld, 99, 121, 138, 159, 181, 184

Gahagan, 298, 299, 300, 301, 302, 303, 305
Gibbs, 295
Glau, 181
Goddard, 212
Goldmann, 145, 181
Goldstein, 352, 363
Goodenough, 82, 98, 121, 185
Goodlett, 125, 181
Göpfert, 145, 181
Gordon, B., 309, 310
Gordon, R. G., 270
Gowers, 298, 299
Greenberger, 106, 107, 181
Greene, 125, 181
Gregory, 182
Griffiths, 270
Grinker, 303, 304
Groff, 182

Habbe, 199, 205
Hadley, 255, 258, 261
Haggerty, 86
Haines, 88, 98, 212, 247
Hall, A. J., 296
Hall, E., 236, 247
Hall, G. S., 210, 247
Hall, P., 137, 182
Hallard, 250
Hallowell, 296
Hardy, 307
Harriman, 304, 305
Hathaway, 261
Hathway, 276, 277, 278
Haüy, 209

Hayes, 88, 90, 98, 213, 214, 215, 219, 221, 225, 226, 227, 228, 231, 233, 234, 235, 237, 244, 247, 248
Head, 351, 352, 363
Healy, 79, 307
Hearon, 259, 261
Heider, F., 142, 145
Heider, G., 142, 145
Heller, 211, 231, 248
Hildreth, 78, 98
Hoefer, 307
Hofsommer, 205
Holland, 182, 224, 248
Hunsley, 334, 361
Hunt, 306

Irwin, 208, 212, 213

Jackson, 351
James, 232, 248
Jastrow, 210, 248
Jenkins, 295, 297
Johnson, B. J., 306
Johnson, W., 330, 361
Jones, 107, 182
Joslin, 291

Kammerer, 274
Kanner, 274
Keller, 210
Kennedy, 334, 337, 362
Keys, 84, 99, 141, 182
Kilpatrick, 110, 182
Kirk, 156, 163, 182, 186
Kitson, 144, 182
Kling, 286
Knotts, 218, 248
Knox, 78
Koch, 217, 248
Köhler, 126
Kohlstedt, 92, 99
Kohs, 78
Kretschmer, 8, 17
Kwint, 297

Lachman, 13
Lamarque, 232, 248
Lange, 297
Lee, 267
Lende, 248, 249
Lennox, 296, 298, 302, 303
Lev, 190, 192, 206
Lincoln, 306
Lindner, 125, 126, 170, 182
Ling, 234, 250
Linogg, 288
Long, 87, 99, 166, 167, 182
Lord, 266
Lorenz, 205
Love, 107, 183
Löwenfeld, 235, 249
Lyon, 158, 170, 183

MacDougall, 232, 249
MacKane, 79, 99, 112, 113, 114, 115, 117, 183
MacMillan, 108, 109, 183
Madden, 190, 194, 195, 205
Makhaeva, 305
Marble, 291
Marks, 291
Marshall, 99
Martens, 171, 173, 174, 183, 280, 281
Mason, 145, 183
Master, 287
Matitch, 307
Matz, 235, 249
Max, 183
Maxfield, 219, 220, 222, 223, 224, 226, 227, 249
McBride, 354, 363
McCollum, 307
McDowell, 329, 336, 337, 361
McGavin, 293, 294

McGrew, 274
McIlvaine, 107, 183
McIntire, 261
McKay, 240, 249
McLeod, 264
Merry, F. K., 218, 225, 249, 250
Merry, R. V., 92, 99, 215, 216, 218, 236, 238, 249, 250, 259, 261
Meyer, 185
Miles, 218, 248, 291
Morrison, 116, 117
Morsh, 168, 170, 183
Mott, 107, 183
Muhl, 216, 229, 250, 308, 309
Myers, E. T., 253, 254, 255, 258, 261
Myers, J. A., 308

Nelson, 284, 285
Newlee, 124, 184
Neymann, 92, 99, 308, 309
Nichols, 306
Nilson, 271
Ninde, 299, 300

Olson, 86
Orleans, 91
Otis, 91

Paskind, 299, 302, 303
Paterson, 77, 79, 99, 110, 111, 112, 122, 124, 129, 138, 140, 170, 184, 185, 296, 307
Patterson, 300, 301, 302, 303
Pearson, 306
Pechstein, 250
Peck, 189, 205, 256, 260, 261
Peden, 293, 294
Pedersen, 84, 141
Peet, 105, 184
Peterson, 121, 184
Petzelt, 250
Phelps, 265
Phillips, 189, 205
Pinard, 9, 17
Pintner, 77, 78, 79, 80, 82, 85, 98, 99, 110, 111, 112, 122, 124, 129, 138, 140, 147, 154, 159, 160, 162, 170, 181, 184, 185, 190, 192, 195, 197, 201, 202, 203, 206
Porteus, 81, 99, 100
Price, 308
Pyle, 124, 185, 237

Rauh, 287
Reamer, 114, 117, 118, 119, 120, 131, 132, 134, 135, 185
Richen, 292
Riddell, 240, 250
Roberts, J. A. F., 270
Roberts, L. J., 307
Robin, 297
Rogers, G. G., 274
Rogers, J. F., 337, 360
Roland, 308
Root, 291
Rosenbaum, 272
Roslow, 157, 186
Ross, 288
Roth, 115, 117, 185
Rowell, 189, 205, 253, 260, 261

Samuelson, 189, 205
Sankey, 368, 380
Sargent, 89, 100, 214, 241, 250
Schick, 185
Schlenkrich, 185
Schmähl, 185
Schultz, 293, 294
Scott, 297
Seashore, C. E., 92, 100, 234, 250
Seashore, R. H., 86, 100, 166, 185
Seidenfeld, 308, 309
Shanahan, 299
Sherman, 297

Shirley, 121, 185
Shrubsall, 297
Sigel, 290
Simon, 131, 180
Smedley, 170
Smith, A. J., 306, 307
Smith, C. H., 287
Smith, J. L., 108, 185
Smith, J. M., 224, 250
Smith, M. B., 268
Solenberger, 280, 310
Spearman, 9, 17
Spence, 296
Springer, 121, 156, 157, 186
Stanton, 87, 100, 168, 169, 186
Sterling, 206
Stevenson, 263
Stinchfield, 328, 360, 365, 380
Strauss, 273
Strecker, 309, 310
Streng, 163, 186
Sullivan, 285, 298, 299, 300, 301, 302, 303, 305
Sutton, 287

Taylor, 107, 130, 186
Templin, 329, 360
Terman, 88, 213, 215
Thomas, 274
Thompson, 143, 186
Thorndike, E. L., 72
Thorndike, R., 286
Thurstone, L. L., 92, 100
Thurstone, T. G., 100
Travis, 338, 360
Turner, 299

Ufkess, 217, 248
Upshall, 119, 135, 136, 137, 186

Van der Kolk, 125, 187
Vertes, 187, 236, 237, 250
Villey, 232, 250
Voelker, 372, 381

Wade, 189, 206
Waldman, 189, 193, 194, 206
Warwick, 192, 206
Weisenberg, 354, 363
Welles, 160, 200, 201, 202, 203, 206
West, H., 292
West, R., 334, 337, 339, 340, 362
Westphal, 335, 362
Whipple, 122, 187
White, 291, 292, 294
Wickman, 86
Wilbur, 251
Wilkins, 298
Williams, 121, 184
Wilson, 288
Witty, 268
Worster-Drought, 303
Wundt, 210

Young, 6, 18

Zeckel, 125, 187

(5)